Manhood in Early

WOMEN AND MEN IN HISTORY

This series, published for students, scholars and interested general readers, will tackle themes in gender history from the early medieval period through to the present day. Gender issues are now an integral part of all history courses and yet many traditional texts do not reflect this change. Much exciting work is now being done to redress the gender imbalances of the past, and we hope that these books will make their own substantial contribution to that process. This is an open-ended series, which means that many new titles can be included. We hope that these will both synthesise and shape future developments in gender studies.

The General Editors of the series are *Patricia Skinner* (University of Southampton) for the medieval period; *Pamela Sharpe* (University of Bristol) for the early modern period; and *Penny Summerfield* (University of Lancaster) for the modern period. *Margaret Walsh* (University of Nottingham) was the Founding Editor of the series.

Published books:

Masculinity in Medieval Europe
D.M. Hadley (ed.)

Gender and Society in Renaissance Italy
Judith C. Brown and Robert C. Davis (eds)

Gender, Church and State in Early Modern Germany: Essays by Merry E. Wiesner
Merry E. Wiesner

Manhood in Early Modern England: Honour, Sex and Marriage
Elizabeth A. Foyster

Gender, Power and the Unitarians in England, 1760–1860
Ruth Watts

Women and Work in Russia, 1880–1930: A Study in Continuity through Change
Jane McDermid and Anna Hillyar

The Family Story: Blood, Contract and Intimacy, 1830–1960
Leonore Davidoff, Megan Doolittle, Janet Fink and Katherine Holden

Manhood in Early Modern England

Honour, Sex and Marriage

ELIZABETH A. FOYSTER

Longman
London and New York

Addison Wesley Longman Limited
Edinburgh Gate,
Harlow, Essex CM20 2JE, United Kingdom
and Associated Companies throughout the world.

Published in the United States of America by Addison Wesley Longman, New York.

First published 1999

ISBN 0-582-30734-1 CSD
ISBN 0-582-30735-X PPR

Visit Addison Wesley Longman on the world wide web at http://www.awl-he.com

British Library Cataloguing in Publication Data

A catalogue entry for this title is available from the British Library

Library of Congress Cataloging-in-Publication Data

Foyster, Elizabeth A., 1968–
Manhood in early modern England : honour, sex, and marriage / Elizabeth A. Foyster.
p. cm. — (Women and men in history)
Includes bibliographical references (p.) and index.
ISBN 0–582–30734–1. — ISBN 0–582–30735–X (pbk.)
1. Men—England—History. 2. Masculinity—England—History. 3. England—Social life and customs—17th century. 4. Men—England—Conduct of life—History—17th century. 5. Men—England—Conduct of life—History—16th century. 6. England—Social life and customs—16th century. 7. Marriage customs and rites—England—History. 8. Sex customs—England—History. 9. Honor—England—History. 10. Sex role—England—History. I. Title. II. Series.
HQ1090.7.G7F69 1999
305.31′0942—dc21 98–42933
CIP

Set by 35 in 10/12pt Baskerville
Produced by Addison Wesley Longman Singapore (Pte) Ltd.,
Printed in Singapore

Contents

Acknowledgements

This book started life as a Ph.D. thesis. My supervisor, Anthony Fletcher, provided much support, was always eager to discuss my ideas, and paid detailed attention to my work. Since the completion of my thesis, he has continued to read my work and give me invaluable guidance and criticism. He has always been an inspiring teacher, and I owe him many thanks. As I have been working on transforming the thesis into book form, I have been helped by the comments of my examiners Christopher Brooks and Bernard Capp, the series editor Pamela Sharpe, and the commissioning editor Hilary Shaw. I have been supported financially by the British Academy for postgraduate and postdoctoral research, and by a one-year Durham University Studentship. While working on this book, I have held a one-year temporary lectureship at the School of History and Welsh History, Bangor, where I was encouraged by many colleagues, in particular Duncan Tanner. I would also like to thank the Master and Fellows at Clare College, Cambridge, for their welcome and support.

I have been extremely fortunate to have worked in some of the most beautiful research environments while I have been writing this book. I started in Durham in the seventeenth-century Bishop Cosin's library on Palace Green, and in 5 The College which overlooks Durham Cathedral. I have also worked in Lambeth Palace Library in London, where the research room adjoins a courtyard in the Palace, and in the summer you can hear the soothing sounds of the trickling fountain. But what has really made these places special has been the librarians and archivists who have worked there. In Durham, I am very grateful to Margaret McCollum, Linda Drury, Joe Fewster and Beth Rainey for sharing with me their expertise of early modern records. At Lambeth, I would like to thank Melanie Barber who has answered numerous questions, and the team of archivists who have collected endless reels of microfilm for me. Away from libraries and record offices, many colleagues have provided me with references, shared their research, read drafts, and asked me pertinent questions. In particular I would like to thank Jeremy Black, Philip Carter, Tony Claydon, Richard Cust, Brian Gibbons, Margaret Harvey, Matthew Johnson, Jenny Kermode, Pete Rushton, Alexandra Shepard, Ceri Sullivan, John Tosh, David Turner, Garthine Walker and Helen Weinstein. Tim Stretton has helped and encouraged me from the start, and has read so many drafts that by now he must know this book by memory. Helen Berry has also been the source of endless critical and intellectual support, as well as much laughter in some of the otherwise serious and sombre surroundings of academic institutions.

The interest which the colleagues listed above have shown in my research, and the friendships which I have made along the way, have counteracted any concerns which I had about the loneliness of an academic career. I am particularly grateful for the loyalty of my friends Sue Lambley and Héloise Lampert. In Durham, the friendship of George and Ghadir Abu-Leil Cooper, Sophia Mavropoulou, Jane Roscoe and Jo Story helped me enormously. I would also like to thank Keith Bartlett and his family for their love and support over the past few years.

Finally, I owe most to my family – Margaret, Richard and Kate – for their absolute faith and trust in me. Without them none of this would have been possible.

Preface

For ease of comprehension all spellings have been modernised except for the titles of printed primary sources. Punctuation and capitalisation have not been modernised.

The year is taken to begin on 1 January for all court records.

The dates of ballads where given are taken from the editors notes to *The Roxburghe Ballads* (W. Chappell ed., vols I–III; and J.W. Ebsworth ed., vols IV–IX), or from the catalogue compiled by H. Weinstein of *The Pepys Ballads* (R. Latham ed., *Catalogue of the Pepys Library at Magdalene College*, vol. II, Part i). These dates are based on when the ballads were printed or registered with the Stationers' Company, or on known biographical details of their authors, printers or publishers. All dates of ballads given are approximate and should be treated with caution, however, since a ballad could be in oral circulation or in illegal printed circulation long before it was officially printed, published and registered.

The dates of plays refer to their composition or earliest known performance. Useful chronological tables are contained in A.R. Braunmuller and M. Hattaway, eds, *The Cambridge Companion to English Renaissance Drama* (Cambridge, 1990), and J. Loftis, R. Southern, M. Jones and A.H. Scouten, eds, *The Revels History of Drama in English: Volume V 1660–1750* (London, 1976).

In an effort to keep footnotes to a minimum, extensive information on secondary sources is given in the guide to Further Reading at the end of the text.

Abbreviations

Manuscript Sources

DDR.V.	Durham consistory court deposition book, 12 vols, Durham University Library. The library of Durham University is currently producing a classified catalogue of Durham Diocesan Records, and detailed lists of consistory court papers.
CA	Court of Arches, Lambeth Palace Library. The numbers of cases are those given in J. Houston, ed., *Index of Cases in the Records of the Court of Arches at Lambeth Palace Library 1660–1913* (London, 1972).
Ee	Court of Arches personal answer
Eee	Court of Arches deposition
J	Court of Arches Bill of Costs

Printed Sources

Euing	*The Euing Collection of Broadside Ballads*, introduction by J. Holloway, (Glasgow, 1971)
M.P.	Martin Parker, ballad author (d.1656?)
Pepys	W.G. Day, ed., *The Pepys Ballads* (facsimile, 5 vols, Cambridge, 1987)
Pepysian Garland	H.E. Rollins, ed., *A Pepysian Garland: Black Letter Broadside Ballads of the Years 1595–1639* (Cambridge MA, 1971)
Roxburghe	W. Chappell, ed., *The Roxburghe Ballads*, vols I–III (London, 1871–80), and J.W. Ebsworth, ed., *The Roxburghe Ballads*, vols IV–IX (London, 1883–99)
Shirburn	A. Clark, ed., *The Shirburn Ballads* (Oxford, 1907)

Journals

CC	*Continuity and Change*
GH	*Gender and History*
HWJ	*History Workshop Journal*
PP	*Past and Present*
TRHS	*Transactions of the Royal Historical Society*

CHAPTER ONE

Discovering Manhood

Do but consider, pray, what is a man,
till such times as he doth marry.[1]

Amongst those worldly Joys, of which
Men equally may have their Share,
Whereof the Poor as well as Rich
most commonly possessors are:
The greatest happiness I find,
Is that which comes from Women kind:
There is no comfort in this life,
Like to a constant loving Wife.[2]

This is a study of gender history. It takes as its premise that ideas of 'manhood' were as much social and cultural constructions as those of 'femininity'. For ideas about what it meant to be a man, as well as how men experienced their gender, have histories. Gender history, as it has been defined, is above all else relational history. It seeks to examine the sexes not in isolation, but rather the relationships between the sexes. It is concerned with discovering how the desirable qualities and attributes for each gender were defined in relation to each other. It is also a history of power relations. By studying men in the context of marriage, this book will show how power relations could be negotiated and challenged, as well as adopted and accepted. Focusing on evidence from the seventeenth century, attention will be drawn to the importance of men's sexual relationships in the formation of their gender identity, as well as to their subsequent social credit or worth. Whilst at first sight the story of early modern gender relations may appear to be one wholly of dominance and subordination, authority and deference, the study of honour will reveal how the interdependency of the reputations of husbands and wives could moderate these relations. Men were all too aware that their honour depended on the actions and words of their wives.

But why, you may well ask, do we need more histories of men? History by its very definition has long been 'his story': the accounts of the lives of men, and the analysis of writings by men. The resurgence of women's history in the 1960s and 1970s has seen a gradual redressing of the balance, but our knowledge of women's experience in the past is still far from complete. It is a measure of the impact of women's history, however, that it has led to a fundamental questioning of the sources, methods, chronologies and categories which have been traditionally employed by historians. Somewhat ironically, by writing histories of women, historians have also exposed the flaws and limitations of previous histories of men. Nowhere has this been more powerfully shown by historians of women than in the examination of the prescriptive literature of the past which taught how patriarchy, the male domination and subordination of women, could be achieved. Early modern English didactic literature ranging from household conduct books to broadside ballads prescribed specific gender roles to men and women. Women were to be chaste, silent and obedient. Men were to be the heads of households, governing over their wives, children and servants. According to this literature, it was essential to the operation of patriarchy that women were confined to the 'private' sphere of the home and excluded from the male 'public' world. Historians of women have exposed this literature for what it was: an expression of the ideal model of gender relations rather than a reflection of its reality. Today it leaves us with evidence of the theory rather than the practice of patriarchy. As Keith Wrightson has concluded from his study of early modern marriage, 'the picture which emerges indicates the *private* existence of a strong complementary and companionate ethos, side by side with, and often overshadowing, theoretical adherence to the doctrine of male authority and *public* female subordination'.[3] In practice, women were able to negotiate their relationships with men and with other women so that their history was not always one of subordination. Instead of reading the advice contained within this literature as evidence of actual women's lives, histories of women have shown how little it could tally with the everyday realities of practical living. Research has revealed that the 'separate spheres' ideology had little relevance to many early modern women. Women from all social groups frequently entered the 'public' sphere, and the 'private' or domestic sphere was rarely completely cut off or isolated from the public world.[4]

It is in the light of this research into women's lives that the inadequacies of our knowledge of men's history become most obvious. For too long historians have assumed that the public lives of men were all that mattered. The private lives of men in the home as sons, husbands and fathers have been forgotten. This is a costly omission, for how will we ever understand how and why patriarchy could endure unless we study men from this perspective? Judith Bennett has called for research on patriarchy to be at the top of research agendas for women's history; we also need to concentrate on the study of patriarchy if we are to understand more about men's lives. Patriarchal ideas are not transhistorical; notions of how men could gain power over women have changed over time and have had different implications depending on the personal, familial or institutional context in which they have been applied.[5] Yet fundamental questions about how men set about achieving dominance over women remain unanswered in the histories that have been written. We need to have a clearer understanding of how individual men in the past shaped patriarchal ideas to suit their needs, and when their behaviour could contest or challenge patriarchy as the dominant ideology. Men may have appeared to have the most to gain from the operation of patriarchy, but what did the ideal of patriarchy mean for the reality of men's lives? This book will demonstrate the importance that power over women had in the formation of a man's identity. But by profoundly affecting men's personal relationships, this book will also argue that the patriarchal ideal had costs for men's as well as women's lives.

Gender Roles and Responsibilities

Patriarchal ideas gained a new force in the seventeenth century, even though by this period they were ages old. Political theorists such as Sir Robert Filmer drew analogies between the power of the king in the state and that of the father in the family. This analogy was extended by royalists when they argued that the contract between a king and his subjects was as irrevocable as the marriage contract between husband and wife. By the end of the seventeenth century the political theory of patriarchy was being challenged by John Locke, but by this time its implications for domestic conduct had become the mainstay of household manuals. Puritan ministers had ensured that patriarchal ideas reached a wider audience when they adopted and adapted them within their sermons and writings on household conduct. For these authors, patriarchy also had a scriptural basis and justification. It was because of Eve's sin that God had made woman subordinate to man. Drawing upon Ephesians 5:21–33 they compared the husband's position over his wife with that of Christ over the Church. William Gouge, one of the most influential of these conduct book writers, quoted verse 22, 'wives submit yourselves unto your divine husbands, as unto the Lord', and verse 23, 'for the husband is the head of the wife, even as Christ is the head of the Church', to explain why women should be subordinate to their husbands. For Puritans, the ordering of the family had both spiritual and political significance: 'the family is a seminary of the Church and Commonwealth', Gouge declared.[6] Men's role as head of the household was so important that it was regarded as an indicator of the ability to govern in the public world outside. As we shall see, in seventeenth-century thinking there was no separation of spheres for men. It was integral to their privilege as the dominant sex that they should be free to move between the spheres, but it was also a test of their manhood that in both they should prove equally capable of managing their affairs. As John Dod and Robert Cleaver explained in the conduct book they wrote in 1612, 'it is impossible for a man to understand how to govern the commonwealth, that doth not know how to rule his own house'.[7]

This patriarchal system was thus a powerful ideology in early modern England which set out notions of appropriate gender roles for both men and women. Whilst for men, as well as women, the patriarchal model of gender relations could remain an ideal pattern that few would achieve in its entirety, as this book will argue, that did not prevent men from attempting to achieve that ideal. Many men adopted particular patterns of behaviour within the household, and within their marital relationships, which they believed would bring them closer to obtaining dominance over women. As we shall see, in the seventeenth century the key to male power in the household was thought to be sexual control of women as well as the self. 'Hegemonic masculinity', as defined by the sociologist R.W. Connell, is the dominant form of masculinity 'which embodies the currently accepted answer to the problem of the legitimacy of patriarchy'. In the early modern period it was by obtaining and maintaining exclusive heterosexual marital relationships that men believed they would come closest to reaching the patriarchal goal. Although many men failed in their bid for sexual exclusivity, some never attempted to gain power in this way, and others gave up trying, that did not detract from the dominance of the hegemonic form. Instead it created 'subordinate masculinities' to which some men were relegated.[8] As John Tosh, a leading historian of nineteenth-century masculinity, has explained, men who belonged to these subordinate groups were those 'whose crime is that they undermine patriarchy from within or discredit it in the eyes of women. Sometimes an entire persona is demonized . . . sometimes specific forms of male behaviour are singled out.'[9] In early modern England, as in the nineteenth century, sodomy between men was abhorred.[10] Amongst heterosexual men, as will be shown, the label of 'cuckold' was attached to those whose lack of sexual dominance had led their wives to adultery. A range of rituals were employed by communities throughout the country to mock and humiliate cuckolds as failures.

The early modern period is a particularly exciting one for the historian because it is so rich in sources in which ordinary men and women speak about their gender, sexual activities and marriages. We can see how abstract notions like 'patriarchy' were put into practice and became tangible realities. Going to the church courts to fight defamation or marriage separation suits, litigants and witnesses spoke and were questioned about the values they attached to a range of male and female behaviours. The term 'manhood' will be used in this book, rather than 'masculinity', since the latter was only employed by contemporaries from the mid-eighteenth century. The language of 'honour' was how men and women talked about their gender roles. By examining the use of this language we can measure the bearing that prescriptive codes had on actual behaviour. From these records we can see how honour, reputation, credit, or a good name could be the rewards for men and women who upheld the ideals of patriarchy. The insults of 'whore' and 'cuckold' were targeted against those who did not direct their relationships towards this ideal. The ideology of patriarchy thus led to the construction of a system of morality which rewarded or chastised those who succeeded or failed to live up to its requirements. The records of marital separation, however, show the difficulties of putting the patriarchal system into place, as well as the costs that could be incurred within marital relationships in the process. Nowhere did the adoption of gender roles appear to have been as straightforward as the authors of prescriptive literature suggested, instead they were open to contest and debate. But the large and increasing numbers of men and women who went to the church courts to defend their good names in this period, in addition to the mass of popular literature which took sexual honour as its theme, should convince us of the overwhelming contemporary interest in and concern with the value of honour earned in this way.

Historians of church court records, in particular Jim Sharpe and Martin Ingram, have analysed the legal processes and thinking which lay behind the production of these records, as well as providing us with the details of their contents.[11] Nobody has done more to increase our understanding of church court records from a gender perspective, however, than Laura Gowing. Her important book, *Domestic Dangers: Women, Words, and Sex in Early Modern London*, has given us a vivid insight into the world of female gossip and slander and has set the study of early modern women on to new and exciting directions.[12] Although this book will suggest alternative interpretations and arguments to those of Gowing since it is a study of early modern men, it will also suggest points of comparison. The work of academics in other disciplines has also confirmed the importance of the concept of honour to early modern thinking. C.L. Barber has found over two hundred plays written between 1591 and 1700 which referred to honour, and C.B. Watson's study of honour in contemporary philosophy and Shakespeare's drama has led him to conclude that men at this time were 'intoxicated' with honour and with 'outward repute'.[13] Honour has also been proved to be of consequence in other early modern countries including France, Germany, Italy and Spain.[14] Archaeologists and historians of English visual culture have found abundant evidence of contemporaries' desire to display their honour on the tombstones, memorials and medallion portraits of parish churches.[15] It would appear that in the early modern period reminders of the importance of honour were everywhere.

Of course, men and women had multiple identities and roles, which were reflected in the way they thought and spoke about their honour. Neither men's nor women's honour depended solely upon how their behaviour was seen in the light of the patriarchal ideal. Both male and female honour was multifaceted. Whilst historians have long recognised the key importance of sexual honour for women, research is now revealing that there were also non-sexual components to a woman's honour. Being a hardworking, industrious housewife was important to a woman's honour, Garthine Walker has argued.[16] When Anne Stoddert declared to her widowed sister-in-law in the parish of Heighington, county Durham, that she 'was the cause of her husband's death and that . . . her husband could have no joyful days with her and that she bore her children but did never take thought for bringing them up', she pointed to another facet of a woman's reputation by claiming that she had been neither a good wife nor a caring, nurturing mother.[17] Women could be as sensitive to slurs on their social status as they were to those on their sexual status. Elizabeth Kendall responded angrily in 1667 when Elizabeth Foote began to spread rumours in Hammersmith that Kendall was from a family of cook-maids and pedlars. Witnesses for Kendall asserted that her father was instead 'a very honest and sufficient man', and that for over thirty years she had been married to 'the greatest and principal Shoemaker at this end of the town'. Provoked in this way, Kendall accused Foote of adultery and bearing bastards, but Foote was even able to turn these words to Kendall's disadvantage, declaring that Kendall's 'vilifying Language and ill tongue show that her breeding was not great'.[18] A reputation for godliness or piety could also be a significant advantage. As we shall see, for the upper sorts, displays of hospitality or charity were often interpreted as signs of godly virtue. For those lower down the social scale, when insults were embellished with the terms 'popish' or 'heathen', both men and women felt compelled to go to the courts to answer the insults and defend their good names.[19]

Although, as this book will show, 'cuckold' was the worst insult which could be directed against a man, male honour could also be damaged by non-sexual insults. Indeed, the insults most frequently directed against men were accusations of dishonesty, of being a thief or a drunk. Drunkenness was an insult which will be discussed more fully in Chapter 2. When a man's good word and honesty were vital in so many daily business transactions, calling a man cheat, liar or thief was a powerful way to damage reputation. Craig Muldrew has shown us how most buying and selling in early modern society was done on credit, and that although the literate and wealthier wrote down these transactions, the majority relied on oral promises. A man's word had to be his bond if this economic system was to work. At each transaction a judgement of the other man's trustworthiness had to be made, and evidence suggests that this was usually based on an assessment of his moral worth. Nowhere was the link between a man's 'private' behaviour more clearly linked to his fortune in the 'public' sphere. 'Credit' meant both honesty and solvency in this period: the one affected the other.[20] Amongst the middling and lower sorts, a man's identity was also closely linked to his occupational status, and the honour of certain trades and occupations was often proudly asserted.[21] Slanders directed against this aspect of a man's honour could have devastating effect. A witness declared in 1607 that after Elizabeth Vincent loudly cursed the doctor Thomas Handley in Newcastle, 'God forbid that ever Handley take any work in hand that ever shall prosper' because her child had died in his care, 'his patients by reason of the said Elizabeth her speeches, are gone from him'.[22] Much of the training for these trades and professions was conducted in an all-male setting. For apprentices, journeymen, and students at the universities and inns of court, very different honour and shame systems could be in operation where heterosexual relationships could play little part. Gender history, which can inform us of the dynamics of power relations in the past, is revealing that there were particular contexts and points in the life cycle at which men were more likely to gain power from their relationships with each other, than from those with women. Furthermore, studies have shown that contemporaries believed that if patriarchy was not to be endangered, the disruptive and unruly behaviour of some young men could require as much supervision and control as any threat of female insurrection. Finally, it is worth noting that as some men were members of organisations such as guilds, the experience of honour may have been for them a collective as well as individual one.[23]

As will be shown, the ways that men could both earn and defend their honour could depend on their social status. Indeed, in early modern England the language of honour varied according to social class. 'Honour' was a term used mainly by the upper sorts; for example there is only one reference to honour in the defamation cases which were brought by the middling and lower sorts to Durham consistory court between 1604 and 1631.[24] It was otherwise more frequently referred to as 'credit', 'good name', or 'reputation'. Each of these terms reflected varying nuances of meaning and were applied in different contexts. As we have seen, 'credit' was a term which implied moral as well as financial worth. In the church courts witnesses in defamation cases often referred to the ways that a person's 'good name' had been affected by the insult in question. 'Reputation', as Cynthia Herrup has recognised, was also concerned with a person's public presentation.[25] Each term served to allow contemporaries a means to describe what was the sum of the composite sexual and non-sexual values which made up every individual. Early modern men and women were eager to find ways of classifying, describing and expressing their relative position in society. A language of 'sorts', Wrightson has explained, was frequently employed to distinguish the 'better sort' from the 'meaner', 'ruder', or 'vulgar' sort.[26] The language of honour can be regarded as another such system of social classification, in which men and women were designated either as 'honourable' or 'dishonourable'. However, rather than confirming the existing systems of power relations, as the vocabulary of 'sorts' tended to do, the language of honour had the potential to create alternative social hierarchies. As we shall see, in the seventeenth century shifting concepts of the make-up of male honour meant that honour was no longer automatically granted to the ruling landed elite. Honour which stemmed from virtuous actions rather than from lineage was such a fragile commodity that the prospect of dishonour was never distant. The dishonour from cuckoldry, as popular literature frequently reminded its audiences, was a leveller which could affect men from all social backgrounds.

It is partly because sexual dishonour could affect men from across the social spectrum that this book concentrates on male sexual honour. Amongst men there was a shared belief in the importance of a worthy sexual reputation which, unlike other non-sexual components of male honour, cut across traditional class differences. This important aspect of men's reputations has been variously neglected, underestimated or even denied by historians. In the only historical survey yet to be published on male honour in the early modern period, Mervyn James confines the concept solely to the aristocracy, and denies that private behaviour could influence public reputation, arguing that 'men of honour could (and did) lie, cheat, deceive, plot, treason, seduce, and commit adultery, without incurring dishonour'.[27] Most research to date based on the defamation records of the church courts has focused on female honour, since in these courts there were always numerically far more female than male plaintiffs. By paying due emphasis to the importance of sexual reputation to women, however, men are too conveniently categorised as 'other' and their reputations are denied a sexual component. In part, this stems from a literal reading of the double sexual standard in which only women were culpable for sexual shame. But as this book will show, it has also arisen from a failure to examine contemporary popular thinking which rested the responsibility for household control on male sexual potency.

What research there has been into the sexual aspects of early modern manhood has often been misguided. Curiously, Susan Amussen, in her recent survey of early modern manhood, chose to examine evidence of rape to measure the importance for male contemporaries of sexual prowess or conquest. Finding that there was an 'absence of allegations of gang rapes', she writes that therefore rape was not 'part of the passage to manhood'. Even though she provides evidence of sexual defamation against men, she concludes as she began by writing that manhood at this time 'was not based on sexual activity'.[28] Certainly, violent sexual behaviour such as rape was never part of the process of becoming a man in early modern England. Instead, young men judged each other's sexual prowess by their ability to be so sexually attractive and skilful that force became wholly unnecessary. But just because male sexual behaviour cannot be conflated with physical force does not mean that the former was unimportant to male identity. In contrast to Amussen's study, this book strongly argues that a man's sexual activities, or lack of them, were central to notions of honourable and dishonourable manhood. It will further show that without the core of a worthy sexual reputation, all other contributing facets to male reputation could be meaningless.

Sources and Methodologies

If a man's sexual honour was contested verbally in this period, he was most likely to go to the church courts if he decided upon legal action as a response. In legal theory, for a defamation case to be heard in the church courts the insult needed to have accused the man of an offence which was within ecclesiastical jurisdiction, and in this period most sexual insults were regarded as spiritual offences. 'Mixed' defamations, for example 'cuckoldly thief', should in theory have been heard in the common law courts. But while the common law courts encroached upon church court jurisdiction during our period, even developing a criminal jurisdiction for slander and libel, the church court records remain the most fruitful for the historian. Despite the attempts of common lawyers, many men continued to go to the church courts after 'mixed' defamation, and even when they had been accused of secular crimes such as theft. Men who were accused of having venereal disease also frequently took their actions to the church courts, despite this being the one sexual offence which in theory should have formed the basis of common law suits. The records of the quarter sessions courts can also be frustrating to use, as recognisances often do not record the words of the insult. Although cases which were appealed to Star Chamber have left us with more detailed records from which some stimulating case studies of male honour have been written, litigants to this court tended to be mainly of high social status. As we shall see, the church courts not only produced records which contain a wealth of detail about the operation, language and defence of male honour, but also present us with a more socially representative picture of honour as litigants and their witnesses were drawn from a wider social spectrum including servants, labourers, yeomen, husbandsmen and tradesmen, as well as the occasional gentleman. The dramatic increase in the numbers of defamation cases heard in the church courts in the late sixteenth and early seventeenth centuries shows that this was by far the most popular legal form of action after sexual defamation.[29]

The witness statements, or 'depositions', recorded for 225 defamation cases and four marriage separation cases from Durham consistory court are bound in volumes for 1604–31, and consist of loose papers for the years 1633–34, 1636–37, 1662–63 and 1664–65. Deposition papers were presented by lawyers to the judge along with the other formal documents relating to the case. During 'instance' cases, which were disputes between parties, these documents usually consisted of the 'libel' brought by the plaintiff, to which the defendant could reply, point by point. The defendant would sometimes produce a counter case known as the 'allegation', which the plaintiff could then answer. Witnesses answered to the facts alleged in the libel or allegation. Either party could also pose questions to the witnesses known as 'interrogatories'. Once a judge had the depositions and all the other papers in front of him he would issue a sentence. Disputes concerning defamation could also be brought to the church courts as 'office' cases. Court officers, parish ministers or churchwardens would inform the bishop or his representatives of those who had transgressed against church law and the court judge would then issue a formal list of 'articles' or charges to the defendant. In most cases if the defendant denied the charges on oath he would be ordered to undergo 'compurgation' when he would have to find a specified number of neighbours to swear to his honesty. As Amussen has recognised, this process 'gave reputation a legal standing', for if enough people could testify to a man's good name, then a case in the church courts could proceed no further.[30] In more serious cases, however, the judge could decide to call witnesses and prosecute the case through the same number of procedural stages as an instance case. Office cases for defamation were far rarer than instance cases. Whatever the procedure followed, if found guilty the defendant could be admonished by the judge, and as a punishment undergo penance or, in the worst cases, excommunication.[31] In defamation cases the motivation to use church courts may well have lain with the punishments which they administered. Penance was a humiliation to suit the crime. It could take different forms: in 1692 a York man was sentenced to go to the house owned by the kinsmen of the man he had slandered, and in front of several members of the town elite admit that he had acted 'wrongfully, rashly and unadvisedly', and that he was sorry to have uttered the slanders. More frequently, those found guilty would be dressed in a white sheet and made to stand barefoot in a church or market place. Penance was an effective shaming ritual, admission of wrong, and a public vindication of reputation.[32] The large numbers of men and women who went to the church courts to fight defamation cases throughout the period help to show that the grievances which some voiced about the operation of the church courts were not shared by all.[33]

If a party wanted to appeal a decision made in a consistory court, he or she could have their case heard at York if they resided in the northern dioceses, or in the court of Arches for the province of Canterbury. This book draws upon the records of the latter court, which was based in London, and from which documents surviving after 1660 have been catalogued.[34] For cases of appeal in the court of Arches, some written appeals from the late seventeenth century survive, as do substantial numbers of process books, which were the copies of the proceedings from the lower court. Other cases came directly to the court of Arches by letters of request, in which the plaintiff gave reasons why his case should be heard in the first instance within the Arches. A group of letters of request survive from 1701–13, and this procedure became increasingly popular from the eighteenth century as litigants saw it as a way of bypassing the cost of pursuing a case in both courts, and as a way of ensuring that the expertise of skilled London advocates would be employed to settle the case. In the seventeenth century, appeal from a lower church court remained a frequent point of entry into the Arches. The majority of cases were brought by proctors of litigants who lived in London or its immediate counties. Once an appeal case had been admitted by the court of Arches, the judge could decide the case simply by reading the documentation contained within the process books, or he may have required the parties to submit further evidence. The subsequent 'personal answers' of the parties to the libels, allegations and articles, and the 'depositions' by witnesses in answer to the interrogatories, are the records examined in this book. Some 192 defamation cases reached the personal answer and/or deposition stage between 1660 and 1700.[35]

A further ninety-two cases for marital 'separation from bed and board' also reached the personal answer and/or deposition stage in the court of Arches during this period. These often lengthy records reveal detailed evidence of married life, and show how male honour was affected by marriage breakdown. Full divorce which allowed for remarriage was not widely available until the Divorce Reform Act of 1857. Whilst couples could remarry if they secured an annulment, this became an unpopular course of action after the grounds for proving that a marriage had been invalid were restricted following the Reformation, and because it left the woman without her dower rights and made any children illegitimate. Parliamentary divorce was too expensive for most, and before 1700 only two private acts for divorce were introduced. Instead couples who came to the church courts could lawfully separate 'from bed and board', but not remarry, if they could prove adultery and/or life-threatening cruelty.[36] Matrimonial suits, which were fought either to dispute the formation of a marriage or to end a marriage, only formed about 10 per cent of all the suits which were brought to the court of Arches.[37] Many suits which were initiated were resolved out of court before they reached the personal answer or deposition stage. Since litigants would often have to fund the case both in the lower court and in the appeal court, the cost of bringing these cases may have encouraged many to pursue more informal means of marriage separation. Unfortunately, only two 'bills of costs' which list the expenses owed by the litigants survive among the ninety-two records studied. Eustace Hardwicke was left with the incredibly high bill of £43 0s 8d in 1671 after he had disputed the amount of alimony he had to pay his wife following her separation suit for cruelty. Martha Butler was charged £13 7s 8d after her separation suit for adultery in 1697, a fee for which her husband would be legally liable to pay.[38] Since litigants' costs increased at each stage of the court procedure, and the appeal of a marital dispute to the Arches was evidence by itself that it was unlikely to be readily resolved, perhaps we should not be surprised to find that in contrast with the lower church courts, litigants of gentry status in the court of Arches who could afford to sustain such costs were not uncommon. Their witnesses, on the other hand, were often their domestic servants. This book draws upon the evidence submitted to the court of Arches between 1660 and 1700 from forty-three marriage separation cases brought on grounds of adultery, forty-two cases on grounds of cruelty, and seven cases brought for adultery and cruelty.

The ground-breaking study by Natalie Zemon Davis on the narrators of pardon tales in the courts of sixteenth-century France has led historians to recognise that court documents cannot be regarded simply as records of the voices of litigants and witnesses. Court records are instead the product of many voices. For when litigants came to the church courts their arguments were framed by proctors, and their witnesses were prompted by the clerk to recall events which had occurred in the past. These oral accounts then became written texts shaped by the clerk to suit legal convention and ensure comprehensibility. The result is that the language of the records is frequently formulaic and stock phrases are often repeated. As Gowing has shown in her study of London church court records, we need to consider how far plaintiffs or defendants, and their witnesses shaped their stories to give meaning to a pattern of behaviour, and to present a convincing story of damaged honour to the judge. Furthermore, by selecting the personal answers and depositions from these records for our study, we need to be aware that we are left with an impression of only several stages in the building of a multi-layered story; proctors, advocates and court officials had more direct input into the making of that story at other stages of the legal process. With the possibility of different stories of the same event being told at each stage, varying due to individual experience and interpretation of the same event, the church courts could not hope ever to establish a definitive true account of a particular incident. Instead, they sought to determine the most convincing interpretation of an event. The aim of this study is also not to attempt to discover 'that mythical beast "the Truth"', but to try to understand what insults and behaviour litigants and witnesses thought most damaging to male honour, and in the more detailed cases, what method of story-telling they believed needed to be employed to produce a convincing case to the court.[39]

If court records are deemed useful historical documents, even though they may be interpreted as 'fictions' which may not guide us to the 'truth', then traditional objections to the use of fictional literature in writing history because it is partial and not factual, also no longer stand. The development of 'new historicism', in which literary criticism has seen a 'return of history', has forced scholars to give more thought to the meanings and significance of the written sources with which they work. According to new historicists, all written documents of the past are 'texts' which can only be read subjectively. The differences between 'factual' history and 'fictional' literature break down, so that the court deposition and the fictional story simply become different forms of narrative discourse, each structured by literary conventions. Works of literature can be seen as historical events which had a material existence, and in performance were reproduced in institutions such as the theatre. For historians the implication of new historicism is that rather than relegate fictional literature as background information, or as an optional extra in the study of the past, it should, along with other written sources, be at the forefront of our thinking.

It is because literature plays a crucial role in the making of history that I have used contemporary plays and ballads in conjunction with legal sources in this book. The power of literature has been recognised by Jean Howard: 'rather than passively reflecting an external reality, literature is an agent in constructing a culture's sense of reality'.[40] Contemporaries in the seventeenth century knew that literature had the power to construct ideas and influence behaviour. The playwright Thomas Heywood defended his art by arguing that plays with a moral subject were written 'to persuade men to humanity and good life, to instruct them in civility and good manners, showing them the fruits of honesty, and the end of villainy'.[41] The influence of fictional literature, however, need not have been always so directly didactic. Evidence of the 'continuous interplay between real and fictional worlds' in the early modern period is not difficult to find.[42] As we shall see later in this book, men were able to draw upon the language and linguistic conventions of popular literature to aid them in their accounts of marital discord when they talked in the courts.[43]

The work of other academics has also shown the overlap between the worlds of fiction and reality. David Lindley, in an excellent book on the fate of Frances Howard, who in 1616 was found guilty of murdering Sir Thomas Overbury, has shown how 'the matrix of assumptions' about women within early modern fictional culture conditioned the way that contemporaries in reality reacted to, and later represented her crime. 'The same ideologies structuring dramatic plots also structure the dramas of the courtroom', Frances Dolan has concluded from her study of the trial of the second Earl of Castlehaven. Tim Stretton's discussion of the many examples of Elizabethan plays in which characters were depicted at law has revealed how playwrights frequently integrated sophisticated legal terminology and procedure into their scripts. The composers of libellous verse, Adam Fox has argued, wrote their own 'homemade ballads', whose format, distribution and performance techniques were shared, and may have been influenced by those of the commercially available broadside ballads.[44] History and literature cannot be seen as binary opposites, rather each created the other.

But, however tempting, we must never see literature as a mirror of reality. One writer in 1656 was horrified at the prospect that historians 'in future ages should make all England in ages past to be a Bartholomew Fair, because Ben Jonson hath writ it. Or that the condition of all our English women may be drawn out of Shakespeare's Merry Wives of Windsor.'[45] Instead literature can only provide us with clues of some of the many different assumptions, beliefs and attitudes of the past. Play and ballad writers had a market to attract and please, and the most obvious way to achieve this would have been to write about issues which were of current interest and import. The repeated male stereotypes in literature, as Philip Carter has shown in his study of the 'fop', can give us indications of 'desirable' and 'deviant' forms of manhood.[46] As we shall see, writers were not always in agreement about what constituted desirable manhood, and their points of difference can highlight tensions and unease with how honourable manhood could be achieved. Whilst it is an added benefit for the historian of early modern manhood that so many of the surviving sources were written by men, fictional sources may also provide us with what other written sources so often lack: a route into the otherwise hidden depths of the male psyche. Tosh has highlighted the gap in our historical knowledge of this aspect of men's lives, and it is perhaps from fictional sources that our search for the 'inner man' may prove most fruitful.[47] So much of our evidence in the early modern period tells us about men's social identity – how they wanted themselves and their relationships to be interpreted – but as this book will show, contemporary drama and broadside ballads can reveal the fears and anxieties which could underlie these public presentations of self. If we neglect to look at these sources we can miss out on how men in the past conceptualised emotions such as love or jealousy. We are still a far cry from understanding how individual men experienced these emotions, but with a knowledge of the cultural world in which they lived, we can at least see how men could learn a language with which they could express themselves, and we can begin to explain better the actions which some men subsequently took.

As with all historical evidence, it is important that we are aware of how fictional sources were produced, their intended and actual functions, as well as the social status and gender of those who participated or witnessed their production and performance. For plays, to a certain extent the social composition of the audience depended on the type of theatre in which the play was performed. Amphitheatres, for example the Swan and the Globe which were completed in 1595 and 1599, were open-air theatres which offered standing room around the stage in the 'yard' and seating in the galleries for a total of some 3,000 people. In contrast, the indoor hall playhouses, such as Blackfriars and the Cockpit, were built in the early seventeenth century to accommodate only about 750 people.[48] The minimum price of admission to the hall playhouses in 1596 was 6d, compared with 1d for entrance to an amphitheatre. The cheapest seat in a hall playhouse could buy the best seat in an amphitheatre, a fact that must have encouraged those with minimal incomes only to patronise the amphitheatres.[49] An observer in the 1590s, when only amphitheatres were open, noted the social diversity of a crowd leaving a theatre:

> For as we see at all the play house doors,
> When ended is the play, the dance, and song:
> A thousand townsmen, gentlemen, and whores,
> Porters and serving-men together throng.[50]

There is much evidence to suggest that although the hall houses may have attracted a greater proportion of audience from the middling to upper stratas of society, theatre audiences remained socially heterogeneous groups. It is highly unlikely that, as Ann Jennalie Cook suggested, playgoing before the civil war was ever restricted to the privileged and idle rich. Ben Jonson noted 'sinful sixpenny mechanics' in the audience of hall houses in the 1630s, the gentry were known to patronise both amphitheatres and hall houses, and acting companies such as the King's Men continued to play the same repertoire at both types of theatre.[51]

In 1660 English theatres were reopened after the civil war. Charles II's active interest and patronage of the theatre, and his friendship with many of its playwrights such as John Dryden, George Etherege and William Wycherley, has led academics to consider how far theatre audiences became dominated by the court elite, and plays came to be written solely to please this aristocratic audience. Certainly, it would appear from the comments of diarists such as Pepys that the aristocrats who went to the theatre were a highly visible clientele, but numerically they were probably never in the majority since the new theatres which were built, such as Drury Lane, seated between 500 and 1,000 people. From evidence based on the physical size and structure of theatres, and the collection of anecdotal comments that contemporaries made, probably all we can conclude is that while the audience of theatres remained socially heterogeneous throughout the seventeenth century, the overall social profile of Restoration audiences was less varied than before the civil war.[52]

Women were regular theatregoers throughout the period. Their social status ranged from vagrants and whores, through to royalty and the ladies of the court.[53] The actors of pre-civil war theatre were all male, but from the 1660s actresses began to share the stage. Elizabeth Howe argues that giving women a voice in such a public arena would have been deeply threatening to the gender order if playwrights had not given actresses female roles which reinforced traditional images of womanhood – the virgin maid in search of marriage, the chaste wife guarding her husband's honour, and so on. An actress was also regarded and treated as a whore, for 'as a sexual object she was no danger to the patriarchal system, but rather its toy'.[54] Whilst the majority of playwrights and their patrons continued to be male, women's status on the stage remained poor, and their representation was shaped by male perceptions and prescriptions. As this book will show, the result is that from seventeenth-century drama we learn much about male honour, and of what men thought female honour should consist.

But what do we know about how contemporaries, male and female, reacted to the plays that were performed? We have to be cautious in our use of written texts, for today we are left with texts of plays which were designed for oral and visual performance. As Michael Hattaway has explained, 'the act of translation from text to performance . . . could well have been an act of transformation'.[55] Furthermore, once the manuscript of a play was sold to a publisher he was free to make minor alterations as he saw fit. In other words, what we study today may well differ from the text of the play that was originally performed.[56] We do have some contemporary accounts about the experience of playgoing. Evidence suggests that early modern audiences may have had advanced listening skills which enabled them to recall passages of plays and remember the words and tunes of long ballads. These skills were encouraged by the practice of rote learning in elementary schools, and were fostered by the presence of a strong tradition of oral culture.[57] But as Andrew Gurr's study has shown, the surviving accounts of playgoing are often disappointing for the scholar, as writers usually followed a conventional pattern of briefly describing the plots of the plays, with little or no comment on what reaction this plot provoked for the writer or other members of the audience.[58] Whereas at the theatre the audience may have acted collectively, clapping and applauding or jeering and hissing, it is likely that within that audience there would have been many different individual interpretations of each play which was performed. Different interpretations of the same performance may have depended upon class, gender, marital status, education, and so on, with each individual 'appropriating' from the performance according to his or her needs.[59]

We do know that for many members of the audience playgoing was concerned with far more than simply watching a play. Audiences were rarely quiet during a performance, but instead exchanged the latest gossip, argued, and even occasionally fought duels. Pepys 'lost the pleasure of the play wholly' when 'two talking ladies and Sir Ch. Sidly' talked all through a play.[60] Playgoing was a social occasion which provided opportunity for ostentatious show and defence of honour, in addition to any discussion of the matter on the stage. Audience reactions to individual performances are difficult to assess, but what is undeniable is that sexual honour was an extremely popular theme. Just a brief survey of the plays over the period reminds us how crucial the subject of honour was to their content. William Shakespeare's *The Merry Wives of Windsor* (1597) is the humorous story of Ford's attempts to protect his sexual honour; *Othello* (*c.*1604) is so wracked with jealousy that he kills his wife who he believes has cuckolded him; Bassanes in John Ford's *The Broken Heart* (*c.*1629) is another jealous husband who tries to imprison his wife in their house to protect his honour; as is Pinchwife in William Wycherley's *The Country Wife* (1675), and the drunken Sir John Brute in John Vanbrugh's *The Provoked Wife* (1697).

There were so many ballads, or stories in song, written about men who had lost their sexual honour in the seventeenth century, that when Pepys came to organise his collection of them he entitled one large group 'Marriage, Cuckoldry etc.'. From the study of broadside ballads we can begin to discover the meaning of male honour within the mental world of the lower and middling orders in seventeenth-century England. Some 138 ballads have been consulted from the *Pepys*, *Roxburghe*, *Euing* and *Shirburn* collections. This number of ballads represents a significant proportion of ballads concerning marriage which survive as many of the same ballads are reprinted in these collections. Ballads were printed in Gothic script on a broadside, or a single sheet of flimsy paper with printing on one side only. The price of a ballad ranged between half a penny and a penny, the cost of half a loaf of bread, a pot of ale, or a standing place to view a play in an amphitheatre.[61] They were written by men who were either professional ballad authors such as Martin Parker and Thomas Deloney, or by occasional writers with an eye for a good story. Few biographical details are known about these writers, other than that ballad writing was not regarded as a highly profitable trade.[62] Ballads were distributed in rural areas by country chapmen, and by specialist ballad sellers on street corners, market places and in alehouses of urban centres. Pedlars such as Shakespeare's Autolycus were familiar figures in early modern England, and often also carried ballads within their stock-in-trade.[63] The successful sale of a ballad depended to a great extent on the performance of the ballad seller who acted as a showman singing the ballad to one of some 1,000 popular tunes.[64] In contrast to theatre audiences, this method of sale and the relatively cheap price of ballads made them a form of culture which was accessible to a socially and geographically diverse audience. A network of ballad sellers who travelled from the publishers in London reached areas as wide apart as York, Berwick, Preston and Carlisle, establishing between them a national market for this form of cheap print.[65] When an Act was passed in 1696–97 to license all hawkers, pedlars and chapmen travelling on foot, over 2,500 of them were licensed within the first year from all over the country.[66] The numbers of ballads produced was enormous; as well as the thousands of ballads which were printed by unlicensed presses, we know of 3,000 titles which were registered with the Stationers' Company between 1557 and 1709.[67] Tessa Watt has estimated that there may have been a total number of three to four million copies of ballads in circulation in the second half of the sixteenth century.[68]

In 1595 Nicholas Bownde commented on the audience of ballads, and wrote that,

> In the shops of Artificers, and cottages of poor husbandmen . . . you shall sooner see one of these new Ballads, which are made only to keep them occupied . . . then any of the Psalms, and may perceive them to be cunninger in singing the one, then the other.[69]

Some fifty years later Izaak Walton referred to 'An honest ale-house where we shall find a cleanly room, lavender in the windows, and twenty ballads stuck about the wall'.[70] How many of the occupants of these cottages and alehouses would have been able to read these ballads? David Cressy has examined evidence from those who could sign their names in this period and has concluded that roughly 30 per cent of men in rural England could sign their names by the 1640s, with a slightly higher percentage in London. In all the geographical areas which Cressy studied, the literacy of women lagged behind that of men. But Margaret Spufford has shown that reading was a skill that was taught and learnt in elementary schools before writing. A boy could be taught to read within the first year of his schooling before the age of six or seven when he might have to join the family workforce.[71] So it is likely that ballads were within the reading skills of considerable numbers of husbandmen and labourers. But for every ballad sold, far larger numbers of people were likely to hear its message because ballads were designed primarily to be sung, not read. As Christopher Marsh has recognised in his recent production of audio tapes featuring performances of seventeenth-century ballads, the music of these ballads could powerfully convey aural messages. Furthermore, most ballads also featured a woodcut picture, which must also have aided comprehensibility to the non-literate or semi-literate. So as Marsh has argued, a distinction must be drawn between the market and the audience for ballads. Literacy was 'a supplementary form of access rather than a vital password without which the door to print remained firmly closed'.[72] Hence women, as the most illiterate group within this society, could be heard singing ballads when Dorothy Osborne, wife of Sir William Temple, walked on a common in 1653, 'where a great many young wenches keep sheep and cows and sit in the shade singing of ballads'.[73]

There is also evidence that ballads were enjoyed by those from the upper echelons of early modern society. Some ballads were directed to those of high social status, for example the ballad entitled, 'A Lanthorne for Landlords'.[74] Chapbooks (cheap books produced by folding broadsides into pages) were often the childhood reading of the social elite, and it seems likely that ballads may also have served this purpose. Adults from the upper sorts also purchased and read or sang ballads. This type of literature was not always used with respect; Sir William Cornwallis kept 'pamphlets and lying-stories and two-penny poets' in his privy to be first read there, and then used. The ideas purveyed in ballads were clearly not restricted to the lower sorts.[75] We have the wealthier members of seventeenth-century communities to thank for the survival of many ballads today, since it was men such as Pepys who collected and saved the ballads of his time.

Audiences of ballads and plays in the seventeenth century cannot be polarised into elite and non-elite groups; the presence of the lower sorts in theatres and the evidence for elite participation in ballad culture shows us that social groups shared many of the same cultural experiences. Nevertheless, ballads can be said to represent 'popular' culture as their authors, distributors and audiences were mainly non-elite, as opposed to theatre audiences in which the elite were a more visible presence, especially after the Restoration. As this book will demonstrate, however, repeated story lines featuring the fate of cuckolded or jealous husbands in both genres ensured that all social groups had access to common understandings of what constituted male sexual honour. Rather than witnessing an increasing divergence of cultures into elite and non-elite, it will be argued that the seventeenth century saw social classes united in their desire to gain and protect sexual honour.[76]

By concentrating on men who married, this book will be a study of a particular cohort of the male population. There were men for whom marriage was not a possibility. Before the 1851 census we can only estimate very roughly how many men and women never married. We cannot calculate rates of celibacy from English burial registers as they did not consistently record marital status. Using methods of back projection to calculate the numbers of those never marrying, the demographers E.A. Wrigley and R.S. Schofield in their *Population History* admitted that they were 'only capable of producing estimates subject to a substantial margin of error'. More recently, Schofield has calculated that as many as 20 per cent of women born between 1604 and 1654 never married. Statistics for the numbers of men who never married are even harder to find. Richard Wall's estimates show that between 3 and 27 per cent of men aged 50–59 in three rural communities between the years 1599 and 1684 never married. In two urban centres, Lichfield and Stoke, in 1692 and 1701 respectively, 8 and 15 per cent of men aged 50–59 had never married. While remaining extremely difficult to calculate, it does appear that numbers of those who never married may have varied over the course of the seventeenth century, and between rural and urban communities.[77] Such patterns could have produced the phenomenon suggested by Peter Laslett, who has calculated that one-fifth of households in early modern England were headed by women, either as spinsters or widows.[78] Of course, if a man remained unmarried, this did not exclude him from heading a household of servants, or even from regarding these servants as part of his 'family'.[79] But there were quite clearly households where the ideals of patriarchy held different meanings, or even little relevance. Relations between homosexual men were obviously conducted along different lines from those described in this book, although the idea of homosexuality as an identity had no meaning in the seventeenth century. The abhorrence for sodomy as an 'unnatural' act, however, was derived from a world in which heterosexual relationships were seen as the norm in the formation of manhood.

Chapter 2 of this book will show how sexual relationships with women could play a crucial part in the process of becoming an honourable man at this time. It will discuss how changing notions of honour amongst the upper sorts during the early modern period meant that they began to share ideas about sexual honour with other social groups. It will examine the experiences of men before marriage, and show how youth could be a period of experimentation and intense competition as men tested the limits of their bodily and sexual control. Chapter 3 will show that once married, few men could afford to rest easy. Adult manhood required continuous assertion and protection, as the talk and behaviour of women was popularly thought to have the power to undermine honourable manhood at any time. The shame which could follow for men who could not maintain sexual control over their wives is discussed in Chapter 4. Fear of the loss of sexual honour could have implications for men's relationships with each other as well as their wives. As the final chapter will show, those faced with sexual dishonour responded by taking action within the courts and outside them. Both legal and extra-legal options held pitfalls. The conclusion will address the issue of change and continuity in the meanings of manhood during the seventeenth century. By looking forward into the eighteenth century and beyond, it will demonstrate how ideas about manhood, sex and marriage in the seventeenth century held unique solutions to the problem of how men could gain and retain power over women both inside and outside the home.

Notes

1. 'The Benefit of Marriage', *Euing*, no. 18, p. 24.
2. 'The Married-mans best portion', *Pepys*, vol. IV, p. 84.
3. K. Wrightson, *English Society 1580–1680* (London, 1982), p. 92.
4. For excellent discussion of many of these issues see, A. Vickery, 'Golden age to separate spheres? A review of the categories and chronology of English women's history' *Historical Journal* 36, 2 (1993), pp. 383–414.
5. J.M. Bennett, 'Feminism and history' *GH* 1, 3 (1989), pp. 251–72; see also her 'Medieval women, modern women: across the great divide', in D. Aers, ed., *Culture and History 1350–1600: Essays on English Communities, Identities and Writing* (London, 1992), pp. 164–5.
6. W. Gouge, *Of Domesticall Duties*, 3rd edn (London, 1634), pp. 15, 17, 28.
7. J. Dod and R. Cleaver, *A Godlie Forme of Householde Government* (London, 1612), p. 16.

8. R.W. Connell, *Masculinities* (Cambridge, 1995), pp. 76–9; see also R.W. Connell, *Gender and Power: Society, the Person and Sexual Politics* (Cambridge, 1987), pp. 183–6.

9. J. Tosh, 'What should historians do with masculinity? Reflections on nineteenth-century Britain' *HWJ* 33 (1994), p. 191.

10. The best introduction to this is A. Bray, *Homosexuality in Renaissance England* (London, 1988).

11. J.A. Sharpe, *Defamation and Sexual Slander in Early Modern England: The Church Courts at York,* Borthwick Papers 58 (York, 1980); M. Ingram, *Church Courts, Sex and Marriage in England, 1570–1640* (Cambridge, 1987).

12. L. Gowing, *Domestic Dangers: Women, Words, and Sex in Early Modern London* (Oxford, 1996).

13. C.L. Barber, *The Idea of Honour in the English Drama 1591–1700* (Göteborg, 1957); C.B. Watson, *Shakespeare and the Renaissance Concept of Honour* (Princeton, 1960).

14. See, for example, N.Z. Davis, *Fiction in the Archives: Pardon Tales and their Tellers in Sixteenth-Century France* (Cambridge, 1987), pp. 38–40, 96–101; R.A. Nye, *Masculinity and Male Codes of Honor in Modern France* (Oxford, 1993), pp. 1–71; L. Roper, *Oedipus and the Devil: Witchcraft, Sexuality and Religion in Early Modern Europe* (London, 1994), ch. 3; E.S. Cohen, 'Honor and gender in the streets of early modern Rome' *Journal of Interdisciplinary History* 22, 4 (1992), pp. 597–625; and M.I. Millington and A.S. Sinclair, 'The honourable cuckold: models of masculine defence' *Comparative Literature Studies* 29, 1 (1992), pp. 1–19.

15. K.A. Esdaile, *English Church Monuments 1560–1840* (London, 1946); N. Llewellyn, *The Art of Death: Visual Culture in the English Death Ritual* c.*1500–1800* (London, 1991), and 'Honour in life, death and in the memory: funeral monuments in early modern England' *TRHS* Sixth Series, VI (1996), pp. 179–200.

16. G. Walker, 'Expanding the boundaries of female honour in early modern England' *TRHS* Sixth Series, VI (1996), pp. 235–45. The importance of this aspect of a woman's honour was to continue, see A. Clark, 'Whores and gossips: sexual reputation in London 1770–1825', in A. Angerman, G. Binnema, A. Keunen, V. Poels and J. Zirkzee, eds, *Current Issues in Women's History* (London, 1989), p. 236.

17. DDR.V.10B. f. 300v.

18. CA, Case 3392 (1667), Ee3, ff. 225–6, 257v–258v, Eee2, ff. 274v–276v, Eee3, ff. 105r–111r, 127v–129r. For the importance of social or economic status to women see also F. Dabhoiwala, 'The construction of honour, reputation and status in late seventeenth- and early eighteenth-century England' *TRHS* Sixth Series, VI (1996), pp. 208–9.

19. For examples of men and women being called popish or heathen see DDR.V.9. f. 176r, DDR.V.9. f. 262r, and DDR.V.11. f. 292r. The relationship between masculinity and religious faith is only just beginning to be explored, for examples see S. Hardman Moore, 'Sexing the soul: gender and the rhetoric of puritan piety' *Studies in Church History* (forthcoming); and J. Gregory, 'Homo-religiosis: masculinity and religion in the long eighteenth century', in T. Hitchcock and M. Cohen, eds, *English Masculinities, 1660–1800* (forthcoming from Longman).

20. S.D. Amussen, *An Ordered Society: Gender and Class in Early Modern England* (Oxford, 1988), pp. 152–5; C. Muldrew, 'Credit and the courts: debt litigation in a seventeenth-century urban community' *Economic History Review* 46, 1 (1993), pp. 23–38, and 'Interpreting the market: the ethics of credit and community relations in early modern England' *Social History* 18 (1993), pp. 163–83.

21. See, for example, T. Adams, *The Souldiers Honour* (London, 1617), and N. Newbury, *The Yeoman's Prerogative Or, The Honor of Husbandry* (London, 1652).

22. DDR.V.8. f. 241.

23. M.E. Wiesner, *Gender, Church and State in Early Modern Germany* (London, 1998), ch. 10; R.C. Davis, *The War of the Fists: Popular Culture and Public Violence in Late Renaissance Venice* (Oxford, 1994), esp. pp. 90–109; Roper, *Oedipus and the Devil,* p. 65, and ch. 5. I am grateful to Alexandra Shepard for bringing these issues to my

attention, and for allowing me to read sections of her forthcoming Ph.D. thesis, 'Meanings of manhood in early modern England with special reference to Cambridge *c.*1560–1640' (Cambridge University), which promises to increase significantly our understanding of manhood in these contexts.

24. DDR.V.8. f. 24r.

25. C. Herrup, '"To pluck bright honour from the pale-faced moon": Gender and honour in the Castlehaven story' *TRHS* Sixth Series, VI (1996), p. 139; for an interesting discussion of the meanings of these different terms of honour see also Dabhoiwala, 'The construction', pp. 201–4.

26. K. Wrightson, 'Estates, degrees, and sorts: changing perceptions of society in Tudor and Stuart England', in P. Corfield, ed., *Language, History and Class* (Oxford, 1991), pp. 30–52, and 'Sorts of people in Tudor and Stuart England', in J. Barry and C. Brooks, eds, *The Middling Sort of People: Culture, Society and Politics in England, 1550–1800* (London, 1994), pp. 28–51. Of course, as Wrightson points out, this division of sorts became tripartite with the emergence of the 'middling sorts'.

27. M. James, *English Politics and the Concept of Honour 1485–1642*, Past and Present Supplement 3 (The Past and Present Society, 1978), p. 28.

28. S.D. Amussen, '"The part of a Christian man": the cultural politics of manhood in early modern England', in S.D. Amussen and M.A. Kishlansky, eds, *Political Culture and Cultural Politics in Early Modern England: Essays Presented to David Underdown* (Manchester, 1995).

29. Ingram, *Church Courts*, pp. 295–300; Sharpe, *Defamation*, pp. 3–11; for a summary of the difficulties of using quarter sessions records to study slander see Dabhoiwala, 'The construction', pp. 208–9, footnote 24; for work on slander which does use evidence from the secular courts see for example A. Gregory, 'Slander accusations and social control in late sixteenth and early seventeenth century England, with particular reference to Rye (Sussex), 1590–1615' (unpublished Ph.D. thesis, Sussex University, 1984); and R. Cust, 'Honour and politics in early Stuart England: the case of Beaumont v. Hastings' *PP* 149 (1995), pp. 57–94.

30. Amussen, *An Ordered Society*, p. 99.

31. For consistory court procedure see R. Houlbrooke, *Church Courts and the People During the English Reformation* (Oxford, 1979), pp. 38–54; Ingram, *Church Courts*, pp. 43–58; R.A. Marchant, *The Church Under the Law: Justice, Administration and Discipline in the Diocese of York 1560–1640* (Cambridge, 1969), pp. 60–5.

32. J.A. Sharpe, '"Such disagreement betwyx neighbours" Litigation and human relations in early modern England', in J. Bossy, ed., *Disputes and Settlements: Law and Human Relations in the West* (Cambridge, 1983), pp. 180–1; for examples of the different forms that penance could take see Ingram, *Church Courts*, pp. 53–4; R.H. Helmholz, 'Canonical defamation in medieval England' *American Journal of Legal History* 15 (1971), pp. 266–7; for an excellent example of the shame and humiliation that could be instilled by performing penance see E.P. Thompson, *Customs in Common* (London, 1991), pp. 502–3.

33. C. Hill, *Society and Puritanism in Pre-Revolutionary England* (London, 1964), pp. 298–343.

34. J. Houston, ed., *Index of Cases in the Records of the Court of Arches at Lambeth Palace Library 1660–1913* (London, 1972); in this book case numbers and dates are taken from Houston's index.

35. For introductions to the court of Arches see M.D. Slatter, 'The records of the court of Arches' *Journal of Ecclesiastical History* 4 (1953), pp. 139–53, and 'The study of the records of the court of Arches' *Journal of the Society of Archivists* 1 (1955), pp. 29–31; M. Barber, 'Records of marriage and divorce in Lambeth Palace' *Genealogists' Magazine* 20, 4 (1980), pp. 109–17, and 'Records of the court of Arches in Lambeth Palace Library' *Ecclesiatical Law Journal* 3 (1993), pp. 10–19.

36. For general surveys on the history of divorce see L. Stone, *Road to Divorce: England 1530–1987* (Oxford, 1990), and R. Phillips, *Putting Asunder: A History of Divorce in Western Society* (Cambridge, 1988).

37. Stone, *Road to Divorce*, p. 34.

38. CA, Case 4177 (1669), J1/6, 19; CA, Case 1544 (1697), J4/59; Stone, *Road to Divorce*, pp. 187–90; the costs of defamation cases will be discussed in Chapter 5 below.

39. Davis, *Fiction in the Archives*, passim; Gowing, *Domestic Dangers*, esp. ch. 7; Stone, *Road to Divorce*, pp. 29–33.

40. J.E. Howard, 'The new historicism in renaissance studies', in R. Wilson and R. Dutton, eds, *New Historicism and Renaissance Drama* (London, 1992), p. 28.

41. As cited in M.J. Johnson, *Images of Women in the Works of Thomas Heywood* (Salzburg, 1974), p. 161; the power of drama to affect popular morality was the subject of much contemporary concern, see J.E. Howard, *The Stage and Social Struggle in Early Modern England* (London, 1994).

42. D. Lindley, *The Trials of Frances Howard: Fact and Fiction at the Court of King James* (London, 1996), p. 3.

43. See Chapter 5 below; Gowing has made similar conclusions in her *Domestic Dangers*, pp. 56–8, 189, 204–6, 244–5.

44. Lindley, *The Trials of Frances Howard*, p. 3 and passim; F.E. Dolan, *Dangerous Familiars: Representations of Domestic Crime in England 1550–1700* (Ithaca NY, 1994), p. 79; T. Stretton, *Women Waging Law in Elizabethan England* (forthcoming from Cambridge University Press), ch. 3; A. Fox, 'Ballads, libels and popular ridicule in Jacobean England' *PP* 145 (1994), pp. 47–83.

45. As cited in K. Thomas, *History and Literature* (Swansea, 1988), p. 3.

46. P. Carter, 'Men about town: representations of foppery and masculinity in early eighteenth-century urban society', in H. Barker and E. Chalus, eds, *Gender in Eighteenth-Century England* (London, 1997), p. 33.

47. M. Roper and J. Tosh, 'Introduction: historians and the politics of masculinity', in M. Roper and J. Tosh, eds, *Manful Assertions: Masculinities in Britain since 1800* (London, 1991), pp. 11, 15; Tosh, 'What should historians do', p. 194; J. Tosh, 'The old Adam and the new man: emerging themes in the history of English masculinities, 1750–1850', in Cohen and Hitchcock, eds, *English Masculinities 1660–1800.*

48. A. Gurr, *Playgoing in Shakespeare's London* (Cambridge, 1987), pp. 13–22; R.A. Foakes, 'Playhouses and players', in A.R. Braunmuller and M. Hattaway, eds, *The Cambridge Companion to English Renaissance Drama* (Cambridge, 1990), pp. 1–52.

49. Gurr, *Playgoing*, pp. 4–5, 26–7, 75.

50. As cited in Gurr, *Playgoing*, p. 66.

51. A.J. Cook, *The Privileged Playgoers of Shakespeare's London, 1576–1642* (Princeton NJ, 1981); Foakes, 'Playhouses and players', p. 37; see also the varied social status of known playgoers in Gurr, *Playgoing*, Appendix 1.

52. E.L. Avery, 'The Restoration audience' *Philological Quarterly* 45 (1966), pp. 54–61; P. Holland, *The Ornament of Action: Text and Performance in Restoration Comedy* (Cambridge, 1979); A.H. Scouten and R.D. Hume, ' "Restoration Comedy" and its Audiences, 1660–1776', in R.D. Hume, ed., *The Rakish Stage: Studies in English Drama 1660–1800* (Carbondale IL, 1983), pp. 46–56; R.W. Bevis, *English Drama: Restoration and Eighteenth Century, 1660–1789* (London, 1988), pp. 31–6.

53. Howard, *The Stage*, ch. 4; D. Roberts, *The Ladies: Female Patronage of Restoration Drama 1660–1700* (Oxford, 1989).

54. E. Howe, *The First English Actresses: Women and Drama 1660–1700* (Cambridge, 1992), pp. 32–6, 171–7.

55. M. Hattaway, 'Drama and society', in Braunmuller and Hattaway, eds, *The Cambridge Companion*, p. 94.

56. S. Orgel, 'What is a text?', in D.S. Kastan and P. Stallybrass, eds, *Staging the Renaissance: Reinterpretations of Elizabethan and Jacobean Drama* (London, 1991), pp. 83–7.

57. Gurr, *Playgoing*, pp. 80–1; M.C. Bradbrook, *Themes and Conventions of Elizabethan Tragedy* (Cambridge, 1980), pp. 72–3.

58. Gurr, *Playgoing*, pp. 105–14, Appendix 2; and G. Salgado, *Eyewitnesses of Shakespeare: First Hand Accounts of Performances 1590–1890* (Sussex, 1975), part I.

59. R. Chartier, *The Cultural Uses of Print in Early Modern France* (trans., Princeton, 1987); for an excellent case study of the appropriation of texts see C. Ginzburg, *The Cheese and the Worms: The Cosmos of a Sixteenth Century Miller* (trans., London, 1980).

60. As cited in Howe, *The First English Actresses*, p. 7.

61. T. Watt, *Cheap Print and Popular Piety, 1550–1640* (Cambridge, 1991), pp. 11–12; N. Wurzbach, *The Rise of the English Street Ballad 1550–1650* (Cambridge, 1990), p. 20; J. Wiltenburg, *Disorderly Women and Female Power in the Street Literature of Early Modern England and Germany* (Charlottesville VA, 1992), p. 30; for ballads which state that they cost one penny see for example, 'A Groatsworth of Good Counsel', *Roxburghe*, vol. VI, part III, pp. 480–1; and 'Half a dozen of good Wives: All for a penny' (1634), *Roxburghe*, vol. I, pp. 451–6.

62. Wurzbach, *The Rise of the English Street Ballad*, pp. 21–3; B. Capp, 'Popular literature', in B. Reay, ed., *Popular Culture in Seventeenth-Century England* (London, 1985), pp. 199–200.

63. W. Shakespeare, *The Winter's Tale* (*c.*1609), ed. J.H.P. Pafford (London, 1990), IV.iii–iv; M. Spufford, *The Great Reclothing of Rural England: Petty Chapmen and their Wares in the Seventeenth Century* (London, 1984), pp. 85–9.

64. Wurzbach, *The Rise of the English Street Ballad*, pp. 13–17; Watt, *Cheap Print*, pp. 23–5, 33–7.

65. Watt, *Cheap Print*, pp. 6, 27–9.

66. M. Spufford, *Small Books and Pleasant Histories: Popular Fiction and its Readership in Seventeenth-Century England* (London, 1981), pp. 116–21.

67. V.E. Neuburg, *Popular Literature: A History and a Guide* (Harmondsworth, 1977), p. 62.

68. Watt, *Cheap Print*, pp. 11, 42.

69. As cited in Spufford, *Small Books*, pp. 10–11.

70. As cited in Wurzbach, *The Rise of the English Street Ballad*, p. 279.

71. D. Cressy, *Literacy and the Social Order: Reading and Writing in Tudor and Stuart England* (Cambridge, 1980), pp. 72, 128–9; M. Spufford, 'First steps in literacy: the reading and writing experiences of the humblest seventeenth-century autobiographers' *Social History* 4, 3 (1979), pp. 407–35; Spufford, *Small Books*, pp. 19–33.

72. C. Marsh, *Songs of the Seventeenth Century* (Belfast, 1994), pp. 8–9, 25, 27, 41–8; Watt, *Cheap Print*, pp. 131–77.

73. K. Parker, ed., *Letters to Sir William Temple* (London, 1987), p. 89.

74. As cited in Marsh, *Songs*, p. 21.

75. Spufford, *Small Books*, pp. 48–9, 72–4.

76. For the debate over the polarisation of culture in this period, and discussion over the meaning of popular culture, see P. Burke, *Popular Culture in Early Modern Europe* (London, 1978), and his 'Introduction' to the revised reprint (Aldershot, 1994), pp. xiv–xxvii; T. Harris, 'Problematising popular culture', in T. Harris, ed., *Popular Culture in England,* c.*1500–1850* (London, 1995), pp. 1–27; M. Ingram, 'Ridings, rough music and the reform of popular culture in early modern England' *PP* 105 (1984), pp. 79–113; and Marsh, *Songs*, pp. 30–8.

77. E.A. Wrigley and R.S. Schofield, *The Population History of England 1541–1871: A Reconstruction* (Cambridge, 1989), pp. 257–65; R. Schofield, 'English marriage patterns revisited' *Journal of Family History* 10 (1985), p. 14; R. Wall, 'European family and household systems', in Société Belge de Démographie, *Historiens et Populations: Liber Amicorum Etienne Hélin* (Limoges, 1991), pp. 634–5; I am very grateful to Roger Schofield for his assistance with this reading.

78. P. Laslett, 'Mean household size', in P. Laslett and R. Wall, eds, *Household and Family in Past Time* (Cambridge, 1972), pp. 77–8; for more conservative estimates see R. Wall, 'Women alone in English society' *Annales de Démographie Historique* (1981), pp. 303–4.

79. N. Tadmor, 'The concept of the household-family in eighteenth-century England' *PP* 151 (1996), pp. 111–140.

CHAPTER TWO

Constructing Manhood

Manhood

'Having a penis does not make the man', Thomas Laqueur has explained, describing the period before the eighteenth century as one in which men's reading of the body favoured the one-sex model, and physiological difference between male and female was not clearly defined. According to this model, the human body was thought to be made up from four humours – blood, phlegm, yellow bile and black bile – and it was their relative heat or moistness which determined maleness or femaleness. Men had a propensity to be hot and dry; women cold and moist. Men and women were anatomically the same, it was just because women were colder that their penis and scrotum were inverted inside their bodies as the uterus and the womb. A wide range of medical texts subscribed to this humoural or Galenic interpretation of the body. Men and women, according to this line of thinking, were not different, rather the female body was an inferior or imperfect version of the male. 'The boundaries between male and female' were those 'of degree and not of kind'.[1]

Today it is hard to imagine that our predecessors thought in such radically different ways about their bodies. Laqueur, and those historians who draw upon his findings, have often been criticised for failing to distinguish between elite male medical thinking or theory, and popular belief or practice. Lyndal Roper and Laura Gowing, for example, have pointed to the ways in which women experienced and talked about their bodies, showing how women were fully aware of their difference from men.[2] Women who menstruated, became pregnant, gave birth and were menopausal went through demonstrably different bodily experiences from men. Men's shunning of women who were menstruating, and women's celebration of childbirth in women-only rituals, are both signs of a popular awareness of female bodily difference.[3] The ways in which men experienced their bodies still remain little explored. But then, as now, the one-sex model provoked reaction. The assertion of 'difference' was as common in the past to men as it was to women. For men constructed gender identities to make them appear fundamentally different from women. They labelled certain behaviours as 'male' and others as 'female'. The two key 'male' characteristics were reason and strength. Men and women were defined in relation to each other's qualities: 'a woman is not as strong as a man', explained Lemnius in the 1630s, 'nor hath so much reason'.[4] It was thought that once men had learnt the essential qualities for their gender, they could then use them to maintain and justify a position of power over women. God had meant to give the male 'great wit, bigger strength, and more courage to compel the woman to obey by reason or force', Sir Thomas Smith wrote in 1583.[5]

In Western philosophy there was a long tradition of thought stemming from Plato which associated reason with men. Men were different from beasts because of their reason, but women were thought nearer to the animal state than were men.[6] Hence Bassanes in John Ford's play *The Broken Heart* (*c.*1629) reflects that whilst beasts are 'only capable of sense', men are 'endowed with reason', and thus are 'verier beasts than beasts'.[7] The contemporary philosopher Descartes (1596–1650), whose ideas were to be so important to the Enlightenment, developed this model further by distinguishing the mind from the body, the male from the female.[8] In practice male reason was contrasted with the 'weaker vessel's' susceptibility to passion, lust and temptation. The 1562 homily on marriage, read aloud from the pulpit, taught how, 'the woman is a weak creature not endued with like strength and constancy of mind; therefore they be sooner disquieted and they be the more prone to all weak affectations and dispositions of mind, more than men be, and lighter they be and more vain in their fantasies and opinions'.[9]

Men used their claim to reason to legitimise their authority over women. Thus William Gouge in 1634 explained the subordination of women because, 'as an head preserveth, provideth for the body, so doth the husband his wife'. Here Gouge associates the head with reason and manhood, the body with the female and the wife, who should obey her husband 'because she is set under him, as his body under his head'.[10] This argument for male domination continued through the period, and is shown in a letter the first Marquis of Halifax wrote to his daughter in 1688. He explained, 'that there is

Inequality in the Sexes, and that for the better Economy of the World, the Men, who were to be the Law-givers, had the larger share of Reason bestow'd upon them . . . Your Sex wanteth our Reason for your Conduct, and our Strength for your Protection.'[11] Having more reason not only legitimised male control of those with inferior reason, but also required men to show self-control over their own passions and emotions. 'Teach him to get a Mastery over his Inclinations, and submit his Appetite to Reason', John Locke advised in his 1693 treatise on the upbringing of sons.[12] The ability to reason was a skill to be learnt. 'What wast thou, being an infant', asked Lewis Bayly, 'but a brute having the shape of a man?'[13] The 1630 ballad 'Tis not otherwise' tells the story of a young man who used to preach against marriage, but it is said that 'had years but given him man-like thoughts, he'd not been so unwise'. Once he matures wisdom makes him a man and he is persuaded to marry.[14] William Shakespeare's *King Lear* (*c.*1605) powerfully shows how an old king who loses his sense of reason and good judgement also jeopardises his manhood. As Lear's madness sets in he fears that his manhood is shaken when, unable to master his emotions, he is subject to 'women's weapons' or 'hot tears'; his crown is replaced by a garland of wild flowers; and when reunited with Cordelia she observes her 'child-changed father'. If Lear's daughters can show that their father has no reason, they know that he will no longer be judged a fit king worthy to rule others. So a man's reason can be dependent on age; it is absent in a child, has to be learnt to obtain full manhood, but is in danger of being lost in old age.[15] Manhood is at risk at any point if there are signs of lack of reason; *Macbeth* (1606) is 'unmann'd' when his guilt about the murder of Banquo causes him to lose his grip on reason, and he imagines that he has seen Banquo's ghost.[16]

Physical strength was an obvious characteristic which men believed made them different from women. According to the humoural model women had naturally less strength than men; their coldness made their bodies frail and function less efficiently, literally rendering them the 'weaker vessel'.[17] But as with reason, physical strength also had to be nurtured in boys and young men. As one writer of advice to parents put it, a young man was merely a 'stripling' who needed strengthening.[18] Just how parents should encourage that physical strength was a matter of some debate. Few probably went as far as John Locke suggested in 1693 and made holes in their sons' shoes to let in water, and gave their sons hard beds to sleep upon.[19] Many boys and young men probably learnt the importance of physical strength during their recreation time. Football and wrestling matches tested the courage and strength of those from the middling and lower sorts, whilst the social elite engaged in sports such as hunting, fencing and running.[20] As Paul Griffiths has recognised in his work on youth, 'physical strength, which was paraded in bouts of fighting, taunting, aggressive language, vandalism, and posturing was one aspect of a developing sense of manhood. It helped young men to distance themselves from children and young women, and to identify with older men.'[21] Courageous endurance of physical pain could also be part of this gender training, as boys tended to receive more physical punishment than girls at school and at home.[22] In these ways the upbringing of boys marked their separateness from their sisters: 'the breeding of men were after a different manner of ways from those of women', Margaret Cavendish, Duchess of Newcastle, observed.[23] Parents who detected precocious physical strength and courage in their young sons could rarely contain their pride. 'He died at the age of five years, yet had the courage and resolution of a man', Hugh Cholmley wrote of his son Richard in 1630; 'he was a beautiful child, and very manly and courageous', recalled Adam Martindale of his two-year-old son in 1663.[24]

Manhood in the early modern period was a status to be acquired and then asserted to others. It was concerned with a rejection of 'feminine' qualities through a display of the 'masculine' qualities of reason and strength. Even if many did not adhere to the medical thinking of the seventeenth century which held that men and women were anatomically the same, as Linda Pollock has shown, there was a widespread recognition that boys could possess both male and female attributes. It was a parent's duty, and that of the individual himself when he reached adulthood, to ensure that his female attributes were kept in abeyance.[25] Masculinity as well as femininity was socially constructed. In practice, as this book will show, sexual difference in seventeenth-century England was founded and constructed in the daily social interactions and relationships between men and women.

Honourable Manhood

Honour, reputation, credit, or good name could be earned if men exercised these male qualities of reason and strength in an approved way. Approval was most likely to be forthcoming if through reason and strength a man could demonstrate self-control and control over the inferiors in his household. But a number of studies of men in the upper echelons of this society have posited that the honour attached to male behaviour varied according to social class. The upper classes, in particular, were assigned codes of behaviour which distinguished them from men in other social groups. It has even been stated that, 'the gentry's code of honour . . . set them apart from other men' and that honour 'is a matter for the upper classes; ordinary people have no pretence to it, and can't afford such a luxury'.[26] Mervyn James was the first of these historians who thought that gentry honour merited separate treatment. His seminal studies argued that in the fifteenth and sixteenth centuries honour was not regarded as an individual possession, but as belonging to the collective entity of the family. James demonstrated how in this period an affront to one member of a family was seen as an insult and challenge to the honour of the whole household. Within the gentry honour descended through lineage from one generation to the next. As male honour was inherited by blood, and concerned with public or political behaviour, James believed it was unaffected by the private or sexual roles which men chose to adopt.[27] With lineage of primary importance to the landed gentry, displaying the male qualities of reason and strength would appear to have little relevance.

James and others based their conclusions on the prescriptive literature addressed to the upper sorts which concerned honour and was written throughout the seventeenth century, from Robert Ashley's *Of Honour* written between 1596 and 1603, to Jean Gailhard's *The Compleat Gentleman* of 1678. The ideas about honour in these tracts were derived from the Christian tradition and from classical sources by writers such as Aristotle and Cicero. A number of works concerning honour were also translations of foreign texts.[28] The authors of these tracts never dispute the importance of a man having honour; it is to be 'more desired than life', and preferred 'above all other good things'.[29] Many writers cite the proverb 'A good Name is to be chosen above great Riches'.[30] The need for honour has become so fundamental to men of this social group that it is even argued that men seek honour and shun shame from natural instinct.[31]

The wealth of visual evidence which remains in today's churches shows that the gentry continued to take pride in their lineage throughout the early modern period. Eulogies on church monuments and family chapels testify to the collective honour of ancient families. In gentry houses examples survive of armorial glass, and of paintings that demonstrate the importance of lineage to these families. Sir John Ferrers painted his parlour at Tamworth Castle with shields to show his pedigree, which he dated back to the Norman Conquest. We also have evidence of gentry interest in lineage from their attempts to trace their ancestry. Sir Richard Grosvenor, for example, employed a local antiquary to investigate his family's history. Some families were even prepared to invent genealogies to win honour. The Wellesbourne family of Hughenden, Buckinghamshire, who were descended from a Wycombe clothier, tried to substantiate their claims that their line actually originated from Wellesbourne de Montfort, illegitimate brother of Earl Simon, by forging medieval seals, carving their coat of arms on a genuine fourteenth-century tomb in their local church, and by constructing a series of effigies of their thirteenth- and fifteenth-century ancestors.[32] That gentlemen saw honour as status accrued beyond the immediate household is shown by evidence that kinship ties continued to have practical importance for many gentry households. Peter Clark has argued that in Kent kinship was an 'important ingredient in the complex web of a gentleman's reputation', and Alan Everitt has substantiated the same point. Blood ties held special duties and loyalties and could provide social and political opportunities for the gentry.[33]

The concept of honour remained a useful political tool for the gentry to enforce and explain the social order. It was the gentry who had the power to bestow honours as rewards on others, and they themselves could owe their positions to the crown. Some treatises described society as a hierarchy of honour with the crown and the gentry at its top. Social groups of inferior status were expected to honour those above them. In this way honour was essentially anti-egalitarian and could be used to justify social difference. As Ashley explained, 'for the dignity and order of the Common wealth there ought to be degrees of Honour, Lest the Common people and the nobility, private men and magistrates ... a King and a Captain should be all of one Accompt'.[34] Writers of these tracts conveniently ignored the competitiveness which could ensue between men in the fight for honour, and instead wrote of how honour acted as a motivator to inspire men to perform good deeds.[35]

But although they may have had the economic means and ostentation to display their lineage visually, concern for social status and the assertion of inherited family honour was by no means confined to the upper ranks of this society. Records of defamation cases show that aspersions on family honour could be taken very seriously much lower down the social scale. In midsummer 1606 in Miles Jefferson's yard in Norton, Durham, Robert Law in the presence of several others of his neighbours openly challenged Ralph Pattenson's good name by asking, 'What art thou?' Ralph Pattenson replied, not giving his occupation as we might expect, but by simply stating that 'he was an honest man's son'. This provoked a torrent of abuse from Robert, 'Nay . . . thou came of a horse stealer, and a sheep stealer and such was thy father thou came of.' Another case heard in the Durham church courts twenty years later may show how an insult was perceived to have greater force if it also involved the slandering of a man's kin. When Ann Strawe called Francis Maltby of Cornforth thief, mainsworne rascal and a beggar, she followed each insult with the words 'and all thy kind'. In the Restoration period, Robert Bendish, a merchant of Eastham, Essex, believed that he could defend himself against his wife's charges of cruelty by claiming that he was 'highly provoked' by her insults against his family. He claimed that she had called his sisters 'whores', and his family 'base mean and beggarly'. Insults against a man's family were clearly not expected to be borne lightly.[36]

The idea that honour or shame could be inherited from one generation to the next is seen in the case of Timothy Barnes against Mary Barnes, wife of Emmanuel. A complex series of events one evening in January led to Mary bringing a defamation suit against Timothy in March 1605, and Timothy bringing a case against Mary in July of the same year. On intelligence that there were papists in Wolsingham, Timothy Barnes in January 1605 had gone to Emmanuel Barnes's house accompanied by a constable. Mary was enraged to see Timothy in the house and ordered him to leave. An argument then broke out. It is obvious from the way that Mary and Timothy interact that this case only reveals a glimpse of a long-term quarrel between the pair. What is most interesting is how their name-calling led to a questioning of the status of their parents. According to the churchwarden Thomas Wright, when Mary called Timothy a rogue, he questioned this and asserted 'I am descended of honour', 'of honour, said she, no', and claimed that he was a priest's bastard son. Another witness said that Timothy also claimed that 'he was a lord's son . . . and he was comed of better parents than she'. In a society of social change and upheaval it could be important for men to assert 'where they came from' and to compare their reputation with others. Whilst Timothy Barnes was probably at the upper end of the 'middling sort' as he was 'employed about the king's business', what these cases show is an awareness of the concept of a man's reputation being inherited through lineage within social groups well below the landed gentry.[37]

The concept of gentry honour was also changing. James argues that over the period 1485–1642 state involvement in traditional gentry politics, together with social and religious change, had a profound effect upon gentry notions of honour. In particular, honour came to be regarded as a reward for individual virtue as well as, or increasingly rather than, an attribute gained through lineage. Writers of conduct books for gentlemen, influenced by the ideas of humanists and Puritans, argued that honour could be claimed by either blood or birth; or virtue or quality; or blood and virtue. It was men who fell into the third category, blood and virtue, who were owed the most honour, and those in the first the least.[38] The relative importance of virtue over lineage was expressed with greater clarity as the seventeenth century progressed. In *The Praise of a Good Name* (1594) Charles Gibbon asserted that 'it is not the Name, but the qualities, not dignity or descent, but the disposition and good demeanour, that makes any renowned and famous'. Richard Braithwait wrote in 1630 that 'Virtue the greatest Signal and Symbol of Gentry: is rather expressed by goodness of Person, than greatness of Place'. By the time Gailhard wrote his treatise in 1678, it was conduct and good breeding which made a man honourable; 'he who is but a Countryman, and lives well as such, seems to me more commendable, than he who is a Gentleman born, and doth not the actions of a Gentleman'.[39] That these ideas were having an effect may be seen by the gentry's loss of interest in gaining formal recognition of their status from heralds' visitations after 1660, and in the changes in memorial architecture. Wall tablets with portraits of busts as memorials to individuals became a more frequent sight in churches than the family tomb with effigies of children along the sides emphasising pedigree and lineage.[40]

Significantly, the actions which these writers of conduct books for gentlemen considered virtuous were those which deployed the manly qualities of strength and reason to worthy ends. Most obviously, on the battlefield physical prowess and courage could earn honour. Tracts such as George Whetstone's *The Honorable Reputation of a Souldier* (1585) emphasised that honour won by military pursuit endured well beyond a man's lifetime.[41] Attitudes as to how this military honour could be won also changed. Whereas early works such as William Segar's *Honour Military, and Civil* (1602) concentrated on the more traditional and chivalric codes of knightly behaviour, later tracts emphasised how military virtue and honour could be obtained by service to the state rather than by fighting private feuds between kin groups.[42] These tracts support James's thesis which argues that society changed in the sixteenth and early seventeenth centuries from one that was characterised by tension and conflict between gentry families, to one that was 'civil' and 'ordered'.[43]

During the relatively peaceful years of the early Stuart period, Roger Manning has argued that hunting 'came to be viewed as a more chivalrous alternative to sixteenth-century land warfare'. It made men 'strong and lusty', argued Gailhard, who was a tutor to young gentlemen. For many young men its rigours and tests of bravery represented an adolescent rite of passage. Gailhard also recommended horsemanship as a 'very manly thing', as well as running, wrestling and leaping. Such sports were extolled for their hardship, and participation was recommended to men who wished to avoid the charge of an over-tender or 'effeminate' education.[44]

Other virtuous actions for gentlemen were the display of piety, charity and justice, all of which required the exercise of wisdom or reason to be employed appropriately. 'Let reason be thy schoolmistress, which shall ever guide thee aright', Sir Walter Raleigh instructed his son.[45] Books of advice for young men gave instructions on suitable conduct for every detail of daily life from rules of speech and dress, to table manners and letter writing. 'Let thy whole carriage, thy very thoughts and desires, be suitable to thy condition, for fear of bringing thy self into danger, harm, shame, and infamy', Gailhard advised.[46] Gentlemen were to be 'professors of civility', wrote one Jacobean commentator. Bodily deportment and demeanour were thought to reflect and enhance social status. The virtuous gentleman was expected to learn how to use his reason to conquer the bestial and present an image that was mannered and ordered. Good manners were increasingly concerned with bodily self-control.[47] In the grammar schools which many sons attended, boys also learnt that it was the Christian virtues of piety and charity which would earn them nobility. Erasmus's teaching on the virtues of Christian belief became a grammar school commonplace: 'let it not move thee one whit when thou hearest the wise men of this world . . . so earnestly disputing of the degrees of their genealogy or lineage . . . thou, laughing at the error of these men . . . shall count . . . that the only most perfect nobleness is to be regenerate in Christ'.[48]

When these boys entered adulthood they were expected to demonstrate in their households the Christian virtues they had learnt.

As Charles Gibbon wrote, 'it is not the glorious show of the house, but the godly actions of the owner that makes him renowned'.[49] Being a godly household head involved showing hospitality to neighbouring gentry families and giving charity to the poor. Felicity Heal explains that honour and reputation in this period were 'attached to good lordship, generosity and the appearance of an open household'.[50] Hospitality allowed the gentry to display their honour to others, as the household provided the ideal forum for a show of wealth, lineage and generosity. Sir John Strode urged other gentry 'let thy doors be (at all seasonable times) open to thy kindred and friends'.[51]

The gentry also saw public office as a means to gain honour. William Segar's tract described duty in civil government as the alternative to military service as a way to win honour.[52] Anthony Fletcher has shown that for many JPs 'prestige not wealth was the principal reward of office'. The wrangles and disputes that occurred in the localities as gentry sought, and sometimes fought for, positions on the bench, reflect the importance of gaining honour in this way.[53] One seventeenth-century magistrate, William Lambard, believed that it was 'by reason of his learning, wisdom, authority and wealth' that the local gentleman was most suited to the role of JP.[54] Just as Lambard placed wealth as the least important of the manly qualities required for service, so there are also signs that election to office became more dependent upon a man's reputation in the community than upon family roots. When Sir Richard Grosvenor stood for election in 1624 the emphasis of his speech to his Cheshire audience was that he qualified for the post as a godly man, rather than because he came from an ancient lineage.[55] No doubt, many Puritan gentry like Sir Richard saw the exercise of religious virtue as the reason for their elevation to positions of honour, as well as the chief function of their office.[56] The learned philosopher in Ford's *The Broken Heart* (*c.*1629) expressed what many of these gentry must have believed, that 'real honour'

> Is the reward of virtue, and acquired
> By justice, or by valour which for basis
> Hath justice to uphold it.[57]

The idea that honour stemmed from virtuous actions never wholly replaced others that laid more emphasis on lineage. After all, for the landed gentry it would have been too politically subversive to suggest that any man who displayed virtue was worthy of honour.[58]

Debates about the importance of birth or personal merit to claims of honour continued to rage through the eighteenth and into the nineteenth century.[59] Even those who saw the value of honour arising from virtue could rarely resist the opportunity to display the honour they had gained through inheritance as well. Thomas Lyte of Lytes Cary, Somerset, who was keen to claim that his interests in genealogy did not stem from 'any ostentation of birth or kindred', and cited Job on the dangers of worldly ambition, nevertheless wrote two pedigrees of his family and decorated his house and chapel with armorial glass.[60] What is more, as Anna Bryson reminds us, the conduct literature from which we gain much of our evidence about changing notions of elite honour, provides us with a picture of the ideals of manliness, rather than its practice. For youthful gentry 'the solid achievement of virtue and learning' may well have been less appealing than traditional pursuits of 'gambling, drinking and fashion'.[61] But crucially, the inclusion of ideas concerning the importance of individual virtue within this literature for gentry, allowed honour to become an ideal which could have shared meanings across a wider social spectrum. In theory, as honour no longer came to man automatically by right of descent, honour had to be earned. 'Advice to a son' books became a minor literary form, which aimed at coaching young gentry to adopt honourable conduct in their relationships with their friends, wives and servants.[62] With the onus of responsibility on the individual, attention shifted to a man's behaviour within the household. The site for the initial assertion of manhood became the home, and those within this testing ground, a man's family and servants. In particular, as will be argued throughout this book, it was by control over the women within the household that all men could most clearly show their superiority of reason and strength.

The importance of this domestic and familial setting for male honour was aptly illustrated by the experiences of Sir Thomas Hoby, Sir Thomas Beaumont, and the second Earl of Castlehaven, whose honour was held up for public scrutiny in three remarkable, yet telling, court trials heard between 1600 and 1631. Sir Thomas Hoby was subjected to humiliation in his home in 1600 when members of a rival gentry family, the Eures, demanded hospitality from him, and then staged a drunken charivari in front of his wife and servants. Seven years later Sir Thomas Beaumont also brought a suit in Star Chamber. He alleged that Sir Henry Hastings had been spreading defamatory statements about his wife and children. In a *cause célèbre* the second Earl of Castlehaven was accused, convicted and beheaded in 1631 for aiding the rape of his wife and for his sodomy with a servant. The opponents of all three men had recognised that questioning a man's ability to govern his household was the most effective way to damage his honour. Loss of sexual control was at the heart of the explanations proffered for the lack of household rule, and it was sexual reputation which these men were most eager to defend. One of the Eure party had wished that the stag's horns in the hall 'were as hard nailed or as hard fastened upon Sir Thomas his head', and William Eure said he would 'set up horns at his gate and be gone'. Horns were the common symbol of the 'cuckold' – the impotent husband of an adulterous wife. Sir Thomas Beaumont was also accused of being a cuckold. Hastings's story was that Beaumont's wife and daughters had sexual relations with a servant in the Beaumont household. According to the accusations against him, this breakdown in sexual control had progressed furthest in the Castlehaven family, where abuse of sexual control, not its absence, was at issue.

The languages or discourses of honour which were employed by these gentry to defend their position varied. Sir Henry Hastings and the Earl of Castlehaven both stressed their lineage; Sir Thomas Beaumont emphasised his reputation for godliness and public service. The make-up of male honour was clearly multi-faceted. But the means by which they had lost their honour was held in common. Gentry honour may have had different components to that of other social groups, but without the basis of a worthy sexual reputation, all other claims to social status were severely weakened. It was gender, and not social class, which frequently set the benchmark of expectations for male behaviour.[63]

Acquiring Honourable Manhood

At around the age of six years a boy would be given his first pair of breeches to wear.[64] This marked the first of a series of stages or rites of passage through which many men passed before they attained full manhood. Childhood and youth were essential periods of a man's life for acquiring reason and strength, and learning how to exercise self-control and control over women. For many, it was probably by observing the behaviour of their elders and peers, and their own trials and errors, rather than by reading conduct books, that young men learnt the most pertinent lessons of manhood. Contrary to the arguments of the influential historian of childhood, Phillipe Ariès, evidence suggests that boys were not segregated from adults as they grew up, but were often witnesses to the adult world around them. From this, boys could learn the essentials of the gender codes, and how relationships could be most effectively negotiated and managed.[65] It was to their friends that young men were most anxious to display what they had learnt. Assertion of newly acquired manhood was all-important, since the force of peer pressure to perform could not be readily avoided.

Learning to exercise bodily self-control was vital to the acquisition of honourable manhood. Drinking tested the limits of that self-control. As an important feature of male friendship and 'good fellowship', the alehouse was a popular site for male sociability. Drinking songs represented a large percentage of the ballads that were circulated throughout the seventeenth century.[66] As Chapter 4 will show, refusal to accept to 'pledge' or drink to someone was considered an insult. Drinking was so important to male conviviality that a man could be mocked for not joining his friends in the alehouse, as William Bell of the city of Durham found when John Sheffeild taunted him in 1631 'that it was a shame for him' to be so 'awebound to his wife in that he durst not drink a cup of ale with a friend'.[67]

Being able to hold one's drink and remain convivial was essential. As Daniel Defoe wrote, 'an honest drunken fellow is a character in a man's praise'.[68] For if a man became so intoxicated that his behaviour became anti-social, then he risked his manhood. Moralists warned that men who were drunk lost their reason and could slip into a bestial state, becoming little different from the 'brutish Swine'.[69] This equation of lack of reason with drunkenness was accepted by eighteenth-century doctors, who believed that heavy drinking could be a cause of madness. Drunkenness could also affect a man's physical strength. 'Intemperance will exhaust his spirits, weaken his parts, and drown his wisdom', one conduct book writer believed.[70] Another wrote in 1727, highlighting more graphically the disorder which accompanied drunkenness, where 'the vile obscene talk, noise, nonsense and ribaldry discourses together with the fumes of tobacco, belchings and other foul breaking of wind . . . are enough to make any rational creature among them almost ashamed of his being'.[71] A man's sexual potency could also be affected. The porter in *Macbeth* (1606) compares the effects of drink with lechery and says that drink is similar for it 'provokes the desire, but it takes away the performance'.[72]

These literary ideas had basis in practice for drunkenness could be a powerful insult against men. Slanderers focused on the lack of self-control which had resulted from drinking. For example, when

Fortune Matthew of South Shields named John Patteson a 'foresworn drunken fellow' in February 1607, she also called him 'spewbleck', a term which powerfully described how the excess of drinking led to uncontrollable vomiting and expulsion of dirt. Richard Porrett also drew attention to the way that drink left men incapacitated when in midsummer 1610 he told Jane Whitefield how he knew that her husband was a 'drunken fellow' because he had to be carried home one Saturday after drinking in Newcastle. John Fleare, a churchwarden of Rainham in Essex, slandered the JP John Lowen in front of all those present at the quarter sessions in July 1664, by claiming that Lowen was so drunk on one occasion that he 'could not sit upon his horse' to read a warrant.[73] Women could be slandered as drunk, but the insult probably did not have the same implications as when it was directed against men. It was widely accepted that women held little control over their bodies, but it was a precept of manhood that men should.[74] Those men who tried to regain control over their drinking habits clearly knew what was at stake. George Hilton, a Catholic gentleman from Westmorland, kept a diary in the first years of the eighteenth century. George was a frequent drinker, and marked his 'fuddle days', as he called them, with elaborate asterisks in his diary. But at the start of 1702, after he had been involved in a drunken brawl at Appleby in which he had knocked out a man's eye, he had resolved to reduce the amount of time and money he spent on drinking. He was persuaded to make this resolution, he argued, because 'I have often lost my reason by my immoderate drinking and am then too provoked to passion', drawing him into fights. Thus he claimed, 'I am most passionately resolved to have so punctual a guard over my inclinations as never to lose my reason by immoderate drinking.'[75]

The alehouse was also often the site for male talk about sex. 'To be a man was to have the power to take a woman', Lyndal Roper has suggested of Reformation Augsburg, and evidence suggests that the same criteria were applied to Englishmen.[76] From the Restoration ideas about sexual libertinism gained currency amongst English elite male circles, encouraging the notion that sexual conquest was one way to acquire honourable manhood. The social pervasiveness and cohesiveness of libertine ideas remains open to debate, as does the extent to which men actually put these ideas into practice.[77] Indeed, at any point during the seventeenth century, it is almost impossible to judge just how many men engaged in premarital sex, and what forms this took. The average age of seventeenth-century marriage was relatively late, with most men marrying in their mid to late twenties. For all but the social elite, it often followed a period of service or apprenticeship.[78] Much evidence suggests that men from at least the lower and middling sorts had freedom to meet with the opposite sex, and to have several relationships before entering into any serious commitment. It was once a couple began marriage negotiations that the constraining pressures of family, kin and the wider community could come into play.[79] We know that both Roger Lowe and Leonard Wheatcroft, who have left us with the best surviving accounts of courtship in this period, had relationships with several women before they married. But whether these relationships were sexual is difficult to tell.[80] Certainly, once marriage was on the horizon the probability of premarital sex increased. Whilst our best source of information about premarital sex may at first appear to be the records of the presentments of couples for fornication, prenuptial pregnancy or bastardy to the church courts, detailed studies of these records have shown that they will never reveal a complete or accurate picture of actual sexual practice. For toleration, or the gap between illicit practice and prosecution, always depended upon local custom or economic, religious and individual circumstances.[81] Nevertheless, the evidence we have of unmarried men bragging or boasting about sex may suggest that many deemed it important enough to make others believe that they had experience of sex, even if their claims had no basis in actuality.

In August 1608 in an alehouse in Gateshead Thomas Claxton said that if he wanted he could have sex with the wife of the alehouse owner, telling her 'where may not I have the use of your body'. His claim to be sexually irresistible then became more exaggerated when he told his friends 'if he would he could procure any gentlewoman in Newcastle to come to his bedside that night'. In a house in Silver Street, Durham city, during November 1615, Nicholas Smith called a widow Elizabeth Whitfield whore, said she had been pregnant, and then claimed to have had carnal knowledge of her body over forty times in three different rooms of her house.[82] William Daine told his friend John Nicholson that he had sex with the unmarried Alice Teasdell of Wearmouth six times in one night in 1619; and in 1622 the Durham court heard how Thomas Laburne, talking of 'Venus sport' one morning with his friends, said that a married woman had paid him 3d to have sex the previous night, and that he had been left 'somewhat raw'.[83] Finally, a married man, Edward Arnold, often told his drinking companions that 'he could not leave off his wenching . . . [for] . . . he could and would have a wench anywhere'.[84]

Why did these men boast about sex? Clearly the alehouse setting of many of these cases must have contributed to the exaggeration of stories by the narrators and the likelihood of the intoxicated audience finding the talk credible and enjoyable. Tim Meldrum's study of London church court records has led him to argue that male boasting about sex reveals that men were 'far from worrying about their sexual reputation' and instead 'positively revelled in their notoriety'.[85] Certainly, there were occasions when single men did not seem to be guarded in their talk when it concerned illicit sex, and their talk could display a freedom of speech and fearlessness of punishment for fornication, which was generally not exhibited by women.[86] But this does not mean that they were unconcerned about their sexual reputation. In fact, boasting about sex was all about attempting to win approval and admiration from others, about gaining the reputation of a man who could 'have a wench anywhere'. It was if male talk about sex spilled out beyond its original audience and became gossip amongst a wider circle of the community that it could be troublesome to a man's reputation. Nicholas Smith told only two of his male friends about his encounters with Elizabeth Whitfield; William Daine claimed he 'had reported to John Nicholson but to none other' of his experiences with Alice Teasdell; Thomas Laburne was with two of his male friends when he first boasted of his 'Venus sport'. For Nicholas Smith and William Daine it was when their talk was reported back to the women involved that they found themselves in trouble; William Daine was so fearful of Alice Teasdell's father's reaction that he fled to nearby Washington at night to escape his fury. Thomas Laburne was subsequently so concerned about Christopher Stephenson spreading gossip about his sexual experience with a married woman that he launched a defamation suit against Christopher to try and stop the talk.

For unmarried men such as Thomas, a reputation for fornication could have very serious material consequences. A male friend of George Fenwick's of St Nicholas', Newcastle, for example, reported in 1626 how when George heard that a fellow servant, Margaret Sharpe, was spreading gossip that she had committed fornication with him on several occasions, he was 'highly discontented that any such report should rise of him'. George confronted Margaret and told her to stop spreading what he claimed were false rumours, 'suggesting unto her that if she did not so it would be to his utter undoing for he should thereby be utterly ashamed and lose his freedom'. Since celibacy was a condition of apprenticeship, George feared that if his master knew of his premarital sexual activities, he would be dismissed without qualifying as a freeman, and his six years of apprenticeship would have been wasted.[87] There were other penalties for male fornication. In Leicestershire, when William Wells's bride-to-be heard rumours that his incontinent bachelor lifestyle had previously led to him being treated for venereal disease, she withdrew her promise of marriage. A village blacksmith in 1670 believed the gossip that Thomas Hubbard had sex with a married woman, 'being a young man, is a disparagement unto him amongst his neighbours'.[88]

What becomes apparent is that it was the location of male talk about sex which was crucial in determining whether it enhanced or diminished a man's reputation. If a young man related his sexual experiences in an environment which was commonly all-male, and jovial, such as an alehouse, then his talk was likely to be well received and boost his reputation, even if in strictly legal terms the relationship was illicit. But if others repeated his words outside the alehouse context, and a man lost 'ownership' of his story, then shameful consequences could follow. For married men, as we shall see in the next chapter, the situation could be more complicated and their boasts of extra-marital sex could be used against them by their wives in marriage separation suits. Whether married or unmarried, sexual relationships could clearly bear much relevance to a man's reputation.

Men's need to prove themselves sexually competent before marriage, and their sensitivity about sexual reputation at this stage in their life cycle, is shown by their reaction to rejection during courtship. Occasionally, a man who had been rejected threatened or attempted suicide.[89] More frequently, his response was to insult angrily the woman he had been courting. When Roger Lowe, an apprentice to a south Lancashire mercer in the mid-seventeenth century, was rejected by Mary Naylor in May 1664, he called her a 'false dissembling hearted person'.[90] J.R. Gillis has found a 1591 London church court case which describes how the rejected Gabriell Holt told his neighbours that 'he did defile [her] body' and tried to have his ex-lover presented as an immoral woman.[91] Nicholas Smith's slandering of Elizabeth Whitfield as a whore after he had sex with her in Durham city in 1615 also bears the behavioural hallmarks of a jilted lover.[92] When Samuel Truett loudly declared in a street in Gravesend in 1675 that 'I have done my endeavour as far forth as any man to get Nan Collins . . . with child, and if she proves with child, I will keep the bastard, but let the whore . . . go and be damned', one passer-by later commented that he 'conceiveth the said Truett spoke [the words] in spite, because the said Ann would not have him'.[93] The anger of these men was more than just a reflection of personal disappointment, but was a sign of concern about what others would think. By publicly degrading a woman by insulting her, the man was making her a prize not worth having, and so diminished the seriousness of his loss. It was also a means of openly distancing his reputation from hers.[94]

There can be little doubt from fictional evidence that rejection was popularly regarded as a humiliating experience. In the ballad 'Poor Robin's Miserable Misfortunes', when Robin, a musician, goes to court 'young Kate', she laughs at him, makes him break his fiddle, and when he tries to kiss her she threatens him with a knife, which forces him to 'run for his life'. Robin is made to look a fool and Kate's treatment of him leaves him 'with loss and disgrace'. Robin was a name frequently given to characters in popular literature who were meant to represent the 'common man'. In another ballad a country gallant pleads with his love to marry him saying, 'let not my suit be now disgraced'.[95] As Wilding warns Mrs Wittwoud whilst he tries to woo her in the 1692 comedy *The Wives' Excuse*, there was so much honour at stake when a man went courting that, ''tis a very difficult matter . . . to refuse a man handsomely'.[96]

In many ways, a man's youthful experiences set the pattern of relationships in later life. His behaviour was determined by the need to first establish, and then continually prove his manhood to himself and others. Male friendships could be extremely competitive; drinking in alehouses and bragging of sexual exploits was all about one-upmanship. But the underlying insecurity that some men felt is revealed by their need to seek continually the approval of their peers as they took their first steps towards manhood. Male friends could play important roles in the courtship of women, providing advice as well as approval of choice of partner. Leonard Wheatcroft, who was a tailor by trade, often mentioned the presence of friends during his courtship of Elizabeth Hawley in Derbyshire over the years 1655–57.[97] Roger Lowe spent much of his diary describing his wooing of Mary Naylor and Em Potter. He often went to the alehouse and talked to his male friends about 'how to get wives'; and on a walk with John Hasledon he described how they 'talked of wenches', with Roger then offering to write a love letter to John's lover in Ireland. Roger accompanied his friends when they visited their lovers, and when his fellow apprentice John Chadocke was married, he visited John's house early one morning less than a fortnight after the marriage, sat at the 'bed's feet and we talked of everything, something about his marriage, and about what had happened upon the Lord's day about clothes for me'.[98]

The approval of friends for a man's choice of marriage partner was even more vital. Manhood was a stage in life which was only reached at around the age of twenty-eight when youth ended with marriage, the writer of *The Office of Christian Parents* believed.[99] 'An unmarried man is but half a man' taught Matthew Griffith.[100] Even on the Restoration stage, where the libertine rake was one of the most popular male figures depicted, marriage to the heroine remained the ultimate conquest of the rake, and marked the conclusion of many plays.[101] For marriage was indeed an 'honourable state of life' in this period, which allowed a man to pass on his good name to his children. The honour that a man gained through marriage was recognised by others in his community; from modes of address to church seating, marriage brought with it privilege and respect.[102] Marriage conferred status: 'we do not call any a "yeoman" ', observed Sir Thomas Smith, 'till he be married and have children and have as it were some authority among his neighbours'.[103] In one contemporary ballad a wife answers her husband's complaints about being forced to give up a single life by arguing that 'a Wife hath won you credit, a wife makes you esteem'd'. She subsequently recounts that since their marriage the 'chief men of the Parish' request his acquaintance and he has been made a churchwarden.[104]

Puritan writers of conduct books taught how parental and community approval for marriage choice was most likely to be won if the couple were equal in age, wealth and faith.[105] An important consideration for a man in his choice of partner, however, was a woman's virtue. For in theory if his marriage partner was not a virgin on the wedding day then the husband could never claim his wife to be his exclusive property. Furthermore, her lack of virtue before marriage could be interpreted as a sign of her behaviour in the future: dishonest maids would make dishonest wives. Thus unmarried women who had been slandered as whores complained that they had their marriage prospects ruined. For example, when Thomas Frinde of Bishop Auckland spread reports in Lent 1615 that Margaret Lever had a child the Christmas before, she told the court how his slanderous stories 'will be a great hindrance of her preferment in her marriage'.[106] With these attitudes in mind,

Claudio's dramatic rejection of Hero at the altar in *Much Ado about Nothing* (1598), after he believes she has been unchaste, is put into context. Don Juan has told Claudio that 'it would better fit your honour to change your mind' about his marriage choice, and Claudio then treats Hero as a woman who would have tarnished his honour, for to marry her would be 'to knit my soul to an approved wanton'.[107]

Claudio's words reflect his concern that his partner's dishonour and sexual reputation will in marriage become indistinguishable from his own; they will be 'knitted' together. In Thomas Middleton and William Rowley's *The Changeling* (1622) Beatrice's first suitor Alonzo tries to dismiss his friend's fears about Beatrice's chastity. However, he admits that her reputation will affect his honour,

> I can endure
> Much, till I meet an injury to her,
> Then I am not myself.[108]

But establishing a woman's honour before marriage was not an easy task. Without a physical examination a man depended on the honesty of a maid's word that she was a virgin. The fear that women's words were not to be trusted is shown in ballads such as 'Children after the rate of 24 in a year', in which a woman feigns virginity to win the heart of a gallant, but within a month of their marriage she delivers another man's baby, leaving her husband to 'rock the cradle . . . when the child's none of his own'.[109] Men's attempts to find a reliable way of testing virginity extended from Pliny into the early modern period. The tests held much popular interest, and Middleton and Rowley feature them in three of their plays.[110] Beatrice in *The Changeling* discovers that Alsemero carries with him a box of potions with which he can test a woman's virginity. As Beatrice fears that Alsemero will kill her if he finds that she has lost her virginity, she fools him into believing that she still has her maidenhead by learning the correct antics of a virgin when the potion is drunk. Even when she puts her servant maid into her place in the marriage bed Alsemero remains woefully ignorant.[111] That men in reality believed women were capable of such deception is illustrated by the evidence given by one witness during the separation suit of Elizabeth and Sampson Bound heard in the court of Arches in 1693. Elizabeth was accusing her husband of adultery and cruelty, he in turn defended himself by accusing her of being a drunk and an adulterer who had given him the pox. He also claimed that she had not been a virgin when he married her because she had already slept with two men. A female servant in their household, however, acted in Elizabeth's defence when she said that she had not heard of any 'contrivance or stratagem' by Elizabeth 'to foish or sham a Maidenhead upon . . . Sampson Bound by the said Elizabeth's using a bladder of Hogg's blood, or any other thing that might . . . imitate . . . that which in virtuous and modest Women is call'd a Maidenhead'.[112] Sampson Bound wished the court to believe his wife capable of devising the most elaborate of schemes to fake her virginity and thus her sexual honesty. The methods he accused his wife of employing were similar to those described in one contemporary medical treatise. Ambrose Parey told his readers in 1634 of how whores learnt to counterfeit virginity by inserting into their vaginas

> the bladders of fishes, or galls of beasts filled with blood, and so deceive the ignorant and young lecher, by the fraud and deceit of their evil arts, and in the time of copulation they mix sighs with groans, and womanlike cryings, and the crocodiles tears, that they may seem to be virgins, and never to have dealt with man before.[113]

By the time Nicholas Venette's *The Mysteries of Conjugal Love Reveal'd* was translated into English in 1703, such techniques of faking virginity had become part of a popular medical lore. He advised a wife who wished to be thought a virgin on her wedding night to insert 'two or three little pellets of dried lamb's blood into her vagina'.[114]

The insistence that all women be virgins on their wedding days was of course impractical. Here a double sexual standard is most apparent for, as we have seen, although women were expected to remain chaste preceding marriage, men frequently proved their manhood by gaining sexual experience before entering into a formal partnership. The mismatch between the requirements of these two honour systems is clear.[115] In fact, about one-third of brides were pregnant on their wedding day, and the decision to marry may have been taken at the point of a woman's pregnancy.[116] But as the case involving Sampson Bound has shown, accepting that a woman had previous sexual experience and had lost her virginity to another could be difficult. From day one of marriage, it seems, men's anxiety about how their wives might affect their honour and manhood could lead to suspicion and distrust.

Notes

1. T. Laqueur, *Making Sex: Body and Gender from the Greeks to Freud* (Cambridge MA, 1990), pp. 25, 115; see also A. Fletcher, *Gender, Sex and Subordination in England 1500–1800* (New Haven, 1995), chs 2–5.

2. L. Roper, *Oedipus and the Devil: Witchcraft, Sexuality and Religion in Early Modern Europe* (London, 1994), esp. pp. 16–18; L. Gowing, *Domestic Dangers: Women, Words, and Sex in Early Modern London* (Oxford, 1996), pp. 6–7, 80–1.

3. R. Porter, 'Bodies of thought: thoughts about the body in eighteenth-century England', in J.H. Pittock and A. Wear, eds, *Interpretation and Cultural History* (London, 1991), p. 97; P. Crawford, 'Attitudes to menstruation in seventeenth-century England' *PP* 91 (1981), pp. 47–73; A. Wilson, 'The ceremony of childbirth and its interpretation', in V. Fildes, ed., *Women as Mothers in Pre-Industrial England* (London, 1990).

4. As cited in M. Macdonald, 'Women and madness in Tudor and Stuart England' *Social Research* 53, 2 (1986), p. 267.

5. As cited in R.A. Houlbrooke, *The English Family 1450–1700* (London, 1986), p. 103.

6. K. Thomas, *Man and the Natural World: Changing Attitudes in England 1500–1800* (London, 1983), pp. 30–2, 43.

7. J. Ford, *The Broken Heart* (*c.*1629), ed. B. Morris (London, 1994), IV.ii.18–28.

8. G. Lloyd, *The Man of Reason: 'Male' and 'Female' in Western Philosophy* (London, 1986), pp. 39–50; V.J. Seidler, *Rediscovering Masculinity: Reason, Language and Sexuality* (London, 1989), pp. 14–15, 18–19.

9. As cited in Fletcher, *Gender, Sex and Subordination*, p. 70; see also M.R. Sommerville, *Sex and Subjection: Attitudes to Women in Early-Modern Society* (London, 1995), pp. 11–13.

10. W. Gouge, *Of Domesticall Duties*, 3rd edn (London, 1634), pp. 28, 77; see also K. Newman, *Fashioning Femininity and English Renaissance Drama* (Chicago IL, 1991), pp. 15–16.

11. As cited in V. Jones, ed., *Women in the Eighteenth Century: Constructions of Feminity* (London, 1990), p. 18.

12. J. Locke, *Some Thoughts Concerning Education* (1693), ed. J.W. and J.S. Yolton (Oxford, 1989), p. 255, see also pp. 107, 166.

13. As cited in P. Collinson, *The Birthpangs of Protestant England: Religious and Cultural Change in the Sixteenth and Seventeenth Centuries* (London, 1988), p. 78.

14. 'Tis not otherwise' (1630), *Pepysian Garland*, pp. 356–60.

15. W. Shakespeare, *King Lear* (*c.*1605), ed. K. Muir (London, 1990), I.iv.294–6; II.iv.275–6; IV.vi; IV.vii.17; see also I.K. Ben-Amos, *Adolescence and Youth in Early Modern England* (New Haven CT, 1994), pp. 28–30.

16. W. Shakespeare, *Macbeth* (1606), ed. K. Muir (London, 1987) III.iv.44–120.

17. Fletcher, *Gender, Sex and Subordination*, ch. 4; Sommerville, *Sex and Subjection*, pp. 10–11.

18. Anon, *The Office of Christian Parents* (Cambridge, 1616), p. 142.

19. Locke, *Some Thoughts*, pp. 86, 98; for one writer who thought that these directions 'probably are never followed' see J. Nelson, *An Essay on the Government of Children*, 2nd edn (London, 1756), pp. 127–31.

20. R.W. Malcolmson, *Popular Recreations in English Society 1700–1850* (Cambridge, 1973), pp. 34–40, 42–3; B. Capp, 'English youth groups and "The Pinder of Wakefield"', in P. Slack, ed., *Rebellion, Popular Protest and Social Order in Early Modern England* (Cambridge, 1984), pp. 212–18; Ben-Amos, *Adolescence*, p. 192.

21. P. Griffiths, *Youth and Authority: Formative Experiences in England 1560–1640* (Oxford, 1996), p. 136; see also L. Roper, 'Blood and codpieces: masculinity in the early modern German town', in *Oedipus and the Devil: Witchcraft, Sexuality and Religion in Early Modern Europe* (London, 1994), pp. 107–24.

22. A. Fletcher, 'Prescription and practice: Protestantism and the upbringing of children, 1560–1700', in D. Wood, ed., *The Church and Childhood* (Studies in Church History, 31, 1994), pp. 325–46.
23. As cited in L. Pollock, '"Teach her to live under obedience": the making of women in the upper ranks of early modern England' *CC* 4, 2 (1989), p. 238.
24. As cited in L. Pollock, *A Lasting Relationship: Parents and Children over Three Centuries* (London, 1987), p. 56.
25. Pollock, '"Teach her to live under obedience"', pp. 231–58.
26. A.J. Fletcher, 'Honour, reputation and local officeholding in Elizabethan and Stuart England', in A.J. Fletcher and J. Stevenson, eds, *Order and Disorder in Early Modern England* (Cambridge, 1987), p. 115; C.L. Barber, *The Idea of Honour in the English Drama 1591–1700* (Götenberg, 1957), pp. 105, 30; see also, R. Kelso, *The Doctrine of the English Gentleman in the Sixteenth Century* (Gloucester MA, 1964), pp. 96–105.
27. M. James, *English Politics and the Concept of Honour 1485–1642*, Past and Present Supplement 3 (The Past and Present Society, 1978), reprinted in M. James, *Politics and Culture: Studies in Early Modern England* (Cambridge, 1986), ch. 8; M. James, *Family, Lineage and Civil Society: A Study of Society, Politics and Mentality in the Durham Region 1500–1640* (Oxford, 1974), pp. 177–94.
28. See, for example, A. Courtin, *The Rules of Civility* (London, 1671), and Count H. Romei, *The Courtiers Academie* (London, 1598); A.C. Bryson, 'Concepts of civility in England *c.*1560–1685' (unpublished D.Phil. thesis, Oxford University, 1984), pp. 249–50.
29. F. Markham, *The Booke of Honour* (London, 1625), p. 1; R. Ashley, *Of Honour* (*c.*1596–1603), ed. V.B. Heltzel (San Marino CA, 1947), p. 24.
30. Proverbs 22:1; for example see C. Gibbon, *The Praise of a Good Name* (London, 1594), p. 4.
31. Ashley, *Of Honour*, p. 40; Gibbon, *The Praise*, sig. B2.
32. K.A. Esdaile, *English Church Monuments 1560–1840* (London, 1946); N. Llewellyn, *The Art of Death: Visual Culture in the English Death Ritual* c.*1500–1800* (London, 1991); F. Heal and C. Holmes, *The Gentry in England and Wales 1500–1700* (London, 1994), pp. 34, 35; R. Cust and P. Lake, 'Sir Richard Grosvenor and the rhetoric of magistracy' *Bulletin of the Institute of Historical Research* 54 (1981), p. 52.
33. P. Clark, *English Provincial Society from the Reformation to the Revolution* (Sussex, 1977), pp. 124–5; A. Everitt, *The Community of Kent and The Great Rebellion 1640–1660* (Leicester, 1966), pp. 33–5; A. Fletcher *A County Community in Peace and War: Sussex 1600–1660* (London, 1975), pp. 44–53; D. Cressy, 'Kinship and kin interaction in early modern England' *PP* 113 (1986), p. 49.
34. Ashley, *Of Honour*, p. 70; for a similar argument see also G. Markham, *Honour in his Perfection* (London, 1624), p. 4; for anthropological observations on the hierarchy of honour see J.K. Campbell, *Honour, Family and Patronage: A Study of Institutions and Moral Values in a Greek Mountain Community* (Oxford, 1964), pp. 264–8, and J. Pitt-Rivers, 'Honour and social status in Andalusia', in J.G. Peristiany, ed., *Honour and Shame: The Values of Mediterranean Society* (London, 1965), pp. 23–73.
35. See for example, D. Tuvill, *Essaies Politicke, and Morall* (London, 1608), f. 119r.
36. DDR.V.8. f. 173; DDR.V.11. ff. 507v, 508; CA, Case 757 (1673), Ee3, f. 59.
37. DDR.V.8. ff. 23v, 24, 28r, 81v.
38. W. Segar, *Honor Military, and Civill* (London, 1602), p. 113; Markham, *The Booke of Honour*, pp. 41–53; Heal and Holmes, *The Gentry*, pp. 9, 17–19, 30–1; for the influence of sixteenth-century humanist ideas on gentry notions of honour see J.P. Cooper, 'Ideas of gentility in early modern England', in G.E. Aylmer and J.S. Morrill, eds, *Land, Men and Beliefs: Studies in Early Modern History* (Oxford, 1983), pp. 43–77.
39. Gibbon, *The Praise*, p. 16; R. Braithwait, *The English Gentleman* (London, 1630), dedicatory; J. Gailhard, *The Compleat Gentleman* (London, 1678), Part I, 'To the Reader', see also, Part II, p. 110.

40. Heal and Holmes, *The Gentry*, pp. 38–9; N. Llewellyn, 'Claims to status through visual codes: heraldry on post-Reformation funeral monuments', in S. Anglo, ed., *Chivalry in the Renaissance* (Woodbridge, 1990), p. 149.

41. G. Whetstone, *The Honorable Reputation of a Souldier* (London, 1585), sig. Aiii.

42. See, for example, Markham, *Honour in his Perfection.*

43. James, *English Politics*; and *Family, Lineage and Civil Society*, especially pp. 177–94.

44. Gailhard, *The Compleat Gentleman*, Part I, pp. 79, 85; Part II, pp. 50–1; R. Manning, *Hunters and Poachers* (Oxford, 1993), pp. 4–17, 35–7; see also M. Vale, *The Gentleman's Recreations: Accomplishments and Pastimes of the English Gentleman 1580–1630* (Cambridge, 1977).

45. *Sir Walter Raleigh's instructions to his son and to posterity* (London, 1632), in L.B. Wright, ed., *Advice to a Son: Precepts of Lord Burghley, Sir Walter Raleigh, and Francis Osborne* (Ithaca NY, 1962), p. 20.

46. Gailhard, *The Compleat Gentleman*, Part I, p. 58.

47. A. Bryson, 'The rhetoric of status: gesture, demeanour and the image of the gentleman in sixteenth- and seventeenth-century England', in L. Gent and N. Llewellyn, eds, *Renaissance Bodies: The Human Figure in English Culture* c.*1540–1660* (London, 1990), pp. 136–53.

48. As cited in James, *Family, Lineage*, p. 101; see also, J. Simon, *Education and Society in Tudor England* (Cambridge, 1966), ch. 14.

49. Gibbon, *The Praise*, p. 23.

50. F. Heal, *Hospitality in Early Modern England* (Oxford, 1990), p. 13.

51. As cited in Heal and Holmes, *The Gentry*, p. 288.

52. Segar, *Honor Military, and Civill.*

53. Fletcher, 'Honour', in Fletcher and Stevenson, eds, *Order and Disorder.*

54. C.B. Herrup, *The Common Peace: Participation and the Criminal Law in Seventeenth-Century England* (Cambridge, 1989), p. 54.

55. Cust and Lake, 'Sir Richard Grosvenor', pp. 51–2; for the importance of godliness and public office to gentry honour see also Heal and Holmes, *The Gentry*, pp. 168–75; and R. Cust, 'Honour and politics in early Stuart England: the case of Beaumont *v.* Hastings' *PP* 149 (1995), pp. 70–4.

56. See Fletcher, 'Honour', pp. 95, 104 for other examples of godly magistrates.

57. Ford, *The Broken Heart* (*c.*1629), III.i.37–40.

58. For discussion of this idea see W. Hunt, 'Civic chivalry and the English civil war', in A. Grafton and A. Blair, eds, *The Transmission of Culture in Early Modern Europe* (Philadelphia PA, 1990), pp. 204–310.

59. P. Corfield, 'The democratic history of the English gentleman' *History Today* 42 (1992), pp. 40–7.

60. Heal and Holmes, *The Gentry*, p. 32.

61. Bryson, 'The rhetoric of status', p. 146.

62. For examples see the three works contained within Wright, ed., *Advice to a Son*; and Anon, *Advice to a Son at the University* (London, 1725). V.B. Heltzel, who edited 'Richard earl of Carbery's advice to his son' *Huntington Library Bulletin* 11 (1937), pp. 59–105, noted how this father's advice to his son was atypical because it did not contain any advice about marriage. Nevertheless, there was still advice about domestic matters such as conduct with friends and servants.

63. For accounts of the Hoby–Eure story see Heal, *Hospitality*, pp. 13–14; Heal and Holmes, *The Gentry*, pp. 3–6; and F. Heal 'Reputation and honour in court and country: Lady Elizabeth Russell and Sir Thomas Hoby' *TRHS* Sixth Series, VI (1996), pp. 161–78; for the Beaumont Hastings case see Cust, 'Honour and politics', pp. 57–94; for accounts of the Castlehaven case see F.E. Dolan, *Dangerous Familiars: Representations of Domestic Crime in England 1550–1700* (Ithaca NY, 1994), pp. 79–88, C. Herrup, '"To pluck bright honour from the pale-faced moon": gender and honour in the Castlehaven story' *TRHS* Sixth Series, VI (1996), pp. 137–59, and C. Herrup, 'The patriarch at home: the trial of the 2nd earl of Castlehaven for rape and sodomy' *HWJ* 41 (1996), pp. 1–18.

64. For contemporaries who recorded this occasion with pride see Pollock, *A Lasting Relationship*, pp. 81–2.

65. P. Ariès, *Centuries of Childhood* (Harmondsworth, 1960); E. Foyster, 'Silent witnesses? Children and the breakdown of domestic and social order in early modern England', in A. Fletcher and S. Hussey, eds, *Childhood in Question* (forthcoming from Manchester University Press).

66. See, for example, 'Good Ale for my Money', *Roxburghe*, vol. I, pp. 412–17; M.P., 'A Messe of Good Fellowes', *Roxburghe*, vol. II, pp. 143–8; see also the large group of ballads in the Pepys collection under the category 'Drinking and Good Fellowship'.

67. DDR.V.12. ff. 290r, 291r; see also P. Clark, *The English Alehouse: A Social History 1200–1830* (London, 1983), pp. 123–44.

68. As cited in R. Porter, 'The drinking man's disease: the "pre-history" of alcoholism in Georgian Britain' *British Journal of Addiction* 80 (1985), p. 386.

69. For ballads with this message see 'The Good-fellow's Advice', *Roxburghe*, vol. III, pp. 261–7; 'The Young Man's Counsellor' (*c.*1681), *Roxburghe*, vol. IV, pp. 74–6; for conduct literature with similar warnings see *Sir Walter Raleigh's Instructions*, pp. 30–1; F. Cheynell, *The Man of Honour* (London, 1645), p. 44.

70. Porter, 'The drinking man's disease', pp. 389–90; Cheynell, *The Man of Honour*, p. 44.

71. As cited in G.J. Barker-Benfield, *The Culture of Sensibility: Sex and Society in Eighteenth-Century Britain* (Chicago IL, 1996), p. 52.

72. Shakespeare, *Macbeth* (1606), II.iii.28–9; for comparison of attitudes in early modern Germany see Roper, *Oedipus and the Devil*, pp. 110–13.

73. DDR.V.8. ff. 223v, 224r, 234; DDR.V.9. f. 241r; CA, Case 5877 (1665), Eee2, f. 4r.

74. For women's bodies see, for example, P. Stallybrass, 'Patriarchal territories: the body enclosed', in M.W. Ferguson, M. Quilligan and N.J. Vickers, eds, *Rewriting the Renaissance: The Discourses of Sexual Difference in Early Modern Europe* (Chicago IL, 1987), pp. 123–42.

75. A. Hillman, ed., *The Rake's Diary: The Journal of George Hilton* (Westmoreland, 1994), p. 28; I am grateful to Jeremy Black for drawing my attention to this diary.

76. L. Roper, *The Holy Household: Women and Morals in Reformation Augsburg* (Oxford, 1989), p. 86.

77. See, for example, J.G. Turner, 'The properties of libertinism', in R.P. Maccubbin, ed., *'Tis Nature's Fault: Unauthorized Sexuality During the Enlightenment* (Cambridge, 1987), pp. 75–87; L. Stone, 'Libertine sexuality in post-Restoration England: group sex and flagellation among the middling sort in Norwich in 1706–07' *Journal of the History of Sexuality* 2, 4 (1992), pp. 511–26; F. Dabhoiwala, 'The construction of honour, reputation and status in late seventeenth- and early eighteenth-century England' *TRHS* Sixth Series, VI (1996), pp. 205–7; and T. Hitchcock, *English Sexualities, 1700–1800* (London, 1997), pp. 21–2. I am grateful to David Turner for bringing these references to my attention and for discussing these issues with me.

78. E.A. Wrigley and R.S. Schofield, *The Population History of England 1541–1871* (Cambridge, 1989), pp. 255, 261–3, 265; the age of marriage varied over time, region and between social groups, see M. Ingram, *Church Courts, Sex and Marriage in England, 1570–1640* (Cambridge, 1987), p. 129 for examples of these variations.

79. Ben-Amos, *Adolescence*, pp. 200–3; D. O'Hara, '" Ruled by my friends": aspects of marriage in the diocese of Canterbury, *c.*1540–1570' *CC* 6, 1 (1991), pp. 9–41.

80. W.L. Sachse, ed., *The Diary of Roger Lowe* (London, 1938); G. Parfitt and R. Houlbrooke, eds, *The Courtship Narrative of Leonard Wheatcroft Derbyshire Yeoman* (Reading, 1986).

81. K. Wrightson and D. Levine, *Poverty and Piety in an English Village: Terling, 1525–1700* (London, 1979), pp. 126–33; Ingram, *Church Courts*, chs 4, 7; P. Laslett, K. Oosterveen and R.M. Smith, eds, *Bastardy and its Comparative History* (London,

1980), chs 2, 5, 6; R. Adair, *Courtship, Illegitimacy and Marriage in Early Modern England* (Manchester, 1996); P. Griffiths summarises the problems of interpreting this evidence in *Youth*, pp. 237–50.

82. DDR.V.9. f. 78; DDR.V.10A. ff. 108, 109r.

83. DDR.V.10B. ff. 415v, 416, 426v, 427r, 447; DDR.V.11. ff. 179, 187.

84. CA, Case 219 (1668), Eee3, f. 211r.

85. T. Meldrum, 'A women's court in London: Defamation at the Bishop of London's consistory court, 1700–1745' *London Journal* 19, 1 (1994), p. 10.

86. J. Kamensky, 'Talk like a man: speech, power, and masculinity in early New England' *GH* 8, 1 (1996), pp. 22–47; Gowing, *Domestic Dangers*, pp. 10–11, 74, 121–2.

87. DDR.V.11. ff. 478v–479r; DDR.V.12. f. 5r.

88. Leicestershire Record Office, Archdeaconry Depositions, 1 D 41/4, Box xvi/28; Box xxxii/30; I am very grateful to Bernard Capp for these references and for discussing these issues with me.

89. M. MacDonald and T.R. Murphy, *Sleepless Souls: Suicide in Early Modern England* (Oxford, 1990), pp. 291–2; Gowing, *Domestic Dangers*, pp. 176–7.

90. Sachse, ed., *The Diary of Roger Lowe*, p. 61.

91. As cited in J.R. Gillis, *For Better, For Worse: British Marriages 1600 to the Present* (Oxford, 1985), p. 40; for more examples from the London church courts of men behaving in this way, see Gowing, *Domestic Dangers*, p. 74.

92. DDR.V.10A. ff. 108, 109r.

93. CA, Case 2160 (1675), Eee5, ff. 623v–624r.

94. For cuckolded husbands who respond by calling their wives whores see Chapter 5 below.

95. 'Poor Robin's Miserable Misfortunes', *Pepys*, vol. IV, p. 97; 'Children after the rate of 24 in a year' (*c.*1635), *Pepys*, vol. I, pp. 404–5.

96. T. Southerne, *The Wives' Excuse: Or, Cuckolds make Themselves* (1692), ed. R. Jordan and H. Love (Oxford, 1988) II.iii.130–1.

97. Parfitt and Houlbrooke, eds, *The Courtship Narrative*, pp. 41, 50, 52, 54, 75.

98. Sachse, ed., *The Diary of Roger Lowe*, pp. 37, 43, 50–1; see also Gillis, *For Better, For Worse*, pp. 36–7.

99. *The Office of Christian Parents*, p. 44.

100. As cited in Griffiths, *Youth*, p. 28.

101. D.M. Turner, 'Rakes, libertines and sexual honour in Restoration England, 1660–1700' (unpublished MA thesis, Durham University, 1994), p. 11; R.D. Hume, *The Rakish Stage: Studies in English Drama* (Carbondale IL, 1983), pp. 138–75.

102. See, for example, D. Rogers, *Matrimoniall Honour* (London, 1642); Anon, *The Court of Good Counsell* (London, 1607); J. Fisher, *The Honour of Marriage* (London, 1695); Gillis, *For Better, For Worse*, pp. 15–16.

103. As cited in K. Thomas, 'Age and authority in early modern England' *Proceedings of the British Academy* 62 (1976), p. 226.

104. 'The Lamentation of a new married man' (*c.*1630), *Pepys*, vol. I, pp. 380–1; for ballads with a similar theme see ''Tis not otherwise', *Pepysian Garland*, pp. 356–60, and 'The Benefit of Marriage', *Euing*, pp. 23–4.

105. See, for example, Gouge, *Of Domesticall Duties*, especially pp. 179–99.

106. DDR.V.10A. f. 10a; see also, DDR.V.8. f. 198r; for further examples see Ingram, *Church Courts*, pp. 310–11.

107. W. Shakespeare, *Much Ado about Nothing* (1598), ed. F.H. Mares (Cambridge, 1988), III.ii.84–5; IV.i.39.

108. T. Middleton and W. Rowley, *The Changeling* (1622), ed. B. Loughrey and N. Taylor (London, 1988), II.i.151–3.

109. 'Children after the rate of 24 in a year' (*c.*1635), *Pepys*, vol. I, pp. 404–5.

110. C. Kahn, 'Whores and wives in Jacobean drama', in D. Kehler and S. Baker, eds, *In Another Country: Feminist Perspectives on Renaissance Drama* (London, 1991), pp. 255–6; D.B. Randall, 'Some observations on the theme of chastity in *The*

Changeling' *English Literary Renaissance* 14 (1984), pp. 347–66; D. Lindley, *The Trials of Frances Howard: Fact and Fiction at the Court of King James* (London, 1996), pp. 109–10, 114–15.

111. Middleton and Rowley, *The Changeling* (1622), IV.i, ii; V.i.

112. CA, Case 1055 (1693), Eee7, f. 681v.

113. As cited in W.C. Carroll, 'The virgin not: language and sexuality in Shakespeare' *Shakespeare Survey* 46 (1994), p. 119.

114. As cited in P-G. Boucé, 'Some sexual beliefs and myths in eighteenth-century Britain', in P-G. Boucé, ed., *Sexuality in Eighteenth-Century Britain* (Manchester, 1982), p. 34.

115. B.J. Gibbons, 'Gender in British Behmenist thought' (unpublished Ph.D. thesis, Durham University, 1993), p. 43.

116. P. Crawford, 'The construction and experience of maternity in seventeenth-century England', in Fildes, ed., *Women as Mothers*, p. 17.

CHAPTER THREE

Asserting Manhood

Once the reputation for manhood had been won, it had to be continually proved and asserted, for manhood was never wholly secure.[1] As this chapter will show, the pivot on which manhood rested was the control of female sexuality, and this gave male fortunes an unstable foundation. Even if men exercised reason and strength, they could never know with certainty whether a woman was chaste, nor could they ever rest easy as the maintenance of female chastity could never be guaranteed. Ironically, by resting manhood on women's sexuality, men had given women the potential for power, as their words and actions could endanger manhood with the most devastating effect.

Dangerous Passions

We have seen in the previous chapter how relationships with women played an important part in the construction of honourable manhood. But a wide range of contemporary literary material also highlighted the dangers which unmarried men could encounter when they embarked upon these relationships. During courtship it was popularly thought that relationships with women could threaten men's ability to reason. Whilst one contemporary proverb ran that 'a man without reason is a beast in season', another taught that 'it is impossible to love and be wise'.[2] Falling in love could lead to a loss of male self-control: as Iago described it in *Othello* (*c.*1604), 'it is merely a lust of blood, and a permission of the will'.[3] Without their hold on reason men could be driven mad with love. *The Mad Man's Morice* was one 1690 ballad which told the tragic tale of a young man who had been regarded as 'the properest Lad' in the parish, but was so driven out of his wits by love that he ended up in Bedlam. It warned other young men,

> If Cupid strike, be sure of this,
> let reason rule affection,
> So shall thou never do amiss,
> by reasons good direction.[4]

The story of this ballad was not far-fetched, for men in reality were admitted to Bedlam and to see the seventeenth-century physician Richard Napier suffering from love-sickness.[5] Of course, women as well as men complained of this malady. But by losing their reason, men in love, unlike women, risked their very gender identity. For when men became irrational they became more closely associated with the female. 'Full of fear, anxiety, doubt, care, peevishness, suspicion, it turns a man into a woman', Robert Burton explained in his analysis of love-melancholy. In their obsession with women, men in love became like women: weak and lacking reason. As Romeo reflects,

> O sweet Juliet,
> Thy beauty hath made me effeminate
> And in my temper soften'd valour's steel![6]

In the seventeenth century 'effeminate' was a term that was applied to those men who were deviant in some way within their heterosexual relationships, it was not until the mid-eighteenth century that it began to connote homosexuality.[7] The deviancy which was typical of men who were in love with women was that they fell so excessively in love that they relinquished their control and power to their lovers. This danger had long been recognised. As Chaucer in *The Franklin's Tale* had illustrated, the gender hierarchy was altered during courtship, so a man might be a woman's 'servant in love, and master in marriage'.[8] These fears about how love could invert traditional gender roles continued, for within seventeenth-century drama there are numerous references to the way in which love disempowered men. Othello's love for Desdemona leads Cassio to recognise her as 'our great captain's captain', and Othello himself realises that 'she might lie by an emperor's side, and command him tasks'. Men who are in love forget their military duty. Othello is concerned that if Desdemona accompanies him to Cyprus he may be seen to neglect his military command.[9] Claudio in *Much Ado about Nothing* (1598) notes how once thoughts of war,

> Have left their places vacant, in their rooms
> Come thronging soft and delicate desires,

and Benedick mocks a man in love who once 'would have walked ten mile afoot, to see a good armour, and now he will lie ten nights awake carving the fashion of a new doublet'.[10]

Men's fears about effeminacy remained as strong at the end of the seventeenth century. In John Vanbrugh's *The Provoked Wife* (1697) Heartfree is so 'wounded' by the love he has for Bellinda that he doubts whether he will 'have courage enough to draw my sword', a sword being a well-known euphemism for a penis.[11] When Horner in William Wycherley's *The Country Wife* (1675) says that 'Good fellowship and friendship are lasting, rational, and manly pleasures', Harcourt replies 'For all that, give me some of those pleasures you call effeminate too'.[12] In a scathing poem 'Upon Friendship, preferre'd to Love', Wycherley continued the theme of his play by claiming that friendship was 'The Manly Virtue of the Soul, that's Great, / Love, is a Vice, Mean and Effeminate'.[13] Heartwell in William Congreve's *The Old Bachelor* (1693) describes love as something that drains away his manhood:

> That ever that noble passion, lust should ebb to this degree – No reflux of vigorous blood; but milky love supplies the empty channels, and prompts me to the softness of a child.[14]

The remarkable autobiography of Thomas Whythorne, a Tudor musician, shows how one man in reality struggled with this unsettling experience of courtship. After one relationship ended he reflected bitterly how 'she would have had me her slave to triumph over'. Whythorne believed that being in love led him to 'embrace Venus' darlings more than reason would have'. As he thought that 'the difference between man the commander, and beasts being by man commanded, is only Reason in men', he resolved in future to 'estrange myself from all loving occasions'. For Whythorne, relationships with women were full of hidden dangers which tempted men to 'follow nature rather than reason after the manner of brute beasts'.[15] Clearly, concern about the dangers of love to manhood was more than just a literary phenomenon. William Stout, a devout Puritan, and perhaps an unlikely candidate for love-sickness, reflected in his autobiography that at the age of thirty-eight, when he 'thought that reason and prudence might have overbalanced affection and passion', he found himself battling 'in a contest betwixt', on the one hand, his 'reason and prudence' which told him that the younger and socially superior Bethia Greene was an unsuitable match, and on the other, his overwhelming 'affections' for her.[16] To Stout, courtship represented a clear choice between manly reason and uncontrolled passion. Allowing such affections to overrule reason could endanger men's power over women, as Francis Osborne advised his son. Love could leave a man 'subject to slavery that was born free and suffering her to command who ought in righter reason to serve and obey', Osborne wrote.[17]

Women's Talk

A man's reputation, regardless of his social class, depended upon the opinion of others. Within gentry families the design and layout of houses still gave limited consideration to privacy, and little went unobserved by servants. In the close-knit village societies of the seventeenth century a man's behaviour was under the constant scrutiny of his neighbours. Church court records confirm that talking about the details of other people's lives was a popular pastime. People talked in kitchens, on doorsteps and in back yards, in market places and in alehouses about those they knew. Anthropologists and linguists who have studied gossip in small village societies and the dynamics of group interaction have taught us much about the way that gossip operates. Gossip is an informal means of communication and a way of gathering information about people and their involvement in events in a community.[18] The subject of gossip may originate with an observed event or with a person revealing a 'secret' part of themselves to another. The 'story' is then passed down a chain, each narrator typically telling the story in a slightly different way. The enjoyment of this type of talk is derived from the belief that the knowledge gained is intimate to its subject and that the information is not shared by the wider community. Arguably, those who participate in the same line of gossip are united and bound together as a group.[19] Revealing details about oneself and sharing the 'secrets' of others has been observed to be an important way of gaining friendship, and a sign of trust and intimacy.[20]

REPRESENTATIONS

Within seventeenth-century popular culture this type of talk only had negative connotations. It was associated wholly with women, and usually married women; the word 'gossip' was derived from the women who would be invited to witness the birth of a child.[21] In popular literature composed by men the gossip is always portrayed as female. In Samuel Rowland's satires gossips are women of different ages who gather to drink and gossip in taverns, and in ballads gossip is portrayed as a favourite female occupation. Most significantly, gossip was viewed negatively because of its destructive potential. Men believed that gossip was talk which evaluated the honour worthiness of others. In other words, they believed that when women talked they were not merely gaining information, but were also being critical and judgemental. Gossip became talk not about someone, but against someone. The reputation of scandalmongering was attached to gossips. Furthermore, it was thought that men were the only topic of conversation for gossips. In *Well Met Gossip* (1619) a maid, wife and widow meet and discuss 'whose choice hath got the kindest man'. They compare the details of the physical appearance of the men they have known from their hair colour to their beards as well as the advantages and disadvantages of a man having wealth or intelligence. The ironically titled *A Crew of Kind Gossips* (1613) portrays the talk of six women, each of whom has a separate complaint about their husbands. The author Rowlands warns married men that 'Your credits are in question' when gossips critically discuss their behaviour. One of the husbands in the story complains bitterly of his wife and how 'she lay me open (as in scorne) / To her companions scoffing at me so'.[22] In one of Rowlands's poems a bride warns other women to avoid the company of gossiping wives because the only function of their conversation is to abuse their absent husbands.[23]

This portrayal of women's talk is also found in contemporary ballads. 'Well met Neighbour' is a song in which two women on their way to a childbirth discuss the faults of the husbands in their neighbourhood. They take it in turn to relate news of different men, beginning 'Know you not Laurence the miller?', 'Know you not Ralph the plummer' and so on. The wives list a variety of faults of the men, one husband beats his wife, another threatens to kill his wife, another keeps wenches. Each wife tries to make her story more shocking than the last. They support each other by their judgements with general exclamations against men such as 'O, fye on these dastardly knaves!' and 'O such a rogue would be hanged!'. They also imagine how they would deal with such dreadful men if they were their wives. The gossips in the 1638 ballad 'The Married Man's Misery' go one step further, using drink to 'arm themselves' to cuckold their husbands.[24] A maid portrayed in an early eighteenth-century satire wishes that she could join the married women at labours and christenings, where she believes wives talk of,

> When 'twas they did at Hoity-Toity play;
> Whose Husband's Yard is longest, whilst another
> Can't in the least her great Misfortune smother,
> So tells, her Husband's Bauble is so short,
> That when he Hunts, he never shows her Sport.[25]

The portrayals of gossips in popular literature reveal male anxieties about female friendship. Women who talk together are shown comparing the reputations of the men they know and condemning those who do not fit their agreed standards of 'honourable' behaviour. Their talk is often about sex. This portrayal of women may have arisen from men's fears about their ability to control and rule their wives. It may also have been a result of men's realisation of the vulnerability of their reputations within married life. The husband in the ballad who complains that his gossiping wife 'lays him open' expresses the fear that his wife does not respect his expectations of privacy within marriage and that she exposes what he thought intimate. It may seem to suggest that men thought women had a different understanding from them as to what was private and personal in a relationship, and what details or events concerning their partnership were fit for public consumption.

The female gossips in popular literature are threatening because of their power. They have power over men, first, because as wives they have gained access to the most personal knowledge of their husbands' bodies and minds, information which they can choose to 'betray' to others. Secondly, by their criticism they appear to control the way that men behave. In literature gossip certainly appears to have this regulative effect upon men's behaviour. In the ballad of 'John Tomson and Jakaman his Wife' the husband wishes he could return to bachelor life. He says he cannot go anywhere without his wife watching him and if he tries to kiss another woman her friends readily tell him 'thy wife shall know of this'. He knows that gossip about his illicit behaviour will get back to his wife, for which he will suffer.[26] In Thomas Harman's 1566 tale of women gossiping, one wife prevents her husband from committing adultery by gossiping to her friends of her suspicions concerning her husband's fidelity. Her friends pounce on the husband as he is about to commit adultery, and with his hose down they beat him. Never again, so the story goes, did the husband stray from the marriage bed.[27] Charles Gibbon in his tract about male reputation bemoaned the fact that men's freedom was hindered by fear of gossip. He writes that a man could be the victim of evil gossip simply by visiting a neighbour's house or by talking with a woman 'upon such honest intent'. Moralists such as the minister Daniel Rogers, writing in 1642, believed that gossip had a positive effect on men's behaviour as it forced them to be faithful to their wives, 'fame and report is well called by some, the married ones Saint'.[28]

RESPONSES

This literary evidence suggesting that men did adjust their behaviour to avoid gossip may seem to be in direct contrast with the conclusion reached by Jim Sharpe's study of church court records, that gossip particularly controlled female behaviour. He argued that in a society which held female chastity to be of key importance, fear that sexual behaviour would be the subject of gossip may have contributed to the regulation of women's conduct.[29] Why popular literature, written mainly by men, should portray male rather than female conduct being governed by gossip is unclear, especially as we also have strong evidence for male determination not to be ruled by gossip. First, men labelled female talk as worthless, trivial and as 'idle talk'. They represented gossips as 'lazy' and as the 'idle Crew'. Women are portrayed as neglecting their household duties by gossiping. In the ballad 'Man's Felicity and Misery' two husbands compare their wives. Edmund's wife is careful to fulfil her duties and 'never comes abroad', but David's wife is so busy spending time with gossips that his children can spend the whole day undressed.[30] By denying the importance of female talk to reputation, and by diminishing its value, men attempted to negate its power.

Secondly, men attempted to control female talk by labelling persistent gossips as scolds. Scolding was an offence which could be prosecuted in the courts and punished in a range of ways, including the use of the ducking- or cucking-stool. Once placed in the cucking-stool the scold could be lowered into a river or pond. The public punishment of scolds must have been a powerful reminder to women of their duty to be guarded in their speech. Steve Hindle's research into the experience of Margaret Knowsley, a maidservant of the Nantwich preacher Stephen Jerome, who in the late 1620s spread gossip that her master had persistently harassed her sexually, eventually attempting rape, has shown the treatment of women who dared to make public male private behaviour. On three market days she was whipped through the town, placed in a cage 'high in the open market' for two hours bearing papers with the inscription 'for unjustly slandering Mr Jerome a preacher of God's word', and then carted through the town still holding this message.[31] In this period language was power, a point made with crystal clarity in Shakespeare's *The Taming of the Shrew* (*c.*1591), in which Petruchio's taming of Kate is complete once she will say that the sun is the moon.[32] Freedom of speech was a privilege restricted to men, and was one way, as Jane Kamensky has shown, in which men attempted to distinguish themselves from women.[33] Women learnt that their honour depended upon not talking about the honour of others, and that virtuous women did not gossip. As Laura Gowing has argued, any public speech, especially about sex, was seen as disreputable for women.[34] Men established a close link between female speech and chastity suggesting that unruly speech implied whoredom. Hence conduct book writers such as Barnabe Rich in 1613 taught that a virtuous woman 'openeth her mouth with wisdom', and Barbaro in his treatise *On Wifely Duties* warned women not to speak in public 'for the speech of a noble woman can be no less dangerous than the nakedness of her limbs'.[35] When searching for a suitable wife a man should note the modesty of a woman's speech, Henry Smith warned in 1591, 'for the ornament of a woman is silence . . . As the open vessels were counted unclean; so account that the open mouth hath much uncleaness.'[36] That such teaching influenced gender training and upbringing is shown by the example of Lady Grace Mildmay, who recalled in her autobiography how both her mother and governess had instructed her as a child always to avoid 'idle talk', and 'ever carry with me a modest eye and a chaste ear, a silent tongue and a considerate heart, wary and heedful of myself in all my words and actions'.[37]

Ironically, the strength and force of men's reaction to women's talk is evidence in itself of their fear of the power of female speech. But how did gossip operate in reality? If we turn now to church court records, we can see that men's anxieties about the effect of gossip on reputation were not entirely ill founded. Gossip was frightening because of the speed at which it could travel: 'nothing fleeth more swiftly than an ill word', wrote Gibbon in 1594.[38] In 1608 the Durham church court heard how Agnes Huntley called her mother whore one Sunday in Sandgate in front of widow Alice Hearon. The very next morning another widow, Isabelle Road, who had not been present at Alice's house, questioned Agnes as to why she had slandered her mother.[39] Susan Amussen's study of Norwich church courts has shown how gossip allowed the reputation of a person to travel with them even when they moved into a new community. In Shropham in 1618 Agnes Ayers called Anne Leight a whore and said she 'was rung out of Hilborough and Swaffham with a basin'. Shropham was at least eleven miles from Hilborough, and fourteen from Swaffham.[40] The 'common voice, fame and report' concerning a person's behaviour could also be remembered for a long period of time. Gossip which had been circulating within a community for a number of years could suddenly be used to discredit the person involved. For example, the rumour that Alice Scroggs, wife of Thomas, had slept with two men before her marriage was raised in Durham consistory court in February 1610, some eight to thirteen years after the supposed relationships had ended.[41]

Those who bore a grudge could deliberately spread malicious gossip and endanger reputation. In 1620, after she had been reproved for her loose living by her vicar William Dixon, Agnes Swale of Osmotherley started to gossip to her neighbours that the vicar had made sexual advances to her. Hindle's case of Margaret Knowsley and the preacher Stephen Jerome has shown how godly officials were open to such charges of sexual hypocrisy.[42] There are also cases that show how people could be bribed to spread false gossip. For example, Andrew Conny of Evenwood discovered in 1616 that his granddaughter had been given a gift for spreading gossip that she saw one Jane Lyndsey stealing milk.[43]

We have some evidence that women did indeed gossip to each other about the differences between their lovers. In 1620 Mary Stringer recalled a conversation she had with Agnes Swale in Osmotherley when they had been walking to a wedding. On their way they 'began to talk of marriage matters' and Agnes said 'that if she could choose she would have one that was a good doer'. She said that she had had several lovers but 'Thomas Twedye pleased her better than any that ever she dealt withall for that he occupied her three times in one night'. When Captain Charles Skelton sued his wife Dorothy for adultery in 1673 a nurse recalled a conversation she had with Dorothy the morning after she had been seen committing adultery. As she talked of her lover Dorothy was reported to have said, 'of all the men that ever I lay with there was never any that meant so dear'.[44]

But there is also ample evidence to suggest that much female talk was not about the opposite sex, nor was it concerned with challenging male authority. Women's talk was just as likely to be about other women's behaviour as men's. Indeed, as we shall see in Chapter 5, women always outnumbered men as those who believed gossip had gone too far, and pursued a defamation suit in the church courts to try and put an end to malicious talk. As Bernard Capp has shown, the network of a married woman's female friends could serve to provide effective practical help, support and advice in a wide variety of ways to meet needs and solve problems which went far beyond those simply of the marital bed.[45] The fears about gossip are also put into context with the evidence that gossips were just as likely to be men as women. There are numerous examples of male gossips in the church court records. Around Candlemas 1604 a yeoman John Hutchinson visited Ralph Wall's house in Wolsingham to purchase a sword. 'Taking occasion to talk of John Wheatley', Ralph Aire, who was also present, told Hutchinson of an argument he had had with Wheatley. Aire then called Wheatley 'an ass, a fool and a pickpurse'. This conversation was overheard by John Oliver through the wall of widow Farrowe's house, and by Henry Jackson who was standing in Ralph Wall's yard. Its wide audience meant that the gossip got back to Wheatley and Aire ended up in court for slander. Further examples of men's behaviour being subject to the gossip of other men include the case of James Noble against Gregory Hutchinson. Gregory spread gossip which James claimed to be false about him committing adultery with Isabelle Moore in 1604. Similarly, John Shipperson's reputation in Wearmouth was put into doubt by the gossip of Thomas Sparrow, who related to several neighbours, including the curate on several occasions, even in church, how he had found John in bed with Isabelle Shipperson, wife of Robert Shipperson.[46] Whilst in reality men did gossip, the sites of male and female talk may have remained gender differentiated. That gossip was thought only to occur when a group was of one sex is shown by a 1774 guide to agricultural techniques, in which the writer advised other farmers to always place one man in a field of working women, for his presence would silence all gossip.[47]

Male suspicion of what women talked about in the 'semi-separate domain outside the family structure and beyond male control' which women's networks of friends constituted ran rife in early modern England.[48] When young men sought to boost their reputations by boasting of their relationships with women, they talked of their own sexual performance. But they feared that when women talked, it was not about themselves, but about their male lovers. Women's talk was popularly regarded as a destructive force to manhood. A stereotypical image of those who judged male reputation can be found in popular literature, which served at this time to reinforce and perhaps even magnify male fears about women's talk. In a way, what women actually talked about matters less to us than what men thought was the content of female gossip. Since it was male conduct in the household and often sexual performance which were imagined to be the subject of most women's talk, this literature is revealing, because it provides us with clues as to what men thought was the most important, and yet the most vulnerable aspect of their reputations.

Married Life

We have seen in the previous chapter that marriage could be an important step in the process of acquiring manhood and enhancing reputation. For most the choice of whom to marry was taken after considerable consultation with friends and family. Without easy access to divorce, marriage in this society was intended to be a lifelong commitment, which few would have undertaken lightly. For many men in their mid to late twenties, the decision to marry came with adult economic independence. For all but the very rich, or the very poor, marriage was an option for men at the end of a long period of service or apprenticeship, or once established in a trade or profession. It was then that a man was thought to have the financial means to marry, set up his own household, and have a family. Theoretically, the married man became master of all those who lived under his roof. Whether wife, child, servant, or apprentice, all were under his command. In particular, as Chapter 1 explained, marriage conferred power to men over women. A 'patriarchal' system of gender relations within marriage, in which men were given supreme authority over their wives and women were expected to be subordinate and obedient to their husbands, held both scriptural and political legitimacy in this society.

But in practice, relations between men and women in marriage were far more complex. The demarcation of roles and responsibilities in the household were frequently not clear-cut, especially since in early modern England many marriages were also business partnerships, with wives of farmers and craftsmen often playing an important part in household economies. It should perhaps not surprise us that advice or conduct books, which taught ways in which men and women could achieve a satisfactory and stable distribution of power within marriage, were in much demand throughout this period. But the advice that the writers of these books offered was riddled with contradiction. On the one hand, men were expected to be rulers over their households; on the other, they were advised to be companions and 'yokefellows' to their wives. According to these writers, men's authority in marriage was not absolute or unconditional, but instead brought with it duties and responsibilities. Since the household was regarded as the basic unit of society, the most fundamental duty for its head was that he should ensure that order was maintained between household members. If a household was known to be disorderly, and relationships broke accepted or conventional bounds, then the spotlight of responsibility would fall on the male head of household.

So by entering marriage a man exposed his manhood to new risks and dangers. It was essential that the honour a man gained on the wedding day was preserved and asserted throughout the course of his marriage. The test of manhood continued through marriage and the stakes were high,

> for whosoever marries a wife may well be called a Merchant venturer, for he makes a great adventure that adventures his credit, his reputation, his estate, his quiet, his liberty, yea many men by marriage do not only adventure their bodies but many times their souls.[49]

A man's credit or reputation was, of course, founded on a range of sexual and non-sexual factors. There were many ways in which 'misadventure' could beset a marriage and undermine a man's honour. Economic misfortune, for example, could devastate families and render redundant a man's ability to provide for his family. The ways in which honourable manhood in marriage could be affected by illicit sexual relationships, however, have been little explored by historians. Yet whether a man or his wife committed adultery, the effects on household order could be catastrophic and widespread, affecting all other facets of male honour, with the finger of blame always pointing back to the man as household head. As we shall see, if a wife committed adultery, contemporaries believed that this provided a clear sign that a man had failed in his duty to maintain household control. A wife who was unfaithful to her husband committed an act of insubordination, which, aside from violence, had no equal. Her adultery destroyed all claims that her husband had to household authority, questioned the legitimacy of his heirs, and affected his credit and standing in the wider community. There could be no more powerful a way to wreck male honour. The remainder of this chapter will show how invariably it was the failure of men to control their wives sexually which was blamed for their wives' adultery. 'Cuckold' was the most shameful name a man could acquire in marriage. Derived from 'cuckoo', the bird that lays its eggs in the nests of other birds, the word came to signify not the lover but his victim, the husband of an adulterous woman.[50]

BECOMING A CUCKOLD

It has been argued both that the term cuckold was not concerned with men's 'own sexuality but that of women for whom they were in some sense responsible', and that it had 'far more potency when it was taken to mean sexual infidelity of wives, instead of their husband's failure to maintain patriarchal control over them'.[51] However, an examination of a range of contemporary sources shows that in the popular mind there was a clear link between a husband's actions and sexual ability, and his wife's behaviour. A woman was not seen to be an adulteress without some fault of her husband. In Count Romei's discourse for gentlemen written in 1598, he discusses why a wife's adultery will dishonour her husband. 'The wife . . . being in her husband's power, and under his government, it appeareth she cannot offend without some fault in her husband . . . and therefore it cannot be that the adulterous wife, should not in some part offend her husband's honour.' A conduct book written a few years later also held that husbands were accountable for their wives' actions. 'For let all men be assured', it warned, 'that the greatest part of the faults committed by wives in this age, take the beginning from the faults of their husbands.' If a wife did offend, a husband was told to examine his own life 'and he shall find how the occasion came from himself, and that he hath not used her, as he ought to have done'.[52]

That 'using' a wife meant satisfying her sexually can be seen from the ballads and drama of the period. In popular medical thinking a woman who did not have adequate sex became ill. It was believed lack of sexual activity would give her an excess of 'seed', and cause 'greensickness'. The joke in the ballad of the 'The Cooper of Norfolk' is that not only is the cooper cuckolded by a brewer, but that the cooper has been such a poor or infrequent lover that the brewer also cures the wife of 'greensickness'.[53] Cuckolds are defined in these sources as men who fail to give their wives sexual pleasure. Thus in the 1685 ballad 'Hey for Horn Fair!' women make their partners cuckolds by 'forsaking their Husbands' dull bed'. In 'A New Western Ballad' a farmer is 'so lazy in bed' that his wife commits adultery with the butcher, and in 'The Cuckold's Complaint' of *c.*1689–91 the husband realises that because he 'cannot ple[ease]' his wife he deserves his fate.[54] In the former ballads women complain about the quality of their husbands' lovemaking, but in others women are forced to look for sex outside marriage because their husbands are impotent. The women in this latter category are portrayed as weary of their maidenheads, and their husbands' inability to consummate the marriage is seen as directly contributing to their cuckold status. So in the 1675 ballad 'Tom Farthing' a 'weary' wife tells other maids to 'try' men first before marriage, and vows 'I'le find out one shall satisfy'. In *c.*1689 'The Scolding Wife's Vindication' featured a wife who commits adultery after two years of marriage 'for nothing at all he'd do', and in another Restoration ballad 'Mirth for Citizens' a husband becomes a cuckold fit for laughter because on his wedding night he remains a 'young puny fool'.[55] In other ballads young wives complain that their husbands are too elderly to satisfy them. The maid in 'The Doting Old Dad' despises her husband for his age, which he argues 'ought to be Honour'd'. When the maid complains, her mother advises her to do as she did 'when my old Dad would deny, to yield me a daily supply', which was to find another lover.[56] If an old man marries a young woman and finds himself a cuckold, 'why . . . the fault is his own', states one writer. Whereas for women sexual energy is perceived as remaining a constant throughout life, older men are seen as having passed their sexual peak and are open to cuckolding. Cuckoldry was considered to be so common a fate for the older man that the anonymous writer of the comic pamphlet *Bull Feather Hall* said that the word cuckold was derived from the initials of the words Cold Old Knave.[57]

The advice given in these ballads is that men would not be made cuckolds if they improved their sexual performance and satisfied their wives. So 'The discontented Married Man' tells another husband to love his wife 'well and make much of her' if he wishes to avoid sharing his fate of being cuckolded, and the husband of 'The Wanton Wife of Castle-Gate' warns other young men to be 'kind to your wives' so that 'God will protect you by night and by day', presumably from the cuckold's horns.[58] 'The Well-Approved Doctor' tells the story of a London physician who was able to cure cuckolds. It is men who are his patients, and those cuckolds who claim that it is their wives' behaviour which is at fault are severely rebuked,

> But some are so wicked that they will exclaim
> Against their poor wives, making 'em bear the blame
> And will not look out in the least for a cure,
> But all the sad pains and their torture endure.[59]

In the drama of the same period husbands who have wives who are unfaithful also look to faults within themselves to explain their partners' behaviour. In Thomas Heywood's *A Woman Killed with Kindness* (1603) Frankford tries to understand why his wife has betrayed him when he discovers her in bed with his friend. He asks her whether he neglected to supply her 'with every pleasure, fashion and new toy'. When she denies that this was her motivation Frankford shows his deepest fear, that there was some inadequacy in himself as a man that was the cause of her adultery:

> Was it then disability in me,
> Or in thine eye seemed he a properer man?[60]

Frankford here assumes that his rival was able to seduce his wife because he was a better lover. 'Proper' in this period meant 'manly', 'handsome' and, in this case, 'sexually attractive'. In *Othello* (*c.*1604) Cassio is referred to as a 'proper man', and such a man is seen as most likely to tempt Desdemona away from the marriage bed. Once more, these sources show the fear that it is a man's sexual inadequacy which makes him a cuckold.[61]

This view is expressed with even greater force in Restoration drama. In John Dryden's *Marriage à la Mode* (1671) Palamede tries to persuade Doralice that if she betrayed her husband by committing adultery it would be a fit punishment for his 'lazy matrimony'. Doralice later complains that she is a widow within marriage, for her husband has 'starved' her of sex. Horner warns the husbands in *The Country Wife* that women 'are like / soldiers, made constant and loyal by good pay rather / than by oaths and covenants'.[62] And in *The Provoked Wife* men are portrayed as getting what they deserve:

> a man of real worth scarce ever is a cuckold but by his own fault. Women are not naturally lewd; there must be something to urge 'em to it.[63]

One of the contemporary explanations for a woman remaining barren in marriage was that she was not being satisfied sexually. For conception to occur, one male medical theory held that both men and women had to produce 'seed'. According to this theory, unless a husband could help his wife to orgasm and so release her seed, she would not become pregnant. The idea that a man could be potent but sterile was not understood by early modern physicians. Mary Fissell's study of the writers of contemporary childbearing guides has shown how they often based their advice on the two-seed model of conception.[64] Several ballads show that the principles of this medical thought were familiar to wider audiences. Awareness of the two-seed theory is shown in the ballad 'Pride's fall'. This ballad relates events which supposedly occurred in Geneva in 1609, with a woman telling us how God punished her for her vanity by scourging 'my seed' so that she produced a two-headed child. In 'The West-country Wonder' William, a serving man, wins the 'admiration of others' when he marries a widow who is nearly sixty-seven years old and manages to get her pregnant. She is given an orgasm, her 'due', and produces the seed necessary for conception. By his wife's pregnancy William 'prov'd himself a Man of Skill', and he is twice referred to as a 'proper' man who 'could Please a Woman well'.[65]

A court of Arches case tells of how in Whitsun 1669 Stephen Seagar of Aldgate suffered the ultimate humiliation of finding that not only had his apprentice Tarrant Reeves made him a cuckold when he was away on business, but that as a result his wife had become pregnant. Stephen found himself the laughing stock of the local community: a mocking ballad was written about his wife Grace and Tarrant, and one man was seen outside Stephen's house holding up a pair of ram's horns to signify a cuckold. Another man who visited Tarrant Reeves after Stephen discovered the adultery asked him how many times he had lain with Grace. When Tarrant said just once, his visitor replied 'that he was a good workman to get her with child by lying but once with her . . . and the said Tarrant laughed thereat'. Pregnancy here is taken to be the consequence of Grace's sexual enjoyment, and it is implied that it was because Stephen could not match the sexual proficiency of his apprentice that he became a cuckold.[66]

Adulterous women such as Grace Seagar were expected to make comparisons between the sexual performance of their husbands and lovers. One witness asked Grace 'whether when she lay with him she found any difference between him the said Tarrant and her said husband'.[67] In a separation case heard in London in 1609 a servant reported how he had overheard Grace Ball say to her lover John Whallie that 'no man living had done that to her which he the same Whallie had done'.[68] Men who were lovers of married women also assumed and flattered themselves that the motivation for their partners' marital infidelity was sexual dissatisfaction. Durham consistory court heard in January 1637 how when Richard Arckley of Burdon suspected his neighbour's wife of adultery he listened to sounds within her chamber by standing outside the window. He said he heard her lover boast to her 'that he had then occupied her better than her husband had done for a year before'.[69] When William Noble, a married man, solicited Ethelreda Baxter in Norfolk in the 1630s, he sought to impress her by boasting as he put his penis in her hand, that 'his pintle was better than her husbands'.[70]

In this context, widows who remarried could be extremely threatening to their new husbands because their experience gave any comparisons between lovers which they made a heightened credibility. Thus the journeyman Thomas Carter overheard Elizabeth Northmore tell her lover in her chamber after they had made love that 'I love thee so dearly for 'tis more than anyone ever did besides my husband Lacke'. Leonard Lacke was Elizabeth's previous husband; when she spoke these lines in 1673 she was married to Edward Northmore.[71] When in 1673 Ellen Charnock brought a cruelty suit against her husband John, he defended his behaviour by claiming that her 'scolding and brawling' and 'abuses of him . . . would have provoked any person'. He recalled how on one occasion when he tried to reprimand her for her lewd behaviour she had declared that he was 'no man, notwithstanding she was assured to the Contrary by having her hand in his Codpiece before the Marriage, and that had she not had two husbands before she should not have known what belonged to a man'. Here we see a woman using her sexual experience to question the manhood of her new husband. Even though her explorations in his codpiece before marriage presumably convinced her that he had a satisfactory penis, which was capable of erection, John's lack of ability to satisfy her since marriage allowed Ellen to claim that he was 'no man'. From their courtship Ellen's seemingly unabashed appraisal of John's sexual assets established her as the dominant partner, her two previous marriages giving her the confidence to take the sexual initiative. She had told John that he was 'too young to catch her', by which she indicated that his youth and therefore sexual inexperience meant that he would be unable to lay claim to her as his own. That this lack of sexual proficiency could also render a man effeminate is powerfully shown by Ellen's words to the servants that, 'if she had not married him . . . he must have worn a Frock'. Her words implied that she thought her husband so unproven in sex that unless she chose to teach him how to be a 'proper' man he would slip into the feminine state. It is hardly surprising that Ellen's public exposure of her dissatisfaction with her marriage left John a figure 'laughed at and scorned abroad'.[72]

A wide range of sources from across the period show that in the seventeenth century 'the honour of the husband dependeth on the wife'.[73] It was a wife's sexual behaviour which most directly reflected on the honour of her husband, as the musician Whythorne lamented, 'a man's honesty and credit doth depend in his wife's tail'.[74] Male and female honour were so closely linked that if a wife committed adultery her husband's sexual reputation would immediately be subject to question. When a husband sees his wife in bed with another man in one popular tale, it is said that he has witnessed 'the act of *his* dishonour'.[75] It is certainly overstating the case to claim that 'all the responsibility for household honour' when it concerned sexual conduct rested solely on women in this period.[76] Instead, the responsibility for the dishonour of wife adultery lay with the husband. It was his sexual impotence which was assumed to be at fault. Hence the shame of cuckoldry. When Thomas Earl of Stamford discovered that his wife had been adulterous in the 1680s, he bitterly told the court of Arches of how he

> found her to be a lewd and adulterous person and had been false to his bed, and the same was public and notorious. And that by her course of living she had ruined him both in reputation and Estate [and he] did wish that he had never seen her face or never married her or that she were dead and so much he hath publicly declared.[77]

The dishonour that he claimed to have experienced was embodied in the frequently cited proverb, 'a virtuous woman is a crown to her husband: but she that maketh him ashamed is as corruption in his bones'.[78]

ATTEMPTING SEXUAL CONTROL

The key to prevention of cuckoldry remained sexual control. It was important for men within sexual relationships to assert a difference or 'separateness' from women in the bedroom if they were able to achieve that control. Here we are entering the realm of men's most intimate emotions and experiences, which for the most part remain obscured from the historical record. But ballads and drama may provide us with clues as to how men thought sexual control could be obtained. In ballads such as 'The Hasty Bridegroom' the husband is shown to be anxious to 'stoutly' make 'bold with his own'.[79] The sexual act is often described by using the terms of male trades and the male role in sex is one of assertive and forceful control: the pedlar will 'pound spice', the taylor uses his 'piercing Bodkin', the cooper will 'hoop her Tubb' and stop her 'lake-hole', and when the farmer is cuckolded his wife is 'plough'd up'.[80] The emphasis is placed on penetrative sex in which men establish their difference from women and their ownership of them. Eric Partridge has found that the bawdy language in Shakespeare's plays displays a similar preoccupation with describing the male role in sex as phallic, assertive, and often aggressive. To cite some examples, women's vaginas are 'cities' or 'forts' to be 'assailed', 'besieged', 'breached' and 'occupied' by penises which are 'darts', 'lances', 'stakes' and 'swords'.[81] When Leonard Wheatcroft, a Derbyshire yeoman, wrote his *Courtship Narrative* in the mid-seventeenth century, he also chose the metaphors of war to describe his experiences; he lay siege to his lover, and she was his commander.[82] In Restoration plays similar metaphors were employed to describe sex, particularly those with a hunting or military emphasis, in which the male role was one of 'hunting for the kill' or 'storming a siege'.[83] During the same period, many writers of contemporary popular health texts used metaphors to which they hoped their audience could relate, as they attempted to describe and explain the reproductive process. From the 1650s these metaphors were increasingly drawn from the male world of work. Fissell has shown how men's active bodies were portrayed as crucial to the reproductive process; women's bodies in contrast were frequently rendered passive. Men 'ploughed' and 'sowed' the female landscape, and 'women's bodies were spaces in which masculine activity reigned'.[84]

How far men in everyday conversations referred to and thought about sex in these terms is difficult to tell. However, witnesses in the church courts did refer to women as being 'occupied' or 'shaken' by men during sex, as well as occasionally women 'occupying' men.[85] Tim Hitchcock has suggested that in the eighteenth century sex was 'redefined', and that a 'sexual revolution' took place in which male penetration became all-important.[86] Examples from seventeenth-century literary and legal sources may prompt us to question seriously the novelty, at least in the realm of male imagination, of this idea.

Drama and poetry sources reveal another aspect of the male role in sex which is not apparent in the ballads. For whilst ballads describe male penetration, they say little about ejaculation. Self-control may have been achievable during penetration, but drama and poetry not surprisingly show that during ejaculation the achievement of 'a simultaneity of release and control' is difficult.[87] Instead, men are portrayed suffering from guilt after sex because they fear that by 'letting go' during sex they had exhibited a lack of self-control which will allow women in future to dominate them. The act of sex itself becomes fearful because it is not rational, and therefore instead of confirming it, may even endanger manhood. As Mark Breitenberg has explained, the moment of male orgasm was seen as dangerous because it generated 'the material of masculinity but also destroys it', and was a 'literal and figurative "emptying out" of the masculine principle'. It also represented what was otherwise seen as a typically 'feminine' inability to control bodily fluids.[88] After Othello has travelled through a storm to Cyprus where he is reunited with Desdemona, he foresees sex with his wife as a 'tempest' which will unleash uncontrollable desires in him. Even within marriage sexual desire can cause men to lose their reason. Othello comes to realise that he 'lov'd not wisely, but too well'.[89] Shakespeare's Sonnet 129 illustrates the guilt and sadness that men could feel after sex:

> Th'expense of spirit in a waste of shame
> Is lust in action, and, till action, lust
> Is perjured, murd'rous, bloody, full of blame,
> Savage, extreme, rude, cruel, not to trust,
> Enjoyed no sooner but despised straight.[90]

This expression of post-coital depression was by no means rare in Renaissance poetry, as C.J. Summers and T-L. Pebworth have shown. 'Doing, a filthy pleasure is, and short: / And done, we straight repent us of the sport', wrote Ben Jonson.[91] When Troilus contemplates sex he asks,

> What will it be
> When that the wat'ry palate tastes indeed
> Love's thrice repured nectar? – death, I fear me,
> Swooning destruction, or some joy too fine,
> Too subtle-potent, tuned too sharp in sweetness,
> For the capacity of my ruder powers.
> I fear it much; and I do fear besides
> That I shall lose distinction in my joys.[92]

Death is the result of sex, and 'to die' is the metaphor Shakespeare uses to describe the male orgasm.[93] As Benedick tells Beatrice in *Much Ado,* 'I will live in thy heart, die in thy lap, and be buried in thy eyes.'[94] For Troilus, who fears that he will 'lose distinction' in sex, male honour is seen as directly threatened by the act of copulation. It may seem little wonder that Othello is persuaded of Iago that,

> An honest man he is, and hates the slime
> That sticks on filthy deeds.[95]

These literary ideas about sex may seem far-fetched to us, but contemporary Christian teaching may have helped men in reality to engender these feelings of guilt at sexual pleasure. Whilst post-Reformation conduct books acknowledged that sex, or 'due benevolence' as it was termed, could be for mutual pleasure as well as procreation, they still urged moderation in love-making. William Gouge warned men against 'excess' in sex, William Whateley taught that too much sex 'doth weaken the body, and shorten life', and Daniel Rogers believed that the marriage bed could be dishonoured by either refusal of sex by one party, or an 'odious' excess of sex.[96] John Calvin had even ministered that the man who showed 'no modesty or comeliness in conjugal intercourse' was committing adultery with his wife.[97] Ministers such as Samuel Hieron in the early seventeenth century continued to teach men that there was an honourable as well as a dishonourable way to love their wives. Couples were to say the following prayer before going to bed, 'Allay in us all sensual and brutish love . . . that we may in nothing dishonour this honourable state.'[98] Since both partners had duties to the marital bed, as Margaret Sommerville has recognised, 'the one area where the wife ruled the husband as he did her was the carnal'.[99]

None of these conduct book writers considered how men were to resolve the central paradox of Puritan thinking concerning male gender roles: how was a man to be a patriarchal head of household as well as a loving, passionate and benevolent husband? Only in fictional sources are the tensions which could arise between these contradictory roles of love and control explored in any detail, but even there, no easy solutions are proffered. The remoteness of some of these conduct book writers from the realities of most men's married lives is illustrated by their belief that men's sexual control of their wives could extend to a control of emotions and desires. Edmund Tilney advised a husband in his relationship with his wife to 'steal away her private will, and appetite, so that of two bodies there may be only one heart'. John Dod and Robert Cleaver argued that 'the husband ought not to be satisfied with the use of his wife's body, but in that he hath also the possession of her will and affections'.[100] But no man could possess the will and affections of his wife, however great his desire for control.

Popular medical thinking also advised men to be moderate in their love-making, and advised that excessive sex could cause ill-health. William Vaughan in his 1600 *Approved Directions for Health*, for example, warned that loss of male seed during ejaculation 'harmeth a man more, than if he should bleed forty times as much'.[101] The writer of *The Office of Christian Parents* believed that lack of moderation in sex could affect the ability of a woman to conceive, so that either she remained barren, or else had 'very weak and sickly children'.[102] *Aristotle's Masterpiece* and Nicholas Venette's *The Mysteries of Conjugal Love Reveal'd* were the most popular manuals of sexual advice in the late seventeenth and early eighteenth centuries. Both were pronatal in their outlook, and saw sex within marriage as natural and pleasurable. But even within this literature which took an essentially positive stance on sex, there was advice to men to be moderate in their love-making. 'The frequent Caresses of women exhaust our Strength and Forces entirely, whereas moderately used, they preserve our Health, and render our Body more free and active than before: I should therefore advise neither to loath Venus with Terror, nor to yield to her Charms too slavishly and effeminately', Venette wrote in 1712.[103] Popular almanacs also advised their readers,

> Neither in labour, meat, or drink,
> In sleep or venery
> Exceed: but keep the golden mean
> To hold thy health thereby.[104]

In popular literature there were numerous accounts of the dire consequences for those who sexually did exceed this 'golden mean'. In one literary defence for men marrying older women, a graphic description of a man exhausted by sex with a young woman is provided:

> show me Hector himself, the stoutest he that lives, who after a week's repose in the bosom of a lusty and youthful Beauty, will not say that he is become a Victim to Venus . . . as his wasted flesh, extenuated Eyes . . . and sneaking behaviour may sufficiently demonstrate, whilst

> she like Aurora looks fresh, bucksome, plump, and lively; her Eyes makes bonfires, crowing and triumphing for the Victory; baffling her Castrated Cavalier with stolen kisses; he mean season returning only a poor and dry salute, and that more to save his Credit, than to serve his Love.[105]

Such literature was written in a blatantly misogynist fashion, and it is hard to believe that in reality many men saw themselves, their lovers, or their love-making in this way. The problem remains, however, that so much of how men thought about their bodies and their sexual experiences is hidden from historical view. By gathering evidence together from literary, theological and medical sources we can attempt to put together a cultural milieu of the world in which seventeenth-century men lived. From this we may deduce ways of thinking about sex which addressed specifically male anxieties, and which some men in reality may have shared. The sources discussed above suggest that although sexual control may have been thought the key to men's subordination of women, contemporaries also recognised that the very act of sex had the potential to disempower men.

A DOUBLE SEXUAL STANDARD?

We have seen how manhood could be endangered by wife adultery, but how far was manhood also threatened by men's own extramarital affairs? Many historians have taken the lead from Keith Thomas's seminal 1959 article on 'the double standard' and have strongly argued that as men's sexual deviance was seen as less morally culpable than women's, the consequences of their illicit sexual relationships did not compare with their wives'.[106] Following this line of thinking, since male honesty depended upon more than just sex, whereas female reputation rested solely on sexual chastity, women's reputation was bound to be more sensitive to accusations of infidelity. Adultery, as Romei explained in 1598, was a greater crime for a woman because it 'offendeth extremely against her own proper and principal virtue, which is honesty'.[107] Records from the church courts which show a preponderance of female plaintiffs fighting sexual defamation suits would appear to support this argument. The consistory court of seventeenth-century Durham, for example, heard 225 defamation cases in the years 1604–65, only 76 of which were brought by men.[108] In the Restoration court of Arches the presence of female plaintiffs was even more striking: only 25 out of

192 defamation cases had male plaintiffs.[109] But how far is this conclusive evidence that married men cared little about their sexual reputations, and that within marriage the only dangers to manhood were from adulterous women?

There is a wealth of evidence to suggest that there was indeed a double sexual standard in place during this period. The most severe act of the seventeenth century against sexual incontinence passed in 1650 embodied the double standard by defining adultery as a crime that could only be committed by women; if a married man had illicit sex it was labelled fornication.[110] Church court records reveal instances of wives discovering their husbands' adultery, and instead of directing their anger against them, they turn on their husbands' mistresses and call them whore.[111] In contemporary ballads wives of adulterous husbands also physically harm their female rivals. A slit nose was the sign of a whore. In 'Have among you! good Women' a Joyner's wife cuts the nose of her husband's lover to give her 'a mark to be known'. In 'Man's Felicity and Misery' David claims that if he even looks at another woman his wife will 'claw her eyes out', and when two wives meet and discuss the marriage fortunes of their friends in 'Well met, Neighbour', one says that if she had an adulterous husband she would ensure that his lover 'should go with no nose on her face'. Gowing has found that women in London threatened to carry out these threats when they suspected their husbands of infidelity. Even if this violence was intended to bring husbands back to their wives, it would appear from these examples that whatever the circumstances, it was a woman who always got the blame and bore the brunt of others' anger.[112]

Separation suits in the Restoration period show that women who dared to question their husbands' behaviour risked being beaten. Hence the court of Arches heard in 1663 how when Cecily Bradley complained to her husband about his mistress widow Anne Cooke living with them, 'telling him it was not fit she should be there under her nose against her will', he responded by beating her and turning her out the house. At a Christmas Eve dinner in their home at Lindfield, Sussex, in 1689 Thomas Holford talked of his mistress in front of his guests and offered his wife a crown to fetch her. The meal ended violently when Mary Holford refused and said that if her husband's mistress was present she would burn her. The enraged Thomas proceeded 'with great violence' to 'thrust or swing her [his wife] round the Room'.[113] When Elizabeth Rich became suspicious of her husband's activities with wenches at the house of Richard Hare in St Martin-in-the-Fields, she went to confront

Richard. She was met with a torrent of abuse. Richard called her an 'impudent woman' and said that 'if he was . . . her husband he would lock her up and go whither he pleased and said further she deserved to be whipped at a cart's arse in offering to hinder her said husband in anything he had a mind to do'. For daring to intrude into her husband's business, and angrily confronting a man who she believed ran a bawdy house, Elizabeth found herself having to defend herself in the defamation case which Richard Hare later pursued.[114] It would seem that these wives would have been wise to have taken the advice of the first Marquis of Halifax, who, writing to his daughter concerning adultery, argued that 'next to the danger of committing the fault yourself, the greatest is that of seeing it in your husband'.[115]

Ballads which tell women to bear with their husbands' faults and tolerate their adultery give us a picture of values and expectations.[116] Clues in these ballads that the physical act of adultery shamed a man in the same way that it did a woman are hard to find. Only two ballads describe how adultery destroys a man's good name, one says that whores take away 'Purse, Person and Fame', the other says of adultery that 'no credit comes on't'.[117] The majority of ballads lay the blame of husband adultery on wicked whores who tempt men away from the marriage bed.[118]

However, conduct book writers taught that men could be shamed by their own illicit sexual activities. Many claimed that sexual incontinence was equally sinful for both men and women, and even that the punishment should be greater for male adulterers than for females due to men's position of authority.[119] At one extreme, Richard Cooke, who published a sermon he gave in London in 1629, wrote that if whoremongers looked at how their reputation was affected by their behaviour they would find that their honour lay 'not in the dust, but even in a dunghill'.[120] Matthew Poole, in his commentary on the Bible, argued that adultery was so damaging to a man, that whoever committed it 'is guilty of self-murder'.[121]

If the ideas of a double standard were wholly accepted, this does not explain why some men were slandered as sexually incontinent, and why these men felt sufficiently concerned by the insult to bring defamation suits. For example, on Whitsunday 1608 Cuthbert Keadland of Newcastle was called a 'whoremaster knave, and a Bastard getter knave' in front of his wife by Margaret Baite, and George Craggs was called a whoremonger according to one witness, a whoremaster according to another, by Christopher Simpson in Gilesgate at Durham in 1625.[122] In the Durham church court records of the early seventeenth century the terms whoremaster and whoremonger were used interchangeably which may suggest that they did not differ significantly in meaning. By the Restoration, the insult of whoremonger was rarely recorded in the court of Arches records, but whoremaster was defined as a man who committed fornication or incontinence with lewd women.[123] It is worth noting, however, that both terms gave men power and control over the women they had sex with: 'whores are always possessed by men'.[124] No distinction is made between men who have casual or long-term affairs. But importantly, from the wording of these insults against men it can be seen that for men it was the consequences of illicit sex, rather than the act of sex or its discovery, that caused shame. We have seen how Cuthbert Keadland was accused of getting bastards; George Craggs was also called a 'beggarly rogue' who had 'spent all his means upon whores and harlots'.[125] By 'keeping' whores, men to their shame disrupt both household economy and order. George Cragg's wife is said to have whipped his whores out of his house; in October 1609 it was heard how Margaret Maire had told her friends that because her husband kept four whores 'she could lead no life with him'; and in July 1628, when Richard Robinson caught Ralph Allanson committing adultery, he angrily told him 'it was more fit for him to be at home with his wife', and threatened to fetch her.[126] Married men who boasted of their extra-marital exploits could also find themselves subject to community censure. Edward Arnold found that his drinking companions testified against him in the marriage separation suit brought by his wife in 1668. His friends repeated to the court the claims that he had made to them that 'he could not be without' his whores, and that 'he could and would have a wench anywhere'.[127]

The ballad called 'The Whoremonger's Conversion' summarises well the shameful consequences for men who had whores. A man describes how he was once a libertine but that his life led him to poverty, to the 'surgeon's hands' with the pox, to being beaten after quarrels over a whore, and to 'disgrace' with the constable and watch.[128] From the sixteenth century venereal disease, or 'the pox', as it was popularly known, had swept across Europe as a terrifying new disease. Until the nineteenth century gonorrhoea and syphilis were not distinguished, but were seen as symptoms of the same disease. The pox caused acute pain, afflicting men with burning scabs, cysts and swelling beginning with the penis and spreading to other parts of the body, sometimes even leading to death.[129] It was seen as a direct consequence of illicit sex, acting as a sign of engagement in extra-marital sex for married men which was as physically visible to the world as pregnancy was for women. The pox was popularly thought to be a punishment from God to teach men to be faithful to their wives: 'men talk never of Continency, and Chastity until the time they see the razor in the surgeon's hands', one contemporary reflected.[130]

Even though in theory accusations of venereal disease should have formed the basis for common law suits, men did bring cases to the church courts after they were slandered as 'burnt' or 'pocky', the insult acting as an 'implicit allegation of past misconduct'.[131] Of course, the slander was not sex specific, and women as well as men were accused of having the pox.[132] Husbands or wives who caught the disease outside the marital bed and then passed it on to their partners were not viewed sympathetically by the courts who determined marriage separation suits. But as the clearest representation of the linkage between love, sex and death, for men the disease powerfully reinforced their fears about the dangers of sex with women.[133] It could inspire male fear and guilt of sex; the surgeon Richard Wiseman published a series of case studies in 1676 which included stories of men who felt so guilty after illicit sex that they imagined they had the pox.[134] It was a disease which carried much stigma. 'The shame of this very thing, I confess, troubles me as much as anything', Samuel Pepys wrote after he discovered that his neighbours were openly discussing the details of his brother's pox.[135]

This shame could have very clear material consequences. Richard and Charity Winckle were both slandered by William Wood with having the pox in 1669. William had boldly declared to Richard, 'you had lost the Bridge of your nose if you had not had a good Chirurgeon', and to Charity that she was a whore who had given her husband the pox and had been to Hampstead to seek a cure. Ignorance of how the disease was transmitted was shown by the reaction of one of the Winckles' customers at their tavern in Wapping. A certain Mr Wollaston, it was reported, would only drink at their establishment if he had a 'Bason of water standing by him, that he might there in wash the glass the producent [Charity Winckle] or her husband drank in, fearing that he should be pockified by them, and swore he would not come into the said Mr Winckle's house until he and his wife had cleared themselves'. Other customers may have been scared away from visiting the Winckles' tavern.[136] Even more frightening was the fact that the pox could affect the very member which had sinned, striking at the core of manhood, often leaving men sexually incapacitated. Two men in the early seventeenth-century Durham courts faced the slander of their neighbours that they had 'half' a prick 'cut off' after contracting the disease, an insult which questioned their very claim to manhood. That one of these men, John Eastmas of Newcastle, faced this taunt from a widow eight years after he had been afflicted with the pox, shows how a single act of illicit sex could haunt and shame a man for years to come.[137]

'Men sued their wives for adultery; women sued their husbands for extreme cruelty. Effectively, only women could be penalised for extramarital sex and only men could be guilty of violence', Gowing has argued, based on her study of marriage separation cases in the London church courts 1572–1640.[138] In the Durham church courts of the early seventeenth century there were only four cases of separation, two brought by women, and two by men. The small numbers of these cases from this court do not allow for any firm conclusions to be made.[139] However, when we turn to Restoration church court evidence we find that male sexual inconstancy was subject to criticism by some wives and was invoked by women in marriage separation cases. In the court of Arches between 1660 and 1700 women brought twenty-one out of the fifty cases heard for separation on grounds of 'adultery' (fourteen female plaintiffs) or 'adultery and cruelty' (seven female plaintiffs). Perhaps what we are seeing here is a change of attitudes over time, and this may be reflected in the views expressed about the double standard on the Restoration stage, as will be discussed below. It may also be that the special nature of the court of Arches as an appeal court meant that women were more likely to present separation suits for adultery in this court than in the lower courts. As women who dared to question their husbands' sexual behaviour, they perhaps had less chance of a successful suit in the lower court and stood a greater probability of needing to pursue their suit further in an appeal court. However, there are features of the separation suits which were heard in this court which would seem to question the notion of a double standard. First, some women who were accused of adultery by their husbands counter this accusation by also charging their husbands with inconstancy, surely an ineffective defence if the double standard was wholly accepted. These women draw attention to the shameful consequences of their husbands' illicit behaviour. For example, Martha Milner, married to John, an upholsterer in St Clement Danes, Middlesex, responded to her husband's allegations of adultery in 1669 by claiming that his infidelities had led to him infecting her with the pox. At the other end of the social scale, the Countess of Stamford defended herself in the separation suit brought by the Earl by arguing that it was his liaisons with 'lewd women' that had driven him into debt. She even said that her husband had an affair with one of his witnesses in the case, Elizabeth Poole, who had tried to 'destroy' her baby when she became pregnant by him. The statements of these women openly defied the notion of a double standard of sexual behaviour.[140]

Secondly, there is further evidence in the cases women brought on grounds of cruelty that adultery of husbands led to a shameful disruption of household order. The pattern of consequences of female infidelity, which, as we will see in the next chapter, was popularly believed to include scolding and even violence as part of wider household disorder, was echoed by that anticipated as following from male adultery. For example, Mary Jones prosecuted her husband George in Cheshire in 1665 after he beat her. She showed the court how household relations had been disrupted after Dorothy Walklate had become her husband's mistress and moved into the house. Mary's story of her husband's adultery clearly shows how her rightful position was usurped by this intruder. Dorothy would bring George a posset in bed, feed it to him, and then climb in beside him. Mary said George had 'never put of[f] his clothes to lie with her since Dorothy Walklate came to live in the house'. In these circumstances, George's beating and expulsion of his wife from the house appear as a further aspect of his generally abusive and disruptive behaviour.[141] The witnesses who spoke for Mary Morgan of Aberhasesp, Montgomeryshire, in her separation suit for cruelty against her husband Matthew in 1680 emphasised how Matthew's cruelty to his wife took place in the context of his adultery with at least three servants and a married woman, Katherine Jones. Matthew's adulterous relationships had also led to Mary's role within the household being displaced; Katherine Jones commanded the servants who were in turn disrespectful to Mary. It was said that Katherine had 'so great a power over him the said Mr Morgan' that if anyone had a request for Matthew, they would first seek Katherine's favour. The story which the witnesses created was one of a husband whose adultery had led to shameful consequences; he was under the 'power' of his mistress who had taken over the control of his household, and he had abused his position as a master, with three maids leaving his house pregnant, and another fleeing from his unwelcome advances. In these circumstances a husband violently beating his wife could be presented as one more indication of a man who had lost control.[142] The blame for disorderly male conduct in these cases may still be attributed as originating with a woman, for example in the Holford case of 1690 one witness remarked how it was 'customary' for Thomas to slander his wife cruelly when he came home from his mistress's house, and Cecily Bradley in 1663 complained how it was her husband's mistress who used to 'instigate her husband against her'.[143] But by indicating that their husbands' behaviour was influenced by other women, these wives were showing how men with mistresses had lost self-control, and thus how adultery could easily become shameful to a man. The result of extra-marital sex for both men and women was shame; but the cause of that shame differed. For men it could be caused by loss of self-control, and more importantly household control; for women it was always the result of compromised sexual chastity.

A survey of the drama of the period reveals that objections to the double standard were voiced by female characters on the stage. Emilia in *Othello* points out that, like men, women have frailties, affections and desires, and that if men treat them ill by pouring 'our treasures into peevish laps', then they should expect similar behaviour in return. She warns,

> Then let them use us well: else let them know,
> The ills we do, their ills instruct us so.

These ideas are expressed in Restoration plays with even greater force. Honour codes which insist on sexual chastity are portrayed as denying women their natural desires, and imprisoning them within loveless marriages. Lucy, Alithea's maid in Wycherley's *The Country Wife*, regards honour as a 'disease in the head' which robs women of their pleasure: 'Men lose their lives by it; women what's dearer to 'em, their love, the life of life.' When Lady Cockwood in *She Would if She Could* (1668) is so cautious of her honour that she is foiled once more in her attempt to make love to Courtall, she realises, 'My over-tenderness of my honour has blasted all my hopes of happiness.'[144] Remaining chaste within marriage is so undesirable and 'so condemned' by men of 'every age', that 'they have thrown it amongst the women to scrabble for', Constant declares in Vanbrugh's *The Provoked Wife.* The argument that fidelity should be reciprocal is voiced by Lovemore in Southerne's *The Wives' Excuse* (1692). He cannot believe that a woman,

> can be contented to have her Honour, much longer than her Fortune in the possession of a Man, who has no fund of his own, to

> answer in security for either.
> Thus, who a Married Woman's Love wou'd win,
> Shou'd with the Husband's failings first begin;
> Make him but in the fault, and you shall find
> A Good Excuse will make most Women kind.[145]

When in *The Provoked Wife* Lady Brute asks Constant why men insist upon chastity for women he explains, 'We recommend it to our wives, madam, because we would keep 'em to ourselves; and to our daughters, because we would dispose of 'em to others.'[146] The motivation for the double standard is represented here as entirely selfish on men's part: marital fidelity is something that they themselves cannot achieve, and is insisted upon purely so that they can claim sexual control over their wives.

It is interesting that men even made a distinction between single and double adultery. Romei stated that a married man who committed adultery with an unmarried woman, 'although he be worthy of some blame, yet looseth not his honour, because he injureth none but his own wife'. On the other hand, double adultery was committed when,

> married or unbound, he useth the company of a woman married. And this man remaineth dishonoured, because he sinneth extremely against the virtue of Temperance, and faileth in justice, he being a grievous injurer or destroyer of another man's honour.

In other words, double adultery was the more serious offence because it harmed another man's honour.[147]

As Faramerz Dabhoiwala has usefully pointed out, 'there existed not one universal standard of male sexual conduct' in this period, but 'several different and conflicting codes'.[148] Whilst some moralists condemned all adultery, regardless of whether committed by husband or wife, legal sanctions reflected much popular thinking which held male adultery to be a far less serious offence. Attempts by wives to expose or control their husbands' sexual activities often met with disapproval, and it took a courageous woman to sue for marriage separation on these grounds. Men could, however, endanger their reputations by their own sexual incontinence. As will be shown in the next chapter, a man's adultery could discredit his subsequent words and actions, and even lead to dismissal from employment. But unlike women's adultery, the shame of men's adultery was neither inevitable nor irrevocable. It was dependent upon the marital status and reputation of the woman with whom they had sex, and upon the extent to which the consequences of their sexual relationship appeared to others to have repercussions for the wider social and gender order. If a man seemed likely to infect others with sexual disease, and was causing disruption in his household by his sexual infidelity, then his behaviour was shameful. It was particularly the public nature of his failure to control his sexual and domestic affairs which was damaging.

Despite being open to debate, the double standard remained deeply and securely embedded within early modern popular culture, and remained crucial to the sexual politics of the period. Although men could be shamed by the consequences of illicit sex, adultery would remain a greater crime for women than men, whilst a wife's adultery 'also staineth the honour of her husband'.[149] A woman's chastity belonged to her husband, 'a woman hath no power of her own body, but her husband', so by committing adultery, she did 'the more wrong to give away that thing which is another body's without the owner's license', wrote Johannes Vives in 1541.[150] Both in reality and on the stage women objected to the double standard, but it would remain in place as long as male honour rested on female chastity.

But we can question how far the double standard is a useful model for explaining the ratio of women to men fighting sexual defamation suits in the church courts. We have seen how some married men were slandered as whoremasters or whoremongers and responded by taking those who defamed them to the church courts. This chapter has also shown that control of women's chastity was of fundamental importance to men's reputations, and that 'cuckold' was the worst sexual insult which could be directed against men. But in the Durham consistory court in the early seventeenth century out of seventy-six defamation cases with a male plaintiff, only three were brought by men who had been called cuckold.[151] In the court of Arches during the Restoration period, there were only three defamation cases brought after the insult of cuckold had been used, and all three cases were initiated as joint actions between the husband and his wife.[152] How can we explain the very small number of these cases? Ironically, part of the explanation may lie with the power of 'cuckold' as an insult. It took a brave man or woman to call a man cuckold, for it was an insult which no other could surmount. It is also possible that some men who were called cuckold would not have dared to have gone to the courts for fear that the insult would have reached an even wider audience. As we shall see, there were other occasions when a man was called cuckold or implied to be a cuckold and his wife ended up being the sole plaintiff in the case which followed. Chapter 5 will discuss these issues further, and show why many of the defamation suits launched by married women may reveal much about their husbands' concerns for reputation. Men cared deeply about their sexual reputations. There was no simple correlation between concern for sexual reputation and the number of defamation suits being fought in the church courts.

HEADING A HOUSEHOLD

The work of demographers in the 1960s and 1970s enabled historians to reject the myth that early modern families were 'extended' in structure, with many generations of the same family living under the same roof. But whereas families were confirmed to be 'nuclear' in size, the presence of domestic servants, apprentices and lodgers in many homes meant that households were on average larger in size than those today.[153] These non-relative members of the household often slept, ate and worked within the same domestic spaces as family members. The work of Naomi Tadmor has shown that contemporaries often referred to these non-relatives as 'family', and interpreted their behaviour as 'familial actions'.[154] It is little wonder, then, that a man's honour depended not only on his wife's behaviour, but also on that of his wider household. Heading a household consisting of servants and apprentices meant more than just providing employment and training in work-related skills, but also setting a moral example. As we shall see, within the household, it was important for a man to show that he was in control of his entire household, for the home was a 'little Commonwealth' in which men were expected to demonstrate their ability to rule.[155] Within the household a man's reputation could also be open to the dangers of non-familial talk and action.

It was deeply insulting to men to suggest that they had lost control over their households. In the week before Whitsuntide 1620 John Yealdert approached Christopher Stoke, who was selling gloves on the Sandhill in Newcastle, and told Christopher that 'he kept a thief' in his house. When Christopher demanded to know what he meant by this, John said Christopher's apprentice William Raine stole from him. John had slandered Christopher by implying that he was unaware that his own apprentice was dishonest. When William Raine appeared as plaintiff against John Yealdert in the defamation suit a few months later, it could be argued that Christopher was reasserting his control over William and demonstrating that he could manage his household.[156] Masters were also expected to ensure the sexual honesty of their maidservants, since any sexual impropriety of a female servant could reflect back on her master. Hence in July 1673 William Colley went up to a glass seller who was standing at his shop door in Cheapside, London, and said 'in a scoffing or jeering manner', 'Dick Clark hath got your maid with child'. As with the Yealdert/Raine case above, the insult was initially directed to the master, and was at least partly intended to damage his reputation. It was also the servant in question, Mary Parry, who later pursued a defamation suit.[157] Just as it will be shown in Chapter 5 that wives fought defamation cases to clear their husbands' names as well as their own, so also servants such as William Raine and Mary Parry could go to court to defend their master's reputation in addition to their own. The pressure on servants such as Mary Parry to go to the church courts to clear their names is evident from the experience of Margery Gregory, who worked at the Red Lion alehouse in Kensington, London. She was slandered as a whore in front of her workplace in 1669 by a man who was believed to be her former master. Her present master and mistress immediately dismissed her from their service, and it was said by one witness that Margery had 'to bring very good testimony of her good and civil behaviour before they would receive her again'. The defamation case in this context can be seen as part of her bid to be re-employed.[158]

The alternative to sending a servant to court was simply to dismiss him or her from the household, thereby distancing a master's reputation from that of his servants. Thus when Alice Richardson was called whore in Michaelmas 1608 she lost her job tending cows in the parish of Chester le Street, and when a rumour began that Elizabeth Joplyn's father and brother had died of the pox, she was dismissed from the Moorecroft household in the city of Durham. Similarly, George Fenwick of St Nicholas', Newcastle, who had served as an apprentice for six years, tried to persuade Margaret Sharpe who was servant in the same household not to tell anyone that they had committed fornication together, for fear of losing his opportunity eventually to qualify as a freeman.[159]

Household heads were expected to ensure that the sexual reputations of their servants were unblemished, and conduct book writers considered it an abuse of masterly control to become sexually involved with maidservants.[160] However, many masters did attempt to have sexual relations with their servants even though, as we have seen, the consequences of this adultery were so often shameful. Keith Wrightson has shown how some 14–23 per cent of women who had bastards in Essex or Lancashire in the seventeenth century named their master, or someone in a 'magisterial position', as the father.[161]

Within the upper classes there could even be a shared male expectation that husbands would seek sexual favours from their servants. Sir Ralph Verney received a letter from his uncle, William Denton, in 1650 announcing that he was sending a new maidservant to the Verney household. William told his nephew that 'I took great care to fit you with a Joan that may be as good as my Lady [Sir Ralph's wife] in the dark . . . Luce [a former servant of the Verney's] is very confident she will match your cock.'[162] Examples of masters from the middling sorts who had sex with their servants are not difficult to find in church court records. Margaret Pigg of Haltwhistle tolerated six years of marriage sharing her house with her husband's mistress who had been a maidservant, and their illegitimate child, before she sued for separation in 1610. In 1621 during a quarrel between two wives in a bakehouse in Gilesgate, Durham, Elizabeth Wilson told Sibell Garrie that her husband was 'a bastard getting Rascal' who got 'bastards with his maids and makes his men take to them'. Sibell and her husband brought separate defamation suits against Elizabeth in the case that followed. What was shameful was the accusation that Humfred Garrie was abusing both his female servants by having sex with them and their partners by leaving to them the responsibility of bringing up his children.

But whilst masters may have frequently tested the sexual chastity of their servants, there is also evidence that on the whole masters saw wider or community knowledge of their sexual relationships with servants as shameful, and that they wished to avoid this slight on their reputations. This is most clearly shown in the records of the 1669 separation suit of Grace Hubbard for adultery and cruelty against her husband John of St Clement Danes, Middlesex. One servant, Elizabeth Malthus, who acted as a witness for Grace, claimed that John repeatedly tried to seduce her when she worked in the Hubbard household. Elizabeth felt so troubled by her master's advances that she told her mother and then got a warrant from one Justice Godfrey for John to appear before the justice. She gained leave of her service, but not before she signed a note to John 'not to trouble him for the uncivil offers or attempts of her chastity he had made, which he said would prejudice his credit and reputation'. Even though John had never actually succeeded in committing adultery with Elizabeth, he felt that without signing the note she would have sufficient information to blackmail him or damage his reputation.[163]

The story of the Seagar marriage told previously in this chapter, in which Grace Seagar committed adultery with an apprentice from her household, has shown how if a mistress committed adultery with a servant her husband could be exposed to incessant mockery. For this transgression showed that a husband was capable of controlling neither his wife nor servant and brought him into disrepute. Similarly, the Earl of Stamford's shame at the discovery of his wife's adultery in the 1680s was probably fuelled by the fact that her alleged lover was one of his servants.[164] When John Coleman, a disgruntled former servant of the Beaumont household, started to spread gossip that he had committed adultery with his mistress in 1607, her husband Sir Thomas Beaumont launched a Star Chamber suit against him for defamation.[165] For relationships between masters or mistresses and servants directly threatened the social hierarchy which household heads were expected to maintain. Even when friendships were formed between mistresses and servants of the same gender, they were subject to critical comment. When Elizabeth Bound accused her husband of adultery in 1693 she found herself subject to the most extravagant of claims by her husband. He and his witnesses told the court that she had tried to prevent her husband from knowing that she had already lost her virginity before their marriage, had gone 'abroad' late at night drinking and dressed in men's clothes ('Hats, Wigs, Breeches and the like'), and had infected her husband with the pox on her return. Witnesses claimed that such lewd behaviour was encouraged by Elizabeth's 'intimacy' with her servant Hannah Hardcastle, who accompanied her on her exploits. One witness commented on how their familiarity was 'not becoming the Decency of a Mistress to her Servant' and that Hannah was 'not fit to be entertained in a civil family'.[166]

Whilst masters and mistresses may have been encouraged to distance their reputations from those of their employees, the comments of servants in separation suits show that the good name of their employers could also exert a considerable influence on their fortunes. Some servants did not wish their masters' reputation to rub off on to their own; such as the London apprentice who told his master 'that he would not tarry with him for he kept a whore in his house'.[167] But for others it was material considerations rather than moral principles which were at stake. If a master or mistress was caught in adultery and a separation suit followed, there was a high chance that the marriage home would be broken up, meaning dismissal for the household servants. Anne Shawe was accused of being an adulterous and scolding wife in 1676. Her behaviour was portrayed as leading to the loss of her husband's customers in his tavern, and the alienation of her servants. Joyce Edwards described her mistress as a selfish woman who left the household with a bag of money, ignoring Joyce's demand as to how she was to secure her wages. Joyce became the spokesperson for all the household servants in the suit which followed when she bitterly complained that 'hath it not been for the said Anne they might have lived well and comfortably and in good reputation'. Joyce's sufferings as a consequence of her mistress's behaviour had made her a valuable and sympathetic witness for Richard Shawe, her master.[168] In June 1696 Dinah Allsop asked her mistress Anne, Countess of Macclesfield, permission to leave her service as she feared the Countess's adulterous liaisons and pregnancy 'would ruin' her, preventing her from getting another post. Dinah's conversation with the Countess was one that was intended to inform her mistress that she was fully aware of her personal affairs, and as such was thinly disguised blackmail. Her strategy proved lucrative, for the Countess promised her 'twenty Guineas and five pounds a Year', and a new post at her sister's household. As the witnesses to many adulterous meetings, servants could become tremendously powerful as the arbiters of their masters' reputations.[169]

FATHERS AND DAUGHTERS

If a man had children it was also important for his reputation as an honourable householder that they learnt to respect and obey his wishes. 'The obedience of children doth most prove the authority of parents, and is the surest evidence of the honour a child giveth to his parent', Gouge wrote. Both Gouge and another conduct book writer, Rogers, reminded children of the commandment to 'Honour thy father and mother'.[170] Fathers were the guardians of their daughters' sexual reputations until marriage; their 'value' in the marriage market was dependent on their chastity. If a daughter had sex before marriage she could no longer be her father's exclusive property, and her damaged reputation reflected back on him. Hence one moralist in 1621 commented that a fornicating man 'wrongs the woman which he polluteth, and brings a perpetual disgrace upon her, and this disgrace redounds to her father, her friends, and the whole family'.[171]

When Hero is accused of fornication in *Much Ado,* her father laments how as she is no longer his he should 'let her die' since she has 'foul tainted flesh'. He wishes in vain that he could detach himself from his daughter's dishonour and say that 'this shame derives itself from unknown loins'. But he knows that the slander against his daughter reflects on himself, 'thou hast so wronged mine innocent child and me' he later tells Claudio. Similarly, in *Othello* Desdemona's father Brabantio comes to see her secret marriage to Othello as a 'gross revolt' against him which amounts to theft. Without her honour Brabantio says that Desdemona is 'dead' to him. A final example is from Ford's *Love's Sacrifice* (*c.*1632), in which Nibrassa disassociates himself from his daughter when she is known to have lost her virginity with Ferentes, a notorious womaniser, telling her 'Get from me, strumpet, infamous whore, leprosy of my blood!'[172]

That fathers did see slanders against their daughters as slights on their good names can be seen in the defamation suit brought in 1619 by Alice Teasdell against John Nicholson of the parish of Wearmouth. John Nicholson had been spreading gossip that his friend William Daine had committed incontinence with Alice. Alice's father Thomas heard the rumours, and this led William to flee to a friend's house in Washington late one night, 'fearing to catch some harm of the said Thomas Teasdell'. Knowing that Thomas was 'offended', both John Nicholson and William Daine also later visited the Teasdell household where William denied in front of Thomas that he had ever confessed to having sex with his daughter. Although it was Alice who eventually brought a defamation case, the men's actions reveal that they expected it would be her father who would interpret their conversation as slanderous and offensive to him as well as his daughter. During their visit, by addressing their denial to him they had attempted to appease Thomas, not his daughter.[173] Some one hundred years later this pattern of addressing the father of a daughter who had been wronged still seems to have been in place. When Edmund Thomas was visited by the father of his servant Anna Giles of Bromley, Kent, Edmund admitted that it was he who had made her pregnant. The two men entered into negotiations, and Thomas Giles later told the court of Arches that Edmund 'promised to come to [me] and make [me] satisfaction for the same'. It was when this financial satisfaction was not forthcoming that Anna Giles took legal action.[174] Since it was recognised that the reputation of fathers could be affected by their daughters' actions, it seems probable that both Thomas Teasdell and Thomas Giles motivated and funded their daughters' law suits. The issue of female plaintiffs fighting cases in which their male relatives had a stake will be discussed further in Chapter 5.

It is also worth noting that in the absence of a father, a brother is portrayed in drama as assuming responsibility for his sister's honour. For example, both Shakespeare's *Measure for Measure* (*c.*1603) and Heywood's *A Woman Killed with Kindness* (1603) tell stories of brothers who try to barter with their sisters' honour. John Ford's *The Broken Heart* (*c.*1629) is a tale of the tragedy and dishonour which follows when a brother marries his sister to a man she does not love. Whether husband, father or brother, the honour of the women a man associated with was closely tied to his own.

All through a man's adult life his manhood was endangered by his relationships with women. Asserting manhood was a task fraught with difficulty. During courtship men in love risked losing their reason and self-control. Whilst the marriage ceremony could mark a key entry point into honourable manhood, it also signified the beginning of the ultimate test of manhood, which was the maintenance of sexual control of the man himself, his wife, children and servants. When male adultery could be linked with a loss of self-control it could be damaging to reputation. Female adultery painfully exposed a man who had failed to control his wife by satisfying her sexually. Illicit sexual unions of children and servants questioned his authority as household head. Honourable manhood depended very literally on the 'carnal knowledge' and ownership of female sexuality. But the irony of this system of gender relations was that women's sexuality was never something that could be 'known' or owned with absolute certainty. For female sexual chastity was, as Iago recognised, 'an essence that's not seen'.[175] Loss of female virginity and chastity was not visible unless women were caught *in flagrante delicto*, or pregnancy resulted and a man could be certain that the baby was not his own. Men were left grappling with virginity tests and potions, and, as will be shown in the next chapter, with interpreting the meanings behind women's speech, dress and actions which might reveal inconstancy.[176]

Possessing the means to test men's sexual potency, and being aware of men's sensitivity regarding their performance, women were potentially capable of questioning manhood. When Troilus courts Cressida, her father warns him of women's ability to reward and take away a claim to manhood. He tells him not to woo with words, but 'give her deeds; but she'll bereave you o'th' deeds too, if she call your activity in question'. Goneril in *King Lear* (*c.*1605), who openly compares her husband with other men, exclaims, 'Oh the difference of man and man', scorns her husband as a 'Milk-liver'd man', and implies he is effeminate, 'your manhood – mew!'[177] Other women in Renaissance drama – Beatrice in *Much Ado*, Lady Macbeth, and Beatrice in *The Changeling* – are all able to influence men's behaviour when they express doubts about their manhood. Benedick, Macbeth and De Flores are all provoked into asserting their manhood to show the falsity of the women's claims and to avoid the shame of their manhood being exposed as 'melted into curtsies'.[178] In reality, it took an outspoken and self-assured woman such as Margaret Cavendish, Duchess of Newcastle, in 1664, to openly admit what few women would have denied: 'we oftener enslave men than men enslave us. They seem to govern the world, but we really govern the world, in that we govern men: for what man is he that is not governed by a woman more or less?'[179] Othello's cry,

> O curse of marriage,
> That we can call these delicate creatures ours,
> And not their appetites!

captures the dilemma of early modern manhood. This was a period which, as we shall see in the next chapter, brought severe penalties for men who failed to uphold the gender order which relied so heavily on male control of female sexuality.[180]

Notes

1. For the importance of the assertion or demonstration of manhood see also M. Roper and J. Tosh, 'Introduction: historians and the politics of masculinity', in M. Roper and J. Tosh, eds, *Manful Assertions: Masculinities in Britain since 1800* (London, 1991), pp. 18–19; and J. Tosh, 'What should historians do with masculinity? Reflections on nineteenth-century Britain' *HWJ* 33 (1994), p. 184.

2. M.P. Tilley, *A Dictionary of Proverbs in England in the Sixteenth and Seventeenth Centuries* (Ann Arbor MI, 1950), M306; L558.

3. W. Shakespeare, *Othello* (*c.*1604), ed. M.R. Ridley (London, 1986), I.iii.335–6.

4. Anon, *The Mad Man's Morice* (1690).

5. M. MacDonald, *Mystical Bedlam: Madness, Anxiety, and Healing in Seventeenth-Century England* (Cambridge, 1983), pp. 88–92; R. Porter, 'Love, sex, and madness in eighteenth-century England' *Social Research* 53, 2 (1986), pp. 217–19.

6. R. Burton, *The Anatomy of Melancholy* (1621), ed. F. Dell and P. Jordan-Smith (New York, 1927), p. 728; W. Shakespeare, *Romeo and Juliet* (*c.*1595), ed. B. Gibbons (London, 1980), III.i.115–17.

7. S.C. Shapiro, '"Yon plumed dandebrat": male "effeminacy" in English satire and criticism' *Review of English Studies* 39 (1988), pp. 400–12; M. McKeon, 'Historicizing patriarchy: the emergence of gender difference in England, 1660–1760' *Eighteenth-Century Studies* 28, 3 (1995), pp. 308, 312–14; A. Bray, *Homosexuality in Renaissance England* (London, 1988), pp. 86–8; P.J. Carter, 'Mollies, fops and men of feeling: aspects of male effeminacy and masculinity in Britain, *c.*1700–1780' (unpublished D.Phil. thesis, Oxford University, 1995), pp. 2–5, 22.

8. As cited in L. Woodbridge, *Women and the English Renaissance: Literature and the Nature of Womankind, 1540–1620* (Urbana IL, 1986), p. 184.

9. Shakespeare, *Othello*, I.iii.261–8; II.i.74; IV.i.180–1; see also II.iii.305–6, 'Our general's wife is now the general'.

10. W. Shakespeare, *Much Ado About Nothing* (1598), ed. F.H. Mares (Cambridge, 1991), I.i.228–9; II.iii.13–15; for contemporary concerns that peacetime robbed men of 'masculine warlike qualities' see also Woodbridge, *Women and the English Renaissance*, pp. 159–63, 279–80.

11. J. Vanbrugh, *The Provoked Wife* (1697), ed. J.L. Smith (London, 1974), IV.iii.128–30; E. Partridge, *Shakespeare's Bawdy: A Literary and Psychological Essay and a Comprehensive Glossary* (London, 1955), p. 199; E.A.M. Colman, *The Dramatic Use of Bawdy in Shakespeare* (London, 1974), p. 217; and M. Gohlke, '"I wooed thee with my sword": Shakespeare's tragic paradigms', in C.R.S. Lenz, G. Greene and C. Thomas Neely, eds, *The Woman's Part: Feminist Criticism of Shakespeare* (London, 1980), pp. 150–70.

12. W. Wycherley, *The Country Wife* (1675), ed. J. Ogden (London, 1991), I.i.209–12.

13. As cited in P. Thompson, 'The limits of parody in *The Country Wife*' *Studies in Philology* 89 (1992), p. 107.

14. As cited in D.M. Turner, 'Rakes, libertines and sexual honour in Restoration England,1660–1700' (unpublished MA thesis, Durham University, 1994), pp. 10–11.

15. As cited in K. Hodgkin, 'Thomas Whythorne and the problems of mastery', *HWJ* 29 (1990), pp. 31, 34.

16. J.D. Marshall, ed., *The Autobiography of William Stout of Lancaster 1665–1752* (Chetham Society, 1967), p. 141.

17. F. Osborne, *Advice to a Son* (Oxford, 1656) in L.B. Wright, ed., *Advice to a Son: Precepts of Lord Burghley, Sir Walter Raleigh, and Francis Osborne* (Ithaca NY, 1962), p. 62.

18. This definition is taken from R. Paine, 'What is gossip about? An alternative hypothesis' *Man* new series, 2 (1967), pp. 278–85.

19. This argument is put forward by M. Gluckman, 'Gossip and scandal' *Current Anthropology* 4, 3 (1963), pp. 307–16, but strongly contested by Paine, 'What is gossip'.

20. D. Tannen, *You Just Don't Understand: Women and Men in Conversation* (London, 1990), pp. 96–122.

21. A. Wilson, 'The ceremony of childbirth and its interpretation', in V. Fildes, ed., *Women as Mothers in Pre-Industrial England* (London, 1990), p. 71.

22. S. Rowlands, *Well Met Gossip* (London, 1619), and *A Crew of Kind Gossips* (London, 1613), sigs A2, D3.

23. S. Rowlands, *The Bride* (London, 1617), sig. E2.

24. 'Well met Neighbour', *Roxburghe*, vol. III, pp. 98–103; 'The Married Man's Misery' (1638), *Roxburghe*, vol. I, p. 152.

25. Anon, *The Fifteen Plagues of a Maiden-Head* (London, 1707), p. 8.

26. 'John Tomson and Jakaman his Wife', *Roxburghe*, vol. II, pp. 137–42.

27. As cited in A.V. Judges, *The Elizabethan Underworld* (London, 1930), pp. 101–5.

28. C. Gibbon, *The Praise of a Good Name* (London, 1594), p. 28; D. Rogers, *Matrimoniall Honour* (London, 1642), p. 168.

29. J. Sharpe, *Defamation and Sexual Slander in Early Modern England: The Church Courts at York*, Borthwick Papers, 58 (York, 1980), p. 20.

30. 'Advice to Batchelors', *Roxburghe*, vol. III, p. 374; 'The Married-mans best Portion', *Pepys*, vol. IV, p. 84; M.P., 'Man's Felicity and Misery', *Roxburghe*, vol. II, pp. 183–8.

31. S. Hindle, 'The shaming of Margaret Knowsley: gossip, gender and the experience of authority in early modern England' *CC* 9, 3 (1994), pp. 391–419.

32. W. Shakespeare, *The Taming of the Shrew* (*c.*1591), ed. H.J. Oliver (Oxford, 1990), IV.v.1–23; K. Newman, *Fashioning Femininity and English Renaissance Drama* (Chicago IL, 1991), pp. 41–5.

33. J. Kamensky, 'Talk like a man: speech, power, and masculinity in early New England' *GH* 8, 1 (1996), pp. 22–47.

34. L. Gowing, *Domestic Dangers: Women, Words, and Sex in Early Modern London* (Oxford, 1996), p. 122.

35. B. Rich, *The Excellency of Good Women* (London, 1613), p. 7; Barbaro is cited in P. Stallybrass, 'Patriarchal territories: the body enclosed', in M.W. Ferguson, M. Quilligan and N.J. Vickers, eds, *Rewriting the Renaissance: The Discourses of Sexual Difference in Early Modern Europe* (Chicago IL, 1987), p. 127.

36. As cited in Newman, *Fashioning Femininity*, p. 11; see also L. Jardine, *Still Harping on Daughters: Women and Drama in the Age of Shakespeare* (New York, 1989), pp. 121–4.

37. L. Pollock, *With Faith and Physic: The Life of a Tudor Gentlewoman Lady Grace Mildmay 1552–1620* (London, 1993), pp. 26–9.

38. Gibbon, *The Praise*, sig. A2.

39. DDR.V.9. f. 61.

40. S.D. Amussen, *An Ordered Society: Gender and Class in Early Modern England* (Oxford, 1988), p. 98.

41. DDR.V.9. ff. 289, 290; unsurprisingly, witnesses differ over when the relationships took place before her marriage.

42. DDR.V.11. ff. 72v, 73, 74, 75, 82v, 83r; Hindle, 'The shaming', particulary p. 401.

43. DDR.V.10A. f. 168r.

44. DDR.V.11. f. 74r; CA, Case 8350 (1673), Eee5, f. 51r.

45. B. Capp, 'Separate domains? Women and authority in early modern England', in P. Griffiths, A. Fox and S. Hindle, eds, *The Experience of Authority in Early Modern England* (London, 1996), pp. 117–45.

46. DDR.V.8. f. 49; DDR.V.8. ff. 78r, 84a; DDR.V.8. ff. 122v, 123, 124; the date of the last case has faded. A. Clark has also found that many gossips were male in her survey of London church courts, 'Whores and gossips: sexual reputation in London 1770–1825', in A. Angerman, G. Binnema, A. Keunen, V. Poels and J. Zirkzee, eds, *Current Issues in Women's History* (London, 1989), p. 240.

47. A. Kussmaul, *Servants in Husbandry in Early Modern England* (Cambridge, 1981), p. 47; I am grateful to Tim Stretton for this reference.

48. Capp, 'Separate domains?', pp. 129–30.

49. Rich, *The Excellency of Good Women*, p. 9.

50. C. Kahn, *Man's Estate: Masculine Identity in Shakespeare* (Berkeley CA, 1981), pp. 120–1.

51. L. Gowing, 'Language, power and the law: women's slander litigation in early modern London', in J. Kermode and G. Walker, eds, *Women, Crime and the Courts in Early Modern England* (London, 1994), pp. 29–30, see also L. Gowing, 'Gender and the language of insult in early modern London' *HWJ* 35 (1993), p. 4; T. Meldrum, 'A women's court in London: defamation at the Bishop of London's consistory court, 1700–1745' *London Journal* 19, 1 (1994), p. 10.

52. Count H. Romei, *The Courtiers Academie* (London, 1598), pp. 126–7; Anon, *The Court of Good Counsell* (London, 1607), sig. C2.

53. M.P., 'The Cooper of Norfolk', *Roxburghe*, vol. I, pp. 99–104; for greensickness see P. Crawford, 'The construction and experience of maternity in seventeenth-century England', in Fildes, ed., *Women as Mothers*, p. 6; for the citation of another ballad which suggests that sex is the only cure for greensickness see P. Crawford, 'Sexual knowledge in England, 1500–1750', in R. Porter and M. Teich, eds, *Sexual Knowledge, Sexual Science: The History of Attitudes to Sexuality* (Cambridge, 1994), p. 95.

54. 'Hey for Horn Fair!' (1685), *Roxburghe*, vol. VIII, part III, pp. 665–6; 'A New Western Ballad', *Pepys*, vol. IV, p. 125; 'The Cuckold's Complaint' (*c.*1689–91), *Roxburghe*, vol. VII, part II, p. 431.

55. 'Tom Farthing' (1675), *Roxburghe*, vol. VIII, part III, pp. 670–1; 'The Scolding Wife's Vindication' (*c.*1689), *Roxburghe*, vol. VII, part I, p. 197; 'Mirth for Citizens' (*c.*1671), *Roxburghe*, vol. VIII, part III, pp. 699–700.

56. 'The Doting Old Dad' (1685–88), *Roxburghe*, vol. IV, pp. 412–13; see also 'The Old Man's Complaint' (*c.*1650), *Roxburghe*, vol. VIII, part I–II, p. 197, and 'The Young Woman's Complaint' (*c.*1665), *Roxburghe*, vol. VIII, part III, pp. 679–81; and J. Wiltenburg, *Disorderly Women and Female Power in the Street Literature of Early Modern England and Germany* (Charlottesville VA, 1992), pp. 150–1.

57. Anon, *Rare and Good News for Wives in City and Country* (London, 1706), p. 7; Anon, *Bull Feather Hall* (London, 1664), p. 4.

58. 'The discontented Married Man', *Roxburghe*, vol. I, pp. 295–9; 'The Wanton Wife of Castle-gate' (1670–89), *Roxburghe*, vol. VII, part II, pp. 369–70.

59. 'The Well-Approved Doctor', *Pepys*, vol. IV, p. 149.

60. T. Heywood, *A Woman Killed with Kindness* (1603), ed. B. Scobie (London, 1991), I.xiii. 112–13.

61. Shakespeare, *Othello*, I.iii.390, see also IV.iii.35; for other references to 'proper man' see Shakespeare, *Much Ado about Nothing*, II.iii.155 and V.i.155–6; W. Shakespeare, *Troilus and Cressida* (*c.*1602), ed. K. Muir (Oxford, 1994), I.ii.183–4; J. Ford, *Love's Sacrifice* (*c.*1632), ed. W. Gifford (London, 1895), V.i; T. Southerne, *The Wives' Excuse* (1692), ed. R. Jordan and H. Love (Oxford, 1988), I.ii.49–50; see also L. Jardine, '"Why should he call her whore?": defamation and Desdemona's case', in M. Tudeau-Clayton and M. Warner, eds, *Addressing Frank Kermode: Essays in Criticism and Interpretation* (London, 1991), pp. 151–2, footnotes 39 and 43; and S.N. Garner, 'Shakespeare's Desdemona' *Shakespeare Studies* 9 (1976), pp. 233–52.

62. J. Dryden, *Marriage a la Mode* (1671), ed. M.S. Auburn (London, 1981), II.i.240; III.i.92–8; Wycherley, *The Country Wife* (1675), I.i.464–6.

63. Vanbrugh, *The Provoked Wife* (1697), V.iv.40–2, see also IV.iv.156–66 and I.i.89–91.

64. Crawford, 'The construction and experience of maternity', and L.A. Pollock, 'Embarking on a rough passage: the experience of pregnancy in early-modern society', in Fildes, ed., *Women as Mothers*, pp. 7, 40–1; R. Porter and L. Hall, *The Facts of Life: The Creation of Sexual Knowledge in Britain, 1650–1950* (London, 1995), pp. 46–7; M. Fissell, 'Gender and generation: representing reproduction in early modern England' *GH* 7 (1995), p. 435.

65. 'Pride's fall', *Shirburn*, no. XXXIII, pp. 134–9; 'The West-country Wonder', *Euing*, p. 644.

66. CA, Case 8136 (1669), Eee3, ff. 603–606, 612v–616v; Eee4, ff. 5v, 6r.

67. CA, Case 8136 (1669), Eee3, f. 605v.

68. As cited in Gowing, *Domestic Dangers*, p. 247.

69. DDR.Box, no. 414 (1636–37), *Thomas Rawdon* v. *Christopher Dickon*.

70. As cited in Crawford, 'Sexual knowledge in England', p. 97.

71. CA, Case 6692 (1676), Eee6, ff. 124v, 128r.

72. CA, Case 1813 (1673), Ee4, ff. 118–122v, 128v; for further discussion of this case see Chapter 5 below, and E. Foyster, 'Marrying the experienced widow in early modern England: the male perspective', in S. Cavallo and L. Warner, eds, *Widowhood in Medieval and Early Modern Europe* (forthcoming from Longman).

73. J. Dod and R. Cleaver, *A Godly Forme of Householde Governement* (London, 1614), sig. L4.

74. As cited in Hodgkin, 'Thomas Whythorne', pp. 35–6.

75. R. Braithwait, *Ar't Asleepe Husband?* (London, 1640), pp. 49–50; the italics are my own.

76. Gowing, *Domestic Dangers*, pp. 101, 106, 109.

77. CA, Case 8648 (1686), Ee6, f. 110v.

78. Proverbs 12.4, cited in, for example, Rich, *The Excellency*, p. 29.

79. 'The Hasty Bridegroom', *Roxburghe*, vol. VII, part II, pp. 458–61.

80. 'The Proud Pedlar', *Roxburghe*, vol. VII, part I, p. 54; 'A New-Fashioned Marigold', *Pepys*, vol. IV, p. 98; 'The Wheel-Wrights Huy-and-Cry' (1693), *Pepys*, vol. IV, p. 115; 'A New Western Ballad', *Pepys*, vol. IV, p. 125; I am grateful to Helen Weinstein for allowing me to read her unpublished paper on this subject, 'Doing it by the book: representing sex in early modern popular literature'.

81. Partridge, *Shakespeare's Bawdy*, pp. 23, 26–7, 30–3; see also Colman, *The Dramatic Use of Bawdy*, pp. 182–224.

82. G. Parfitt and R. Houlbrooke, eds, *The Courtship Narrative of Leonard Wheatcroft Derbyshire Yeoman* (Reading, 1986), pp. 41–2.

83. Turner, 'Rakes, libertines', pp. 14–16.

84. Fissell, 'Gender and generation', pp. 435–40.

85. See for example, DDR.V.8. f. 78r; DDR.V.9. ff. 6v, 10r; DDR.V.11. f. 362; DDR.V.11. ff. 518v, 519r; see also Gowing, *Domestic Dangers*, p. 271.

86. T. Hitchcock, 'Redefining sex in eighteenth-century England' *HWJ* 41 (1996), pp. 73–90, and *English Sexualities, 1700–1800* (London, 1997), esp. ch. 3.

87. L. Danson, '"The catastrophe is a nuptial": The space of masculine desire in *Othello, Cymbeline*, and *The Winter's Tale*' *Shakespeare Survey* 46 (1994), p. 73.

88. M. Breitenberg, *Anxious Masculinity in Early Modern England* (Cambridge, 1996), p. 50.

89. *Othello*, II.i.185; V.ii.345; for sex and the loss of reason see also D. Lindley, *The Trials of Frances Howard: Fact and Fiction at the Court of King James* (London, 1996), p. 102.

90. J. Kerrigan, ed., *The Sonnets and A Lover's Complaint* (Harmondsworth, 1986), p. 141.

91. As cited in C.J. Summers and T-L. Pebworth, 'Introduction', in C.J. Summers and T-L. Pebworth, eds, *Renaissance Discourses of Desire* (London, 1993), p. 2.

92. Shakespeare, *Troilus and Cressida*, III.ii.18–25.

93. Partridge, *Shakespeare's Bawdy*, p. 93; Colman, *The Dramatic Use of Bawdy*, p. 191.

94. Shakespeare, *Much Ado about Nothing*, V.iii.78–9.

95. Shakespeare, *Othello*, V.ii.149–50; for discussion of these lines see E.A. Snow, 'Sexual anxiety and the male order of things in *Othello*' *English Literary Renaissance* 10 (1980), pp. 384–412.

96. W. Gouge, *Of Domesticall Duties*, 3rd edn (London, 1634), p. 224; W. Whateley, *A Bride Bush* (London, 1623), pp. 18–19; Rogers, *Matrimoniall Honour*, pp. 176–7; see also T.N. Tentler, *Sin and Confession on the Eve of the Reformation* (Princeton NJ, 1977), pp. 174–9; K.M. Davies, 'Continuity and change in literary advice on marriage', in R.B. Outhwaite ed., *Marriage and Society* (London, 1981), pp. 58–78; A. Fletcher, 'The Protestant idea of marriage', in A. Fletcher and P. Roberts, eds, *Religion, Culture and Society in Early Modern Britain: Essays in Honour of Patrick Collinson* (Cambridge, 1994), pp. 176–7; Crawford, 'Sexual knowledge', p. 89; and J.G. Turner, *One Flesh: Paradisal Marriage and Sexual Relations in the Age of Milton* (Oxford, 1987), pp. 73–80.

97. As cited in S. Greenblatt, *Renaissance Self-Fashioning* (London, 1984), p. 248, see also pp. 249–52.

98. As cited in Greenblatt, *Renaissance Self-Fashioning*, p. 305, footnote 57.

99. M.R. Sommerville, *Sex and Subjection: Attitudes to Women in Early-Modern Society* (London, 1995), p. 133.

100. As cited in Newman, *Fashioning Femininity*, p. 27.

101. As cited in Breitenberg, *Anxious Masculinity*, p. 50.

102. Anon, *The Office of Christian Parents* (Cambridge, 1616), pp. 28–9; see also Crawford, 'Sexual knowledge', pp. 88–9.

103. Porter, 'Love, sex, and madness', pp. 226–7; R. Porter, '"The secrets of generation display'd": *Aristotle's Master-piece* in eighteenth-century England', in R.P. Maccubbin, ed., *'Tis Nature's Fault: Unauthorized Sexuality during the Enlightenment* (Cambridge, 1987), pp. 1–21; R. Porter, 'The literature of sexual advice before 1800', in Porter and Teich, eds, *Sexual Knowledge*, pp. 145–6; Porter and Hall, *The Facts of Life*, ch. 2.

104. B. Capp, *Astrology and the Popular Press: English Almanacs 1500–1800* (London, 1979), p. 117, see also pp. 118, 120.

105. B.A., *Learn to Lye Warm* (London, 1672), p. 18.

106. K. Thomas, 'The double standard' *Journal of the History of Ideas* 20, 2 (1959), pp. 195–216; M. Ingram, *Church Courts, Sex and Marriage in England, 1570–1640* (Cambridge, 1987), pp. 302–3; Sharpe, *Defamation and Sexual Slander*, p. 28; Gowing, *Domestic Dangers*, pp. 2–4, 65, 112–15, 194.

107. Romei, *The Courtiers Academie*, p. 97.

108. These figures are based on the surviving records of defamation from Durham consistory court bound in volumes 1604–31 (DDR.V. 8–12), and loose papers for the years 1633–34, 1636–37, 1662–63 and 1664–65 (DDR.Box, no. 414); the remainder of the cases were brought as follows: two as joint actions by husband and wife, one as a joint action between mother and daughter, six as office suits in which there was no named promoter of the suit, and 140 cases by women.

109. These figures are based on all defamation cases which had personal answers (Ee) and/or depositions (Eee) for the years 1661–1700; the remainder of the cases were brought as follows: four as joint actions by husband and wife, and 163 cases by women.

110. K. Thomas, 'The puritans and adultery: the Act of 1650 reconsidered', in D. Pennington and K. Thomas, eds, *Puritans and Revolutionaries: Essays in Seventeenth-Century History presented to Christopher Hill* (Oxford, 1978), pp. 261–2.

111. See for example, DDR.V.9. f. 152v; DDR.V.12. f. 71–72; DDR.Box, no. 414 (1636–37), *Margaret Anderson* v. *Isabell Key*; see also Gowing, *Domestic Dangers*, pp. 74–5.

112. M.P., 'Have among you! good Women', *Roxburghe*, vol. I, pp. 435–40; M.P., 'Man's Felicity and Misery', *Roxburghe*, vol. II, pp. 183–8; M.P., 'Well met, Neighbour', *Roxburghe*, vol. III, pp. 98–103; Gowing, *Domestic Dangers*, pp. 103–4 and 'Language, power and the law', p. 10; see also Capp, 'Separate domains?', pp. 133–4; for discussion of possible reasons why the nose was targeted see V. Groebner, 'Losing face, saving face: noses and honour in the late medieval town' *HWJ* 40 (1995), pp. 1–15; for examples of husbands who threaten to mark their wives as whores in a similar way see Chapter 5 below.

113. CA, Case 1127 (1663), Eee1, ff. 57, 62v; CA, Case 4688 (1690), Eee7, ff. 119–121v.

114. CA, Case 4188 (1668), Ee3, ff. 430v–431v, Eee3, ff. 396r–398v; for the punishment of carting see Chapter 4 below.

115. As cited in Thomas, 'The double standard', p. 196.

116. See, for example, 'A Good Wife is a Portion every day' (1673), *Roxburghe*, vol. VI, part I–II, pp. 332–5; and 'The Maiden's Counsellor' (1685–88), *Roxburghe*, vol. IV, pp. 77–9.

117. 'The Father's good Counsel to his Lascivious Son' (1675), *Roxburghe*, vol. VIII, part III, pp. 578–80; 'Nothing like to a good Wife', *Pepys*, vol. IV, p. 80.

118. See, for example, 'The Patient Wife betrayed', *Euing*, p. 473.

119. See, for example, Gouge, *Of Domesticall Duties*, p. 221; *The Court of Good Counsell*, sig. C3; William Heale lamented the injustice of the law which more frequently punished female adultresses than male adulterers, see *An Apology for Women* (Oxford, 1609), pp. 26–7; see also Sommerville, *Sex and Subjection*, pp. 141–5.

120. R. Cooke, *A White Sheete, Or A Warning for Whoremongers* (London, 1629), p. 22.

121. M. Poole, *Annotations upon the Holy Bible* (London, 1683), Proverbs Chapter VI, v.32.

122. DDR.V.9. f. 67v; DDR.V.11. ff. 437v, 446v; for other examples of married men being accused directly of adultery, or being called whoremaster or whoremonger, see DDR.V.8. f. 123r; DDR.V.11. f. 174–176; DDR.V.12. f. 162–165r; DDR.V.12. f. 187.

123. See, for example, CA, Case 7195 (1668), Eee3, ff. 62v–63; Case 7758 (1677), Eee6, f. 128v.

124. Gowing, 'Gender and the language of insult', p. 15.

125. DDR.V.9. f. 67v; DDR.V.11. f. 446v.

126. DDR.V.9. f. 153r; DDR.V.12. f. 163; for examples from the court of Arches of married men who brought defamation suits after they had been slandered as sexually incontinent see CA, Case 4309 (1671), and CA, Case 8344 (1675).

127. CA, Case 219 (1668), f. 211r.

128. 'The Whoremonger's Conversion', *Roxburghe*, vol. III, pp. 122–6; for other ballads that warn men that illicit sex will be paid with the pox see M.P., 'A Messe of Good Fellowes', *Roxburghe*, vol. II, pp. 143–8; 'The Westminster Wedding', *Pepys*, vol. IV, p. 105; 'Nothing like to a good Wife', *Pepys*, vol. IV, p. 80.

129. For descriptions of men with the pox see R.A. Anselment, 'Seventeenth-century pox: the medical and literary realities of venereal disease' *The Seventeenth Century* 4, 2 (1989), pp. 195–6.

130. J. Cleland, *Hero-Paideia, Or The Institution of a Young Noble Man* (Oxford, 1607), p. 208.

131. R.H. Helmholz, *Roman Canon Law in Reformation England* (Cambridge, 1990), pp. 56–7; Sharpe, *Defamation*, pp. 10–11; for examples of men who did pursue slander cases in the church courts after they had been accused of having the pox see DDR.V.9. f. 26, 27r; DDR.V.9. f. 163; DDR.V.10A. f. 83a/v; CA, Case 4620 (1676), Eee6, f. 48r and CA, Case 1393 (1677), Eee6, ff. 261r–263.

132. See, for example, CA, Case 6456 (1665), Eee2, ff. 34r–40r; CA, Case 8212 (1667), Eee2, ff. 380r–383r; and CA, Case 8147 (1669), Eee4, ff. 65v–69r.

133. B.J. Gibbons, 'Gender in British Behmenist thought' (unpublished Ph.D. thesis, Durham University, 1993), pp. 38–42.

134. Anselment, 'Seventeenth-century pox', pp. 202–3.

135. As cited in Anselment, 'Seventeenth-century pox', p. 202.

136. CA, Case 10232 (1669), Eee3, ff. 452r–454r, 460r–467v, 485v–487r; for further examples of ignorance about how the disease was transmitted see Anselment, 'Seventeenth-century pox', p. 193.

137. DDR.V.11. f. 482 and DDR.V.12. ff. 8, 12; DDR.V.9. ff. 163, 185v; also see Gowing *Domestic Dangers*, p. 90 and 'Gender and the language of insult', pp. 12–13; and R. Davenport-Hines, *Sex, Death and Punishment: Attitudes to Sex and Sexuality in Britain Since the Renaissance* (London, 1990), ch. 2.

138. Gowing, *Domestic Dangers*, p. 180.

139. DDR.V.9. f. 196; DDR.V.9. f. 243; DDR.V.9. ff. 249, 250, 257r; DDR.V.12. ff. 283v, 284, 285r, 288.

140. See CA, Case 6292 (1669), Ee3, f. 483r; CA, Case 8648 (1686), Ee6, ff. 98v, 102v–103r; see also CA, Case 9005 (1663), Eel, f. 356; for cases in which the defendants' witnesses claim that the husband had committed adultery see CA, Case 8350 (1673), Eee5, ff. 461–464r, 467r; and CA, Case 9032 (1663), Eeel, f. 192r.

141. G.M. Walker, 'Crime, gender and social order in early modern Cheshire' (unpublished Ph.D. thesis, Liverpool University, 1994), p. 92.

142. CA, Case 6397 (1680), Eee6, ff. 440–445r, 457, 478–486.

143. CA, Case 4688 (1690), Eee7, ff. 121v–122v; CA, Case 1127 (1663), Eeel, f. 62v.

144. Shakespeare, *Othello*, IV.iii.86–103; Wycherley, *The Country Wife*, IV.i.32, 34–6; G. Etherege, *She Would if She Could* (1668), ed. C.M. Taylor (London, 1972), III.i.171–2.

145. Southerne, *The Wives' Excuse*, I.iii.61–7; see also III.ii.32–4 and IV.i.129–31; for a discussion of these themes see also Turner, 'Rakes, libertines', pp. 43–53.

146. Vanbrugh, *The Provoked Wife*, III.i.354–62; for examples of the female critique of the double standard in other literary genres see Breitenberg, *Anxious Masculinity*, pp. 197–201.

147. Romei, *The Courtiers Academie*, p. 96; see also Ingram, *Church Courts*, p. 239; Thomas 'Puritans and adultery', pp. 259–60.

148. F. Dabhoiwala, 'The construction of honour, reputation and status in late seventeenth- and early eighteenth-century England' *TRHS* Sixth Series, VI (1996), p. 204.

149. Romei, *The Courtiers Academie*, p. 97.

150. As cited in N.A. Gutierrez, 'The irresolution of melodrama: the meaning of adultery in *A Woman Killed with Kindness Exemplaria* 1, 2 (1989), p. 271.

151. DDR.V.8. f. 191; DDR.V.11. ff. 69v, 70r; DDR.Box, no. 414 (1633–34), *John Colthird* v. *Roger Story*; one further case was brought as a joint action by the husband and wife after he had been called a cuckold, see DDR.V.11. f. 207v.

152. CA, Case 5417 (1665); CA, Case 3227 (1669); CA, Case 2979 (1670).

153. T.K. Hareven, 'The history of the family and the complexity of social change' *American Historical Review* 96, 1 (1991), p. 104.

154. N. Tadmor, 'The concept of the household-family in eighteenth-century England' *PP* 151 (1996), pp. 111–40.

155. Gouge, *Of Domesticall*, p. 17.

156. DDR.V.11. f. 106.

157. CA, Case 6940 (1674), Eee5, ff. 334, 354v–355r.

158. CA, Case 3936 (1669), Eee4, ff. 72–73.

159. DDR.V.9. ff. 170v, 171r; DDR.V.11. ff. 179v, 180; DDR.V.11. ff. 478v–481, DDR.V.12. ff. 4v, 5.

160. See, for example, Gouge, *Of Domesticall*, pp. 661–2; of course, some masters also had sexual relationships with their male servants, see Bray, *Homosexuality*, pp. 49–51.

161. K. Wrightson, 'The nadir of English illegitimacy in the seventeenth century', in P. Laslett, K. Oosterveen and R. Smith, eds, *Bastardy and its Comparative History* (Cambridge MA, 1980), p. 187.

162. As cited in M. Slater, 'The weightiest business: marriage in an upper-gentry family in seventeenth-century England' *PP* 72 (1976), p. 39.

163. DDR.V.9. f. 243; DDR.V.11. ff. 174–6, 178; CA, Case 4834 (1669), Eee3, ff. 237–9; for other examples of masters being accused by their wives of having sex with servants see CA, Case 6397 (1680), Eee6, ff. 440–5, 457, 478–86; CA, Case 1544 (1697), ff. 494–5, 498–502; CA, Case 9240 (1699), Eee8, f. 635r. For further examples of court cases in which servants claimed that masters sought sexual favours see Ingram, *Church Courts*, pp. 264–7; P. Griffiths, *Youth and Authority: Formative Experiences in England 1560–1640* (Oxford, 1996), pp. 274–8, 284–6; for a printed transcription of a servant's statement in the court of Arches that her master was the father of her child see P.M. Humfrey, '"I saw, through a large chink in the partition . . .": What the servants knew', in V. Frith, ed., *Women and History: Voices of Early Modern England* (Toronto, 1995), pp. 70–1; for a case study of the fate of one servant who dared to question her master's behaviour see Hindle, 'The shaming of Margaret Knowsley', pp. 391–419; and for a fictional account of the consequences of master/maidservant sexual relationships see S. Richardson, *Pamela* (London, 1740).

164. CA, Case 8648 (1686); for other examples of accusations against wives for committing adultery with servants see CA, Case 9032 (1663), Ee1, ff. 600–1, Eee1, f. 192; and CA, Case 8350 (1673), Ee4, ff. 287v–303r, Eee5, ff. 48r–49r, 65–7, 72–3, 300–3; see also L. Stone, *Road to Divorce: England 1530–1987* (Oxford, 1990), pp. 271–2; for examples of cases earlier in the century see Gowing, *Domestic Dangers*, pp. 190–2, 202–4 and Griffiths, *Youth*, pp. 278–81; for a printed transcription of the deposition of a servant who believes that she has witnessed a mistress committing adultery with an apprentice see Humfrey, '"I saw, through a large chink"', pp. 63–4.

165. R. Cust, 'Honour and politics in early Stuart England: the case of Beaumont *v.* Hastings' *PP* 149 (1995), pp. 57–94; in this context the talk of dismissed servants could be very dangerous for their masters' reputations, see for an example of a female servant abusing her former master and family, Capp, 'Separate domains?', p. 117.

166. CA, Case 1055 (1693), Eee7, ff. 713v–720v.

167. As cited in Griffiths, *Youth*, p. 242.

168. CA, Case 8209 (1676), Eee6, ff. 64, 65r.

169. CA, Case 5938 (1697), Eee8, ff. 419v–420v, for a printed transcript of Dinah Allsop's statement see Humfrey, '"I saw, through a large chink"', pp. 67–9; for the role of servants as witnesses to adultery see also Stone, *Road to Divorce*, pp. 30, 211–5, 220–3; Gowing, *Domestic Dangers*, pp. 191–2, 246–8; Griffiths, *Youth*, pp. 171, 338–9; for a scene in a drama which portrays servants gossiping about the sexual reputations of their masters and mistresses see Southerne, *The Wives' Excuse*, I.i.

170. Gouge, *Of Domesticall*, pp. 432, 446, 452; Rogers, *Matrimoniall Honour*, p. 88.

171. As cited in Lindley, *The Trials*, p. 173.

172. Shakespeare, *Much Ado*, IV.i.147, 136, 128; V.i.63; Shakespeare, *Othello*, I.i.134; I.ii.62, 95–9; I.iii.58–60; Ford, *Love's Sacrifice*, III.i.

173. DDR.V.10B, ff. 415v–416v, 426v–427r, 447.

174. As cited in Humfrey, '"I saw, through a large chink"', p. 71.

175. Shakespeare, *Othello*, IV.i.16.

176. Breitenberg, *Anxious Masculinity*, ch. 6.

177. Shakespeare, *Troilus and Cressida*, III.ii.52–4; Shakespeare, *King Lear*, IV.ii.26–68.

178. Shakespeare, *Much Ado*, IV.i.291–307; *Macbeth*, I.vii.35–83; T. Middleton and W. Rowley, *The Changeling* (1622), ed. B. Loughrey and N. Taylor (Harmondsworth, 1988), II.ii.107–17; see also C.B. Watson, *Shakespeare and the Renaissance Concept of Honour* (Princeton NJ, 1960), pp. 245–52.

179. As cited in N.H. Keeble, ed., *The Cultural Identity of Seventeenth-Century Woman* (London, 1994), p. 194.

180. Shakespeare, *Othello*, III.iii.272–4; for a discussion of these lines see Danson, '"The catastrophe is a nuptial"', pp. 69–79; and D. Cohen, *Shakespeare's Culture of Violence* (London, 1993), p. 119.

CHAPTER FOUR

Lost Manhood

Most research on sexual defamation has concentrated on revealing its effects on women's lives. Maids could have their marriage prospects jeopardised, wives could find their marriages disrupted and even face desertion or separation, and widows were unlikely to be able to remarry. Women's economic role was also threatened by sexual slander: maids were often dismissed from service, and alewives and other tradeswomen could lose customers.[1] But even with the large number of women fighting sexual slander suits, there are only rare glimpses of the emotional effect of slander on them. For example, in June 1631 Isabell Taylor of the city of Durham told the court how she visited Elizabeth Bell after a quarrel had broken out between Elizabeth and Margaret Sheffeild. During the quarrel Elizabeth had been called a 'beggarly quean' and the good name of her husband and her kin had been questioned. When Isabell found Elizabeth in the kitchen her eyes were 'red with weeping'.[2] We are even less likely to find evidence of men's emotional response to loss of reputation when contemporary thought held it unmanly and a sign of weakness to cry or show feelings of emotional distress. Thus *King Lear* (*c.*1605) feels 'asham'd' when he is moved to tears, which he describes as 'women's weapons' which can 'shake' his manhood.[3] However, there is a wealth of material within popular culture which can provide clues to the implications of the loss of male sexual reputation in both the private and public spheres. This chapter explores these consequences, and distinguishes between those which were likely to be common to all men, and those which were particular to certain social groups.

The Cuckold's Wife

When a wife committed adultery and thereby shamed her husband, as we shall see the marital discord which could ensue was popularly thought just as likely to be fuelled by anger from the wife as from the husband. In 1607 when Mistress Graunt committed adultery with John Warner in Little Barningham, Norfolk, villagers told the court how her infidelity had led her to 'greatly disagree together' with her husband.[4] For the most obvious consequence for a married man who lost his sexual reputation was that his wife was also seen as an angry scold. This was because it was believed that if a man had no sexual control over his wife all other control was subsequently lost. In numerous ballads of the period cuckolded husbands also find themselves victims of scolds.[5] The connection between sexual and vocal control is made most explicit in the Caroline ballad 'The Discontented Married Man'. Men are warned to rule their wives, otherwise, as the chorus line reminds them, women will find it impossible to keep their 'lips together', a reference to both a woman's mouth and her genitals.[6] The link between female chastity and scolding was also made in statements to the courts. During an argument between Dorothy Dunn and Anne Scott of Sedgefield in June 1629, Anne called Dorothy a whore who was 'burnt' with the pox. She added to the insult by saying that she also had the pox 'dried' within her throat. Sexual disobedience had affected every channel of her body, leaving her, as another witness put it, 'burnt within'.[7]

Whilst courtship was feared to be a period in which men were prone to effeminate behaviour when women ruled their lovers, marriage was intended as an institution in which men and women resumed their rightful places in the gender order. Husbands of scolds are portrayed as men who have been unable to regain a position of dominance. So in ballads these husbands play female roles, washing dishes, cooking and cleaning the house.[8] Their wives wear the breeches and become the masters. Wives show their power by their ability to refuse any sexual contact with their husbands. The wife in 'The Cuckold's Complaint' beats her husband if he happens to 'touch her Toe' in bed, and he tells the audience how if he tries to kiss her 'she'll fling and throw, And call me Cuckold to my face'.[9] In other ballads the husband is literally kicked out of bed.[10] These images of the wife of a cuckold give us a cultural context to the slanderous words of men such as John Lawford, who angrily seized Robert Markham by the throat in the summer of

1675, and declared 'you Pitiful Cuckold you are fit for nothing but to wash your wife's dishes'.[11]

The ballad material is also closely paralleled by the evidence of some of the separation cases that reached the court of Arches. In Alexander Denton's case against his wife for adultery heard in 1688, he and his witnesses told the court of the behaviour which accompanied Hester Denton's adultery. Whilst Hester's behaviour was never described as that of a scold, her actions spoke of the disrespect and lack of reverence that was expected of a woman who was cuckolding her husband. It was alleged by friends and servants that she did not rise from her seat or take notice of her husband when he entered the room, she 'made mouths' at him behind his back and when he was eating, and refused to let him touch, kiss, or allow him his 'conjugal rights' from her for more than sixteen months.[12] Sarah Hooper was a servant to William and Mary Hockmore in the 1690s. Sarah told the court of Arches that when Mary started an affair with Charles Manley, a midshipman, her adulterous behaviour precipitated a complete breakdown in household order. William's lack of control over his wife, once his claim to sexual exclusivity had been lost, led Mary to invite her lover and the crew from his ship to stay in his home in Devon. This company joined in Mary's scolding of her husband, 'calling him base and scandalous names'. William was so afraid of damage to his property that he was forced to keep 'a continual Guard in the fields to prevent the said Crew from burning and destroying his corn'. The threat of damage to his property later extended to a fear of personal injury. Verbal abuse by adulterous wives could turn to physical violence. On one occasion Mary was said to have openly boasted to her husband that 'she was a Whore and had cuckolded him sufficiently'. When William then tried to leave her company she and her female servants forcefully kept him in the house 'against his will', threatening to 'bind him if he would not be quiet'. When he got into the courtyard she said she would 'split his skull' if he did not return to the house. She and the servants derided him, called him a fool, and said they would never obey him. It was only the next afternoon, the story went, that William could make his 'escape out of a window of his said house'.[13]

Of course, Sarah Hooper's story may well have been an exaggerated picture of reality to please her master, which drew upon a tradition within popular culture of narratives telling of violent and even murderous adulterous wives. The story of Arden of Faversham, which was based on real events which took place in 1551, and told of Alice's murder of her husband for her lover Mosby, so fascinated contemporaries that it formed the basis of both a play and subsequent ballads.[14] Another story within this genre, also based on real events, and related in ballads of the late sixteenth century, was that of Mistress Page who murdered her husband for the love of George Strangwidge.[15] Although from the mid-seventeenth century the attention of popular literature shifted more towards husbands who murdered their wives, stories of wives who were murderesses continued to attract an audience. When Mary Hobry murdered her husband in 1688, at least four accounts of the murder were published.[16] Since all available evidence suggests that spouse murder was always far more likely to be committed by men than women, we can speculate that these stories were told not to reflect reality, but to reinforce the view that wives should be kept under control if terrifying and bloody consequences were to be avoided.[17] In the ballads 'The West Country Weaver' and 'Mirth for Citizens' the threat of violence is also depicted as coming from the lover of the wife. Gallants threaten husbands with blows, draw swords, and wish the death of them.[18] Laura Gowing has shown from London consistory court evidence that the danger of gallants to husbands was not just fictitious and that husbands could be beaten by their rivals.[19] Records of the Elizabethan consistory courts and the court of Requests reveal that men believed that their lives could be threatened by their wives' adulterous liaisons.[20] Deposition records of marriage separation cases which reached the courts in the late seventeenth century show that these fears of murderous wives were still very much alive. Richard Shawe and his witnesses told the court of Arches in 1676 how once Anne Shawe had committed adultery she became violent towards her husband and threatened to kill him. Witnesses said that she struck her husband with an axe, kept a sword under the bed, and threw pots and an iron at him so that 'they would have killed him'. In 1669 the court heard a witness for John Hubbard, of St Clement Danes, Middlesex, reveal how Grace Hubbard's lover had entreated his friend to 'beat and abuse' John. When Thomas, Earl of Stamford, heard that his wife's lover, his servant John Jennings, had threatened to kill him, he was so frightened that he had warrants issued for his arrest.[21]

It is clear that the adulterous behaviour of a wife could have a number of consequences, which, because they exposed the cuckolded husband as powerless, served only to shame him further. One husband in a ballad pleads with his wife not to let others know that she commands him because it will bring him 'disgrace', and in another ballad a cuckolded husband laments that the behaviour of his unfaithful, scolding and violent wife leaves him 'hen-peckt to the sight of my friends'.[22] Within this context it is understandable why historians studying the church courts of the early seventeenth century have found that men rarely sued for separation on grounds of cruelty. In Durham of the four cases for separation for bed and board between 1604 and 1631, only one case was brought on grounds of cruelty, and that had a female plaintiff.[23] That we only learn of the cruelty that George Whitehead of North Shields supposedly suffered at the hands of his wife after his death in a case disputing his will in 1625 may be taken to suggest that in a man's lifetime it was too shameful for him to admit to being beaten by his wife.[24] In the Restoration period, of forty-two cases for separation on grounds of cruelty which reached the court of Arches in 1660–1700, only five were brought by men.[25] Of these it is clear that the cases were initiated to dispute the sums of alimony allocated in the lower consistory courts. In only two cases is violence by the wife mentioned, probably with the purpose of adding substance to allegations of wifely disobedience.[26] So when men such as William Hockmore and Richard Shawe did relate stories of their wives' cruelty to the courts, to try to avoid further shame and mockery, they generally presented stories in the context of suits for adultery. Unsurprisingly, at no point do they accept any responsibility for their household disorder. Rather, they may well have tended to exaggerate the degree of violence to which they were subjected to win the sympathy of the court. In this way Sarah Hooper may also have needed to magnify the extent of her mistress's violence before describing her master's escape out of the window of his house. For then his actions could be interpreted as those of a desperate man whose life was at risk, rather than as the behaviour of a fool and a coward.[27]

Community Reactions to Lost Manhood

A community which became aware that a husband had been cuckolded could mock him using horns as symbols. So in 1620 in Chester le Street, Durham, during a dispute between William Wales and Thomas Postgate, a witness heard William tell Thomas 'go thou art a cuckold' and then William 'held two of his fingers towards him importing or signifying a sign of horns'.[28] Historians studying records from across the country have found that real horns could be placed on the door or on the property, or even attached to the church pew of a man suspected of being cuckolded.[29] The long-term consequences of this type of mockery can be seen from a Star Chamber case for libel brought by Robert Reede of Tiverton. In 1610 he had been the victim of a mocking rhyme and a pair of horns were fastened to his door. He told the court how from this point whenever his neighbours passed him or his wife in the street they used their fingers to make the cuckold's sign. This was 'likely not only to cause a separation between them but also were like to have bereaved them both of their lives through the grief, sorrow and discontentment which they conceived at the said scandalous imputations'.[30]

Another form of derision was the use of mocking rhymes which could circulate in a community in oral form, or be written and displayed in prominent places such as on a church door.[31] Even though the secular courts became responsible for the prosecution of the authors of these libels, there are occasional references to mocking rhymes in the church courts.[32] So in the dispute between Thomas Postgate and William Wales in 1620, William not only made horn signs at Thomas, but also wrote a mocking ballad about Thomas which depicted him as a cuckold. William had the affront to hand a copy of the rhyme to Thomas, who had to undergo further humiliation as, being unable to read, he was forced to ask a neighbour to read it to him. Thomas clearly intended to take action in response to this insult for the next day he visited the curate of Chester le Street and asked him to make a copy of the libel. This was a wise decision for when Thomas then tried to get William to put his name on the original in front of his neighbours, William duly tore it up and threw it out of the window. The curate's copy was presented to the court in the defamation case which followed.[33] Similarly, when Stephen Seagar's wife was suspected of making him a cuckold in 1669, he not only had horns held outside his house, but also found that his dishonour was 'so public and notorious' that ballads were written about his wife and apprentice.[34] It appears from this case that a man's loss of honour often did not long remain personal to him, but soon became a matter of public interest and knowledge.

This evidence from court cases gives us the context for the many ballads and dramas of the period which refer to the public rituals employed in dishonouring men for the loss of sexual control. Horns were the visual representations of dishonour that made public what men most desired to keep private. Appearing on the head of the cuckold, horns were phallic symbols which made a man a fool because of their lack of potency and their 'dumb bestiality'.[35] When

'The London Cuckold' feels horns growing on his head he tells his wife ''tis of your making', and in another ballad a jealous husband fears that his wife will make him join the 'shameful sort' that wear horns.[36] Fear alone about being cuckolded can make the buds of horns appear, hence *Othello* (*c.*1604) feels the pain of horns appearing when he begins to believe that Desdemona has cuckolded him, and Sparkish warns the suspicious Pinchwife in *The Country Wife* (1675) that 'cuckolding, like the smallpox, comes with a fear'. One newly married husband in a ballad tells others that it is only if men take care of their wives, in other words, provide them with satisfactory sex, that they will avoid wearing the fully grown horns.[37] Many cuckolds complain of the pain of horns: one is unable to sleep because of the pain, another is forced to 'stoop' under their weight.[38] But this pain is justified in the preface to 'The Jolly Widdower' as due 'punishment' for marrying a shrew and being unable to control her.[39] As men who allowed their wives to rule over them, cuckolds are portrayed in fiction and slander accusations as threatening to household order. Their horns grow so big that they even destroy the structure of their houses, as Anne Phesey indicated in 1609 in her words to William Dynes, 'Go thou cuckoldly slave thou wittal thy horns are so great that thou canst scarce get in at thine own doors, take heed thou dost not break a hole with thy horns through thy neighbours wall.' A 'wittal' or 'wittol' cuckold, as we shall see in Chapter 5, was a man who took no action, even though he knew his wife had been unfaithful.[40]

There were degrees of dishonour which a man could suffer, and to be a target of a charivari was probably the ultimate public disgrace. Charivaris were loud mocking demonstrations aimed at shaming individuals who had offended community norms.[41] They could be directed against men who allowed their wives to rule over them, and often included a 'riding'. For example, in Wetherden in Suffolk in 1604, after the drunken Nicholas Rosyer was beaten by his wife, his neighbour Thomas Quarry was made to 'ride about the town upon a cowlstaff' wearing a gown and apron.[42] Dorothy Bolton of Heighington told Durham consistory court in October 1609 how she heard that Jane Romwhate 'did so abuse her husband, as in reproach thereof her next neighbour was carried upon a stang about the town'. Riding a 'stang' was the northern version of charivari which involved mounting a man on a pole and then carrying him through the streets.[43] We tend only to have records of charivaris when they became troublesome to the authorities, which means that it is difficult to estimate how often they occurred. Martin Ingram has also questioned the extent to which charivaris can be seen as features of 'community' custom, since they so often were closely associated with 'official' shame punishments.[44] But there is no doubt that this public exposure of a man's dishonour often amounted to feelings of utter humiliation, disgrace and rejection from a community. Indeed, the Rosyers were forced to leave Wetherden in shame.[45] These shaming rituals won popular notoriety and charivaris featured in plays such as *The Merry Wives of Windsor* (1597), at the end of which Falstaff is mocked by the wives in a ritual which closely resembles a riding.[46]

The processions which were often part of these ridings could end at a Horn Fair, and these fairs are referred to in the ballads of the seventeenth century. The most [in]famous of these fairs is recorded as having been held annually on St Luke's Day, 18 October, at Charlton in Kent. A crowd met at Cuckold's Point on the south bank of the Thames at Rotherhithe and marched in a procession through Deptford and Greenwich to Charlton. Local legend held that the fair and its association with cuckoldry originated when King John was caught by a miller committing adultery with his wife. To make amends with the cuckolded miller the King granted the miller all the land he could see as far as the bend in the river which was to be called Cuckold's Point. In return the miller had to make an annual pilgrimage to Cuckold's Point (which also came to be known as Cuckold's Haven) wearing a pair of buck's horns. Of course, there is no historical evidence for this story, and it is probable that over time the naming of the fair was related to the selling of horned beasts, and its date associated with St Luke whose emblem is a bull.[47]

However, in the popular mind it is likely that the festive elements of the fair retained their links with cuckoldry. Hence in 1598 a German lawyer Paul Hentzner described how he saw the fair. 'It was an ancient custom for a procession to go from some of the inns in Bishopgate in which procession were a King, a Queen, a miller and his pretty wife, a counsellor and a great number of others with horns on their hats.'[48] The 1605 play *Eastward Ho!* by Ben Jonson, George Chapman and John Marston featured a humiliated, shipwrecked husband who is washed up at Cuckold's Haven.[49] In 1623 John Taylor, a poet and boatman on the Thames, had heard stories about the fair, and was disappointed not to find anything marking Cuckold's Haven. He later remarked with satisfaction that local people had set up a post marking the spot.[50] Samuel Pepys was certainly aware of the Point as he mentioned sailing past it in a diary entry of February 1663.[51]

Fictional stories of the fair continued into the Restoration period. The 1685 ballad 'Hey for Horn-Fair' describes the Charlton Horn Fair as an event which attracts wives who have forsaken 'their Husband's dull bed' and who join with gallants at the fair who know how to please them. Cuckolded husbands have to perform the humiliating task of digging gravel to make a path for their wives to take them to the fair.[52] In other ballads scolding wives threaten to make their husbands dig gravel at the next horn fair.[53] Thomas Southerne's *The Wives' Excuse* (1692) mentions the horn fair as a time when a married man with a good-looking wife is 'put in mind of his fortune'. Fortune in this context could either mean his fate to be a cuckold, or may be indicative of the uncertain future of a man married to a beautiful wife.[54] The fair even became the subject of one popular proverb, 'To send one to Cuckold's Haven'.[55] From the writings of contemporaries it is clear that the fair did win a reputation for promiscuous behaviour, leading to temporary suppression in the late eighteenth century, and it is likely that there were some fairs at which wives cuckolded their husbands.[56] But it seems from the popularity of stories about the fair that to this wider audience the fair's fictional origins and purpose were far more significant than what actually occurred at each fair. The fair which the ballads represented was a public occasion from which men who had lost their sexual reputation were excluded and humiliated. Forcing them to bow to the greater sexual powers of their wives was symbolised by the story of the gravel digging. Both in popular literature and on the actual promontory by the Thames, the carnivalistic elements of the Charlton Horn Fair played out portrayals of the 'world turned upside down' by the cuckold.

A similarly popular story portrayed in ballads was that cuckolded husbands were unable to eat roast ram, an animal whose horns also symbolised cuckoldry. At 'A Banquet for Sovereign Husbands', which was supposedly held on Midsummer's Day 1629, the ballad 'reports' that only husbands who ruled their wives were able to eat the ram, others did not for fear of 'displeasing' their wives. Eating the ram is a test of manhood, and only those who succeed are preserved from cuckoldry:

> [And many a man there] thither came,
> [Swearing he would] his wife rule and tame:
> [And that he s]hould eat up the spit,
> [His wife also] should taste a bit.
> [But all be]held most sure I am
> [That nothing was ea]ten of the Ramme.

The story was retold by John Taylor in 1652 in his *Newes from Tenebris.*[57] In 'Have among you! good Women', another ballad by Martin Parker, one man says that a husband who 'will be his wife's drudge . . . should eat none o' th' roasted Ram'.[58] It appears that there was a whole genre within popular mythology which focused on relating tales of customs which shamed the cuckold.

Of course, in reality community responses to male dishonour did not always vicitimise the husband directly. Women who were thought to be whores could be subject to official punishments by the secular authorities and carted through the streets. When sexual insults were used against women they were often reminded of this degrading punishment. Hence in April 1627 when the married Isabell Wright was called a whore by Isabell Sander in an alehouse in Framwellgate, Durham, she was also called 'a common whore and a carted whore'.[59] In the separation case between William Newton and his wife Alice, heard in the Durham consistory court in 1610, witnesses deposed how Alice was carted through the streets of Durham, and her lover Richard Waules whipped, when they were discovered committing adultery. When they continued to defy the authorities, constables dramatically broke down the door of Richard Waules's house, dragged Alice out from where she was hiding under his bed, and took them both to Durham gaol.[60]

Punishments against disobedient wives could be concerned as much with publicising a man's failure to rule and his subsequent loss of reputation, as serving to shame his wife. When a woman was ducked in Leeds in 1619 she claimed that as a result she *and* her husband were utterly 'disgraced [and] defamed'.[61] Women who were accused of being scolds could be subjected to a range of punishments from bridles or branks – iron collars with bits which cut into the tongue to prevent the woman from talking – to the cucking or ducking stool. Inhabitants of communities such as those of Thunderidge and Waddes Mill in Hertfordshire could be presented to the quarter sessions for not having built a cucking stool. Ingram has convincingly argued that in Elizabethan and early Stuart England there was not an 'epidemic' of scolding as David Underdown initially proposed, and that the pattern of prosecutions for scolding suggests that contemporaries perceived scolds to be women who persistently insulted, abused or 'harassed' those living outside their households.[62] The early seventeenth-century ballad 'The cucking of a scold' supports these findings. The wife in the ballad is punished by a charivari which ends with a ducking after she scolds many of her neighbours, both 'old and young', and even the constable.[63]

For community action to be taken against those who were thought to be whores and/or scolds, wives' disobedience had to disrupt neighbourhood order as well as household order. Such a situation could only arise if a man had lost control over his wife.

Basic to all these forms of charivari 'was mocking laughter, sometimes mild and good-hearted, but often taking the form of hostile derision'.[64] It was being made the butt of other people's jokes which most distressed cuckolds in contemporary ballads. 'The Cock-pit Cuckold' complains that his neighbours laugh at him because his wife commits adultery with a young squire; 'The Merry Cuckold' is jeered at by his friends who taunt him by telling him to 'dine at the Bull or the Ramme'; and the cuckold Simon in 'Household Talk' complains that 'my dearest friends doe scoffe me'.[65] Occasionally, men in reality confessed that they were hurt by this type of derision. When John Charnock was accused of cruelty against his wife in 1673, he defended his actions by telling the court of his wife's adulterous and scolding behaviour. He believed he had 'no Joy Comfort or Content at home, and was laughed at and scorned abroad'. Laughter at cuckolds could be real, as well as imagined or suspected. During Dorothy Skelton's affair in London with Charles Brookes, a servant to Baron Brouncker, she openly frequented alehouses with her lover whilst her husband was at sea. One witness recalled hearing 'some gentlemen' laughing as they saw Dorothy and Charles leaving a tavern in a coach, and joking 'that when Captains are at sea, their wives must be coached about by footboys'. Although in this case Captain Skelton did not admit to being harmed by laughter, the witnesses' statement shows the assumption that if a man lost his sexual reputation, he would easily become a laughing stock.[66]

There are a number of theories explaining why people laugh, and what function laughter serves. The complex nature of humour may mean that the historian will never be able to give a definitive answer as to what lay behind the laughter of those who mocked cuckolds. Laughter may also have been experienced differently depending on whether it was provoked by the presence of a 'real' cuckold, or by the reading, listening or sight of a fictional cuckold in ballads and plays. It is unlikely, however, that people laughed at the cuckold simply because he was an incongruous figure with whom men could not or would not identify themselves. Laughter must have required a degree of empathy, and an understanding of the cuckold's predicament. Furthermore, laughter may have served a purpose of cathartic release, as Ingram has suggested in his study of audiences at charivaris. Men who laughed at the cuckold may have temporarily been able to free their otherwise hidden anxieties and fears about married life.[67] So, as Joy Wiltenburg has argued, explaining the humour of many of the ballads about cuckoldry requires understanding that this comedy 'both reflected male anxieties and helped to ease them'.[68] The seventeenth-century philosopher Thomas Hobbes believed that laughter was 'proof of weakness, indicating pleasure in the misfortunes of others and lack of confidence in one's own abilities'.[69] When Swift watched a crowd at a charivari he observed that,

> Those men who wore the breeches least
> Called him a cuckold, fool and beast.[70]

These men laughed 'nervously' because they lacked confidence in their own abilities as husbands, all the while fearing that they too would share the cuckold's fate.

But Hobbes, drawing upon Aristotle's philosophy, also thought that 'this passion of laughter is nothing else but sudden glory, arising from sudden conception of some eminency in ourselves, by comparison with the infirmity of others, or with our own formerly'.[71] In other words, people may have laughed at the cuckold because they wished to assert themselves as superior to the cuckold. Pleasure was gained at the sufferings of others. Laughter in this way can take on a political function, as those in power laugh at those who have none. In many of the community responses to male dishonour it was women who were temporarily given power over men, and this inversion of conventional gender roles in itself may have provoked more laughter.[72]

How far this laughter then acted as a form of social control is difficult to determine. The contemporary playwright Thomas Heywood certainly believed that comedy could serve a social function, for it encouraged men to 'reform that simplicity in themselves which others make their sport'.[73] The work of modern psychologists has agreed with this point of view, 'in laughter we always find an unavowed intention to humiliate, and consequently to correct our neighbour, if not in his will, at least in his deed', one has argued.[74] When a community came together to mock an individual who did not conform to gender norms, laughter may well have also acted as 'a powerful source of social cohesion'.[75] Charivaris were occasions when a community could display a collective understanding of honour; communities as well as individuals had reputations to maintain.[76]

A charivari may have acted as a corrective to behaviour in so far as it demanded a response from its victim. As one anthropologist has explained, 'to be ridiculous is to lack the recognition for social reputation'.[77] The cuckold, as will be explained in the next chapter, could attempt to regain recognition by altering his behaviour so that he reassumed household control, or, as in the case of Nicholas Rosyner at Wetherden, be forced to leave the community in shame. Most cuckolds could only tolerate the laughter of others for so long.

Occupation and Office

'My house', declared the Earl of Huntingdon in a set of household regulations of the early seventeenth century, 'doth nearest resemble the government in public office which men of my rank are very often called unto . . . if I fail in the lesser . . . I shall never be capable of the greater.'[78] It followed that a man who could not control his domestic affairs could not be held responsible for public office outside the home. It was rare that, as Faramerz Dabhoiwala has argued, a man's sexual reputation could be considered separately from his social worth.[79] Instead, it was more commonly held that if a man lost his sexual reputation he should be, as Thomas Whythorne wrote, 'barred of divers functions and callings of estimation in the commonwealth as a man defamed'.[80] Othello's cry at his 'discovery' of Desdemona's adultery – 'Farewell, Othello's occupation's gone!' – is particularly relevant here. The pun on the word 'occupation' to imply both vocation and copulation shows that notions of 'public' and 'private' reputation were inseparable in this society.[81]

In theory, if a man had been damaged materially by sexual slander then he should have taken his case to the secular courts, rather than the church courts.[82] Hence, in the defamation cases of the church courts there are only occasional cases which give us evidence of how reputation could shape a man's job prospects. One such case is that of the apprentice George Fenwick of Newcastle who tried to prevent Margaret Sharpe from telling others of how they had committed fornication. He believed that if his sexual behaviour became public knowledge 'it would be to his utter undoing for he should thereby be utterly ashamed and lose his freedom'. Even though George had already served six years of his apprenticeship, a poor sexual reputation could bar him from gaining freeman status.[83] Similarly, when Asa Scandover was dismissed from the Earl of Hertford's service in the period 1615–29, he claimed that it was because three women said that he had sex with one Bridget Humphrey.[84] Married men who were suspected of adultery could also face ostracism. When Thomas Mace declared that John Skarre, a waterman who had been married for six to seven years, had committed adultery with the widow Mary Joynes in 1675, one witness declared that Skarre 'hath been and is like to be turned out of his employment as to the Custom house at Gravesend'.[85]

There is evidence from the separation suits which reached the church courts that wife adultery could have material effect. Husbands in their personal answers often argued that their 'credit' status had been damaged and that they had been driven into debt by their wives' adulterous behaviour. So Thomas Middleton claimed in February 1662 that he was 'by reason of the lewd and Adulterous Carriage of [his wife] . . . much indebted'.[86] Several contemporary ballads warned that this was the fate of the cuckolded husband; a merchant complains in one that when his wife is with her lover 'with my treasure his pockets she often will line', and in another ballad the adulterous wife 'spends her husband's treasure' at the dancing school where she meets her lovers.[87] Of course, in the courts statements such as Thomas Middleton's are often stock phrases about indebtedness which may well have been used to try to avoid paying large sums of alimony. But occasionally more detail is given in a case to show and convince the court that a wife's behaviour had affected her husband's trade. For example, witnesses for Richard Shawe, a wine cooper at the Three Tuns in Smithfield, London, claimed in 1676 that his wife's 'fighting and quarrelling' had 'so far disturbed his house and Guests that she brought the house into disrepute and caused his Customers to leave and forsake his house'. Richard's trade suffered so badly that his creditors had come, seized all his goods, and turned him out of his house.[88] Richard Shawe's experience shows that just as marriage often sealed an economic union, so also adultery could serve to destroy it.[89]

It is clear from some of the cases which reached the secular courts that discrediting a man sexually could be seen by rivals as an effective means to threaten his public position. Hence, one Thomas Pride stood outside the home of a JP in Westminster and cried 'Justice Lawrence by God is a pimp' in January 1687. The JP was sufficiently troubled by the accusation that he took Thomas to court to try and clear his name and hold on to his position.[90] William Eure, we have seen, attempted to ruin the political career of Sir Thomas Hoby in 1600, when he mounted a charivari and accused him of being a cuckold. When Sir Henry Hastings heard gossip in 1607 that his rival Sir Thomas Beaumont had been cuckolded by one of his servants, Hastings tried to use the information to have Beaumont dismissed from the bench and shunned by local gentry society. Sensing that their public positions were threatened by accusations of cuckoldry, both Hoby and Beaumont launched Star Chamber suits to defend their reputations. As Richard Cust has pointed out, it is remarkable, given the links made between a wife's sexual behaviour and her husband's reputation, that more instances of men actually losing public office as a result of their wives' adultery have not been found. Nevertheless, Sir George Belgrave's words, when he spoke in defence of Sir Thomas Beaumont, show how a man's public political credibility was closely tied both to his personal worth and to the reputation of the family he governed. Sir Thomas, he said, was a 'gentleman of worthy parts, as well in his wise and religious government of his family and virtuous bringing up of his children as in his upright carriage of himself publicly in execution of justice'.[91]

Historians have found other examples of men in lesser positions of local authority who faced loss of office after sexual slander. In 1630 the corporation of Thetford, Norfolk, decided that Walter Salmon, a burgess, was 'unable for to undergo the said office' since he had 'lately lived incontinently . . . to the great disreputation of the Corporation'.[92] The local version of charivari known as a 'groaning' directed against George Andrews, tenant and bailiff to Sir Richard Holford of Westonbirt, Gloucestershire, after George was accused of sodomy in 1716 was interpreted as an attack on the position and status of both men.[93] It is clear that men who were in positions of public authority, from the humblest parish priest to the most senior statesman, were particularly vulnerable to accusations of sexual misconduct. Those who defamed church ministers hoped to jeopardise their standing in the community by exposing hypocrisy. Steve Hindle has shown how quickly gossip about the sexual antics of the Nantwich preacher Stephen Jerome became public scandal when his maidservant Margaret Knowsley started alleging that he had attempted to rape her.[94] David Turner's study of the extra-marital affair between Robert Foulkes, vicar of Stanton Lacy in Shropshire, and Ann Atkinson, one of his parishioners, has illustrated how once news of their affair became public knowledge, Foulkes became embroiled in a web of gossip and anti-clerical sentiment which ended with his execution for the murder of his bastard offspring in 1679.[95] The Bishop of Rochester's reputation was scandalised in 1667 by rumours of sexual impropriety. According to Pepys, Rochester's enemies spread stories 'of his being given to boys and of his putting his hand into a gentleman (who now comes to bear evidence against him) his codpiece while they were at table together'. Pepys later recorded Rochester's dismissal from office.[96] Sexual scandal could also threaten to topple men down from the very highest points of the political ladder. Robert Cecil, Earl of Salisbury, and the Duke of Buckingham were both notorious victims of libellous accusations of venereal disease and homosexuality in the early seventeenth century. By tarnishing their sexual reputations, the libels directed against them starkly highlighted their inaptitude for government, and denigrated the court and the King who appointed them.[97]

It would appear that even the most mundane of public offices could not be served by men with doubtful sexual reputations. Witnesses who spoke in the church courts could find the credulity of their statements open to question if the opposing party could provide convincing evidence of some former sexual misdemeanour. Hence John Harding, a witness for Mary Conghley during a defamation suit brought by her in 1674, found that his statement was questioned by three male witnesses who spoke for the opposing party, because they claimed that as well as being 'addicted to excessive drinking and swearing', he was 'a company keeper of lewd women', and frequently visited the bawdy houses of Moorefields, 'albeit he hath a wife and children of his own'.[98] As John was sexually incontinent, these men argued that his words could not be trusted and should be disregarded. It seems that the double sexual standard could be readily ignored by men when it suited.

There were many rituals within early modern society which signalled which men had worthy reputations, and which had lost claims to honour. Men of honour could expect others to doff their hats in their presence.[99] This was a custom, as Penelope Corfield has pointed out, which was particular to men, given the 'fixity of women's bonnets and head-dresses'. Whilst it is true that men were traditionally required to doff their hats to women, especially 'ladies', arguably this did not jeopardise the gender hierarchy which rendered men superior to women, since men retained the crucial power 'to extend or withhold the accolade', according to their judgement of a woman's worth.[100] During the seventeenth century there was a market amongst the social elite for books such as Antoine Courtin's *The Rules of Civility* (1671) and Jean Gailhard's *The Compleat Gentleman* (1678) which gave instructions on the appropriate modes of behaviour for those who met and visited men of honour.[101]

An honour ritual which concerned all social groups was seating within churches. A man's pew position in a church reflected his social status and authority within his local community. The closer to the altar, the greater the honour a man held. So in 1637 when church seats were redistributed in a church in Tisbury, Wiltshire, they were done so according to the 'ranks, qualities and conditions' of parishioners.[102] Seating plans could be further complicated by the politics of age, with older men claiming better positions over youth.[103] Pew seating could prove to be a very contentious issue, and men frequently argued over where they ranked on this highly visible scale of reputation. In the early seventeenth century Thomas Fraunceis of Gerberstone, Somerset, was highly offended when his claim to seats in the north aisle of West Buckland church was challenged by the Ley brothers who were clothiers 'of mean and obscure parentage'.[104] Some thought in Swaffham, Norfolk, in 1636 that the seat Robert Theodorick had been given was too high for him, 'he being an oatmeal maker and a man of no great credit'.[105] In one contemporary ballad a wife tells her new husband that he should look upon his marriage favourably because it will allow him a higher position in the church,

> His wife shall then be seated
> in Church at her desire,
> Her Husband he is a sideman,
> and sits within the Quire,
> Then he is made Churchwarden;
> and placed somewhat higher:
> Great joy to a married young man.
>
> Then seeing all this credit
> by marriage you do find,
> Unto your wife tis reason,
> you should be good and kind.[106]

Whilst in this ballad it appears that the husband and wife sit separately, Mervyn James has argued that the usual practice in Durham parishes was for the head of household to sit with his family and servants.[107] However, at about Whitsuntide 1634 a dispute broke out in the Durham parish of West Bowden whilst a group of male parishioners sat drinking and waiting for the wood to arrive for the repair of church seats. They started to argue about 'the placing of the parishioners there', and some suggested that it would be 'convenient for the women to sit by themselves'. Robert Atchinson strongly rejected this idea, saying that it would only allow Richard

Clay to 'make them all Cuckolds meaning . . . the married men of Bowden'.[108] From this case it would seem that pew seating was not only concerned with the display of honour, but also could involve its protection. Even within a church men could feel that their sexual reputation was at stake, and Robert Atchinson needed to sit with his wife to feel secure of his honour.

Another important ritual of honour in this society was pledging. According to the Oxford English Dictionary pledging was 'an assurance of allegiance or goodwill attested by drinking in response to another; the drinking of health to a person, a toast'.[109] Pledging was a popular practice in the seventeenth century. The ballad 'Match me this Wedding' published between 1636 and 1641 features men passing a cup of drink around and taking turns to toast their women. John Evelyn noted the English custom 'to drink to everyone at the Table' in 1659. It was chiefly a male activity: Mirabell in William Congreve's *The Way of the World* (1700) defended pledging, telling the women that they should on no account 'encroach upon the men's prerogative, and presume to drink healths or toast fellows'.[110]

As we will see in the next chapter, pledging could be a useful means of settling a dispute as the parties ended their differences in a drink. But it was refusal to pledge someone which could lead to trouble. As Courtin had reminded his gentry audience, if a man drank your health ''tis your duty to pledge him'.[111] At a gathering of neighbours at Longhorsley in Northumberland in March 1606 William Johnson took up a cup of ale and offered to drink to Thomas Bolton. But Bolton answered that in return 'he would not pledge him for some causes known to himself'. In Johnson's eyes, by rejecting the offer of a pledge Bolton was showing that he did not respect the goodwill which he had proffered. Deemed unworthy and humiliated in front of his neighbours, Johnson responded to this challenge of reputation by slandering Bolton. He claimed that he was 'sorry that he had drunk to any such she Carle as he was and further said to him that he was a Rogue, and a thief and a murderer'. A carle is a Northumbrian word for a peasant or clown; by calling Bolton a she carle he was using both a sexual and a social insult. Johnson then claimed that Bolton had paid a man to cut the throat of his first wife, and that he would pay again to kill his second wife.[112] Such a torrent of abuse shows how seriously Johnson interpreted Bolton's refusal to reciprocate his pledge.

Johnson's words and Bolton's subsequent action for defamation in Durham consistory court must also be partly explained by who was present when they quarrelled. In this case they were surrounded by 'divers other Neighbours'. In other cases it is the quality or honour of those who hear the insult which is significant, since honour was, as Robert Ashley defined it, the praise of the 'better sort'.[113] It appears that a man's dishonour may have increased in proportion to the social status of those who were present when he was shamed. So, for example, Matthew Hinde told Nicholas Briggs that 'he had wronged him very greatly' when Nicholas had called him a 'drunken fellow', for he had done so at a dinner party at Littleburn in the presence of Sir John Calverley. Matthew asked Nicholas 'what reason he had to slander him in such sort as he had done and that before such a worthy man as the said Sir Calverley'.[114] When William Patteson was accused of being a 'mainsworne man' by Agnes Norrish, it was noted by witnesses that it was in the town court of Newcastle in front of the 'Mayor, aldermen, sheriff and Jurors and many more'.[115] In 1624 Henry Collins of Winscombe, Somerset, a wealthy clothier and constable, was victim to a series of mocking rhymes which he claimed were deliberately sung in front of 'the better sort' of the neighbours. The rhymes claimed that he was a bad debtor and that he had committed adultery with many women. The result was that he was shunned from his 'better' neighbours, unable to operate his trade, and since his wife believed the rumours of his infidelities, she became 'frantic'.[116] In another case in April 1625, Michael Heworth was the unfortunate victim of slander at a meeting of 'the whole Corporation' of Gateshead. Richard Grame called Michael 'a backbiting busy fellow and not fit to come in any honest man's company'.[117] Richard's insult boldly suggested what the consequence of Michael's dishonour should be: exclusion from the society of all the honourable men belonging to the corporation.

What these cases show is that although sexual behaviour was not invariably invoked during quarrels between men, a man's reputation in its widest sense depended on his honesty or probity in all aspects of his character. If a man was to have the honour of those below him on the social scale, and the respect of those who were his social equals or betters, then the integrity of his sexual reputation needed to be without question. Without that integrity, no claim to status or prestige within his community could be sustained.

Paternity

Jokes about unchaste women bearing illegitimate children are abundant within ballad literature of the seventeenth century. Their comedy centres on the foolish gallant or husband who ends up supporting a child which is not his own. In 'The Jolly Widdower' the man warns bachelors against marriage, telling them that when he was married 'I often rock'd another man's child'.[118] Maids pretend virginity and trick young men into marriage or into maintaining a bastard in both 'Children after the rate of 24 in a year' and 'The Country Girl's Policy'. The chorus of the former ballad runs,

> Rock the Cradle, rock the Cradle,
> rock the cradle John,
> There's many a man rocks the cradle,
> when the child's none of his own.[119]

Evidence from separation cases suggests that in reality men took this consequence of their failure to exert sexual control over their future brides or wives very seriously. For even though legal theory held that all children born by a married woman were legitimate, in practice when the paternity of a child was in doubt rightful inheritance of property was immediately at stake.[120] It becomes obvious why so many contemporary writers described adultery as an act of theft when we understand that bastards were thought likely to rob other children of estate and property. The double standard of morality is justified by contemporaries because the consequence of a woman's adultery is that, 'she may bring into her Husband's house strange children, to wipe her husband's own children's nose of their share in his goods, and falsify all whatsoever'.[121] Women's power to disrupt the rightful inheritance of property by mixing it with blood of lower social status was recognised by John Taylor, the Water Poet:

> The greatest females underneath the sky
> Are but frail vessels of mortality . . .
> Lust enters, and my lady proves a whore:
> And so a bastard to the world may come,
> Perhaps begotten by some stable groom;
> Whom the fork-headed, her cornuted knight
> May play and dandle with, with great delight,
> And thus by one misbegotten son,
> Gentility in a wrong line may run:
> And thus foul lust to worship may prefer
> The mongrel issue of a fruiterer.[122]

An illegitimate child could also be regarded as the long-term living proof of a husband's shame. Even if, as Chapter 2 argued, ideas of inherited lineal honour were being gradually replaced by those that placed more emphasis on individual virtue, concern about illegitimate children shows that the concept of inherited dishonour continued. As Gibbon wrote in 1594, 'An ill Name doth not only disparage and impeach the Agent, but such as be allied to him; not only the party, but his progenitors, and such as belong or be anyway derived from his lineage.' When Hermione in *The Winter's Tale* (*c.*1609) stands trial for adultery, she points straight to her husband's concerns about his succession when she recognises of honour, ''Tis a derivative from me to mine.'[123]

It is little wonder, given this context of ideas, that when Alexander Denton discovered that his wife had suffered a miscarriage after he claimed not to have had sex with her for eight or nine months, he visited her bedside, 'and asked how she could offer to do herself and him so much injury'.[124] In November 1696 the Earl of Macclesfield was concerned by reports that his wife was pregnant for a second time with an illegitimate child. He visited her sister, where he suspected his wife was seeking refuge, and tried to persuade her to allow two of his female relations to examine his wife to determine the truth of the claims. The Earl told his wife's sister that if they found that 'she was not with Child it would be much to the reputation of his Wife and her Family as well as a great satisfaction to him'. The Earl had reason to be concerned when the Countess had born him no children and when the likely fate of his estates was subject to popular gossip. For despite the Countess's attempts to remain anonymous during the birth of her children by wearing a mask, her infidelity to the Earl appears to have been widely known. The midwife and other female attendants were reported to have speculated that her child 'if a Boy would be a great Heir'. It is unsurprising that on hearing that his wife could be pregnant the Earl admitted to his own sister that he had 'no mind to make a Noise about it'.[125] Husbands such as the Earl may well have found a sympathetic audience in the all-male environment of the courtroom. In 1656 during a parliamentary debate on divorce, members favoured giving Edward Scot a divorce based on his accusations of his wife's adultery, even though he was mentally unstable, since 'it is fit the gentleman should be relieved, that bastards may not inherit his estate'. Another member agreed, arguing 'it is a sad case to have such a wife and to have a posterity put upon him that is none of his own'.[126]

Once pregnancy became visible it could provoke severe anger from husbands who were suspicious of being cuckolded. Hence when William Younger met his wife in a street in Wapping after they had been informally separated for around seven years, he became violent when he saw she was pregnant. He hit her on the belly, called her 'Greenwaye's whore' and cried 'what more bastards coming to Town . . . telling her that it was none of his'. His anger and violence attracted the attention of shopkeepers who sent for constables, but William followed his wife through the streets and attacked her again. This time he claimed that she had another bastard which she 'buried in the kitchen', and threatened to see her hanged for this crime. William's public beating of his wife was probably partly designed to ensure that his neighbours would not hold him responsible for maintaining his wife's child. Similarly, in 1669 after two years of marriage James Whiston claimed 'in a loud voice in the open street' that his wife 'was with a child by another man and not by him, that he would therefore be divorced from her'.[127]

But whilst at first sight pregnancy would appear to provide powerful grounds for marriage separation compared with trying to gain witnesses to adultery which was *in flagrante delicto*, proving that a child had not been conceived in wedlock was in fact fraught with difficulty. One of the greatest pitfalls of a male honour system which rested on female chastity was that it depended on women's words. For as the Roman jurist Gaius recognised, 'Maternity is a fact. Paternity is a merely an opinion.'[128] When Leontes first suspects his wife of infidelity in *The Winter's Tale*, he turns to his son and heir to the throne and asks, 'Mamillius, Art thou my boy?' He stares at Mamillius and remembers that women have said that they share looks, that the boy's nose is 'a copy out of mine'. But Leontes realises with horror that although 'women say so', women 'will say anything'.[129] Similarly, when Miranda learns of her noble origins in *The Tempest* (*c*.1611) she asks Prospero, 'Sir, are you not my father?' To this Prospero can only provide limited assurance, for he too depended on his wife's word: 'Thy mother was a piece of virtue, and / She said thou wast my daughter' he replies.[130] Some early modern writers even argued that mothers were bound to love their children more than fathers, because only the former could be certain that the children were their own.[131]

In practice, the paternity of a child could be always open to question, because its determination was so dependent upon interpretation of a child's visual appearance. 'Thou . . . is John Hedley's bastard . . . see thou art as like John Hedley as if he had spit thee out of his mouth', cried Mary Bryan to the daughter of Anne Hudspeth in Pilgrim Street, Newcastle, in 1629.[132] As Ann Holliday stood holding her child in Love Lane in Stepney in 1671 Margaret Cowper pointed to it and said 'that child . . . is a bastard and like a man in Wapping and you are a whore'.[133] One Norfolk man was left bitterly complaining 'that he had paid for eleven church goings [the thanksgiving after childbirth], but God knew who was the father of his children'.[134] Women, who were in the popular mind so easily capable of deception, had the power to make a mockery of an inheritance system which by primogeniture was intended to ensure that land was passed legitimately from one male to the next. As Calvin had warned, 'What else will remain safe in human society if licence be given to bring in by stealth the offspring of a stranger? to steal a name which may be given to spurious offspring? and to transfer to them property taken away from lawful heirs?'[135] That the pregnant and adulterous Countess of Macclesfield was supposedly advised by her friends to pretend that her husband had 'met her in the Streets, and carried her to a Tavern and there lay with her and had a Child by her', shows how easily women could fabricate stories about the paternity of their children.[136]

It seems probable that men at the upper end of the social scale would have been more sensitive and wary of consequences of sexual dishonour which threatened legitimate inheritance than those from the lower orders. After all, for the gentry there was more land and property at stake. There does seem to have been a commonplace in this society, stemming from the biblical precedent, 'Look how the mighty have fallen', that because the upper orders had more in material terms to lose by dishonour their 'fall' and shame would be proportionately greater. D'Avolos in Ford's *Love's Sacrifice* (*c.*1632) comments on the fate of the cuckold that 'Wherein do princes exceed the poorest peasant that ever was yoked to a sixpenny strumpet but that the horns of one are mounted some two inches higher by a choppine than the other?'[137] The fall of a great man would be of such magnitude that it would be visible to all.

Male Friendships

Ballads, satire and drama provided a context in which men learnt what was manly and honourable. Popular rituals which taunted men who did not fulfil their prescribed gender roles were painful reminders of the consequences for men for whom honourable manhood had been lost. But how were men's day-to-day relationships with each other and their wives affected by this culture of ideas and expectations? The remainder of this chapter will explore how fear of loss of manhood had consequences for both male friendships and heterosexual relationships.

It has already been shown how male friends played an important role in a man's social life before marriage. In village society the alehouse was the focal point for male fellowship and the approval of friends was sought in the choice of lover or marriage partner. The Renaissance had seen the revival of many ancient texts which extolled the virtues of same-sex friendship. As a result, in the Elizabethan period there were circumstances in which men as friends could openly express love for each other in letters, and share close physical intimacy by becoming 'bedfellows'.[138]

It becomes evident from a number of literary sources, however, that the male friendships of childhood and adolescence were idealised to contrast with the heterosexual relationships which most men formed upon sexual maturity. The ballads of the period present unmarried life as a time free from the worries of pleasing a wife and the responsibilities of providing for a family. One typical ballad within this genre, 'Advice to Batchelors; Or, The Married Man's Lamentation', begins,

> You batchelors that single are
> may lead a happy life;
> For married men are full of care,
> and women oft breed strife.[139]

Polixenes in *The Winter's Tale* remembers his childhood friendship with Leontes as a time when,

> We were as twinn'd lambs that did frisk i' th' sun,
> And bleat the one at th'other: what we chang'd
> Was innocence for innocence.

The closeness of male childhood friends is expressed by Othello who, when Cassio's drunken behaviour disturbs him from his marriage bed, promises punishment on the culprit, even if he was 'twinn'd' with him from birth.[140] Male friendships were also described with fond recollection in Montaigne's sixteenth-century essay 'On Friendship' as 'souls that mingle and blend with each other so completely that they efface the seam that joined them'.[141]

But with marriage men's attentions shifted away from their male friends to their wives as they became eager to gain honour by exhibiting sexual prowess and control. A man's sexual potency became all-important, and only men with 'every Husbands proper sign' could enter the adult world of male relationships. So when Horner in *The Country Wife* pretends to be a eunuch he is excluded from the homosocial world. Sir Jaspar Fidget leaves Horner with his female kin while he mixes with other men and attends to his business.[142] Literary texts which praised friendship competed with those which promoted the Puritan notion of the heterosexual relationship within marriage. Marriage provided the setting in which male friendships could be construed as 'unnatural' and even branded as 'sodomitical'.[143] In popular literature male friendships are also portrayed as changing profoundly with maturity because instead of the equality of childhood ('innocence for innocence'), men become competitors and potential rivals. Within the adult world of sexual politics it is men who betray and cuckold other men.[144] Ironically then, whilst men had a common interest in the preservation of patriarchy, this was within a political arena in which men were engaged in a power struggle against each other for honour. Friendship could just become a means of getting closer to a man's wife:

> a rival is the best
> cloak to steal a mistress under, without suspicion;
> and when we have once got to her as we desire, we
> throw him off like other cloaks.

In drama any man who trusts his friend with his wife is shown to be mistaken. Hence in *The Country Wife* Sparkish's belief that his best friend Harcourt will be able to act as a reconciler in 'the differences of the marriage bed' without becoming emotionally or sexually involved with his fiancée is shown to be naive and foolish. Indeed, Horner argues that friendship and love of women cannot mix because ultimately a man will always betray his friend rather than resist the woman.[145]

The risk of being cuckolded and losing honour to one's friend raised a dilemma for men of how to adjust their male friendships to married life. One particular problem was how a husband should entertain his friends when they came to stay. Chapter 2 showed that offering hospitality could be an important way for men to gain and display honour. Yet acting as a host also made a man vulnerable to losing his honour. A common theme of the drama of the early seventeenth century was that male guests who enter the home of a married couple could be disruptive both to the husband/friend relationship and the husband/wife bond. In Heywood's *A Woman Killed with Kindness* (1603) Wendoll causes disaster in the Frankford marriage; Othello's friendship with Cassio has tragic consequences; and Fernando is the Duke's friend who disrupts his marriage in Ford's *Love's Sacrifice*.[146] The husband and his friend have to accommodate a female presence in their relationship when before there was none. There can be a history of emotional attachment between two men of which the wife is ignorant. Hence, Hermione in *The Winter's Tale*, for example, has to enquire about the childhood games and friendship between her husband and Polixenes.[147] But questioning does not necessarily lead to an understanding of the intricacies of a relationship, so that a wife's involvement in her husband's friendships can easily be resented. Othello becomes increasingly irritated when Desdemona interferes with his relationship with Cassio by pleading on his behalf.[148]

Most significantly, however, a male friend within the household can cause tensions between a husband and his wife. The woman has a difficult role to play in both obeying her husband and pleasing the guest. Hermione in *The Winter's Tale* plays her part as hostess too well and by persuading her guest to stay causes Leontes to be jealous. Despite the men's years of friendship, Hermione has a greater power of persuasion over Polixenes than Leontes.[149]

Clearly a key problem for a wife was how far she should or could extend her friendship to her husband's friend. The drama of the period shows that the idea of a husband and wife having mutual friends appears impossible. In Heywood's *A Woman Killed with Kindness*, on the arrival of his friend Frankford orders his wife Anne to 'Use him with all thy loving'st courtesy'. Anne immediately foresees the difficulty of obeying her husband when she replies,

> As far as modesty may well extend,
> It is my duty to receive your friend.[150]

The greatest risk that faced a husband was if his friend decided not to reciprocate hospitality by behaving in an honourable way. Instead, as portrayed in *A Woman Killed with Kindness*, a friend could abuse his position as guest and exploit the uncertainties of the wife/host role by committing adultery, repaying kindness with horns.

Several court cases of the period show that the fears of betrayal by friends depicted in drama could be shared by men in reality. Laura Gowing has shown how Grace Ball responded to her husband's accusations of adultery in 1609 by explaining that he had insisted that she welcome his friends into his house. He then would become jealous if he perceived that 'she was over-familiar with them'. If she tried to avoid confrontation by keeping out of their company, he would 'quarrel with her because she did not bid them welcome'. Grace tried to show the court the difficulties she faced living with a husband whose jealousy meant that he drew a fine line between her showing due hospitality and playing the whore.[151] Both Edmund Clarke in 1676, and Alexander Denton in 1688, accused their wives of adultery with men who they had introduced as their friends. Their wives denied the charges and defended their actions by claiming that they had only entertained the men as their husbands' guests. Martha Clarke said that her husband told her that Mr Millington was his friend, and that she was commanded to be 'civil' to him. When her husband also introduced Mr Conigsby as a kinsman, and willed her to 'respect him accordingly', Martha said she behaved only 'as became her to do to a friend of her said Husband'.[152] Similarly, when Hester Denton was accused of adultery with one Thomas Smith, she claimed that Thomas was frequently at their house because he was a close friend of her husband. She argued that Thomas and her husband often hunted together, went to the horse races, and spent much time with each other's families. Their friendship was so intimate that she claimed that if they spent any time apart her husband became 'very uneasy and dissatisfied'. In this context, it could only be part of Hester's duties as a good wife to entertain her husband's friend.[153]

Undoubtedly, for many men the responsibilities and concerns of married life put an end to the carefree lifestyle of bachelor sociability. As Edward Coxere, a ship apprentice, approached marriage he reflected how 'care began to creep in, which before I was unacquainted with'.[154] On the Isle of Portland there was even a ritual performed at the church door in which a bridegroom would cry to his former friends, 'young men and bachelors I bid you all adieu / Old men and married men I'm coming to you.'[155] Ballads with titles such as the 1670 'No Money, no Friend' reflected anxieties about the instability of the foundation of friendships which centred so much on the capacity to buy oneself and others drink in the alehouse.[156] It seems highly likely that men's satire on female friendship and demeaning of female talk to 'gossip' stemmed at least partly from an envious recognition that female friendships faced no troublesome readjustment upon marriage.[157] To men, women's friendships may also have appeared to have been configured quite differently from their own. Male authors represented the basis of female friendships as the exchange of worries, concerns and complaints, but for men themselves, relationships along these lines ran the risk of being seen as indicative of weakness or lack of self-reliance. Instead of seeking mutuality, men's talk is often featured in the records left to us as highly competitive and concerned with one-upmanship. Rather than ask friends for help, as Helen Berry has shown, men often had to find alternative sources of advice, such as that contained within the popular question-and-answer pages of the 1690s periodical *The Athenian Mercury*.[158]

Jealousy: Fictional Evidence

As jealousy could have been interpreted as a sign of weakness – an admission that a man feared that he was losing the sexual control of his wife – men were unlikely to admit to such an emotion in any public forum.[159] Instead, historians are left with evidence of the actions of jealous men, or the conduct which was the consequence of this emotion, within the court records of marriage separation which women brought on grounds of cruelty. These men exhibited what has been termed as 'reactive jealousy': actions taken once they became convinced that their wives had committed adultery. This behaviour will be discussed fully in the next chapter.[160]

If we are to put these actions in their context, we need to reach to their psychological roots. Playwrights of this period devoted considerable thought to the causes and consequences of male jealousy. They display it as chiefly a male characteristic which originates from men's concern to adhere to honour codes which lay emphasis on male control of women. For women such as Alithea in *The Country Wife*, jealousy has become such a common tendency of men that are in love, that if a man does not exhibit jealousy his true intentions are placed in doubt. She is concerned at Sparkish's 'want of jealousy' when she spends time with Harcourt. She has been told that jealousy is the 'only infallible sign' of love, and suspects that because Sparkish is not jealous, 'you care not for me nor who has me'.[161] If a man loved a wife, and had concern for his honour, it is shown as only natural that he should fear losing her. In this line of thinking, men's desire to maintain authority over the women to whom they form emotional attachments inevitably leads to a jealous zeal to protect and defend reputation.[162]

In contrast, a man who is married to a jealous wife is open to mockery. By allowing their lives to be controlled by their wives, these men have surrendered all claims to male honour. One typical ballad within this genre tells the story of John Tomson, who is married to a jealous and possessive wife. When John is out with his friends his neighbours tease him by pretending that his wife can see him, and then laugh at him when he looks fearful. For seven years he has lived with her but she has remained suspicious and scolds him frequently.[163] Men such as John Tomson who tolerate their wives' jealousy are labelled as henpecked.[164] In Etherege's *She Would if She Could* (1668) Sir Oliver's hesitancy as he enters an alehouse to meet whores, and his fears of his wife's discovery, make him a feeble and comic figure.[165]

Contemporary dramatic depictions of jealous men showed the way that their imagination was thought to centre upon forming images of their wives' betrayal. When Othello first believes that his wife has betrayed him he starts to visualise the 'stol'n hours of lust' and 'Cassio's kisses on her lips'. After Othello's demand to Iago to 'Make me see't', Iago encourages him to imagine Cassio making love to Desdemona. He recalls the words Cassio uttered in his sleep, and says that Cassio has boasted of 'lying' with Desdemona. The latter triggers Othello's outburst,

> Lie with her, lie on her? – We say lie on her, when
> they belie her, – lie with her, zounds, that's fulsome![166]

with each repetition forming a clearer picture in his mind of the sexual act he finds so nauseating. Leontes in *The Winter's Tale* does not need an Iago figure to give rise to his jealousy; he imagines Polixenes as 'Sir Smile' who in his absence 'sluic'd' his wife, opened his 'gate' and 'fish'd' his 'pond'.[167] 'A jealous man's horns hang in his eyes', taught one proverb, for a jealous man could not see anything else but his imagined cuckold's status.[168]

Given that, as one ballad puts it, 'There's no greater plague th[a]n imagined horns', why did men allow their imagination to centre upon such horrifying sexual images?[169] In *Othello* the perceptive Emilia states of jealousy,

> 'tis a monster,
> Begot upon itself, and born on itself,

and Iago declares of his actions to Othello,

> I told him what I thought, and told no more
> Than what he found himself was apt and true.[170]

Jealousy stems from a man's insecurity about himself and from his innermost fears and anxieties. It can be caused when 'the eye looks curiously into his own heart, and spies some fault in himself, which [is] displeasing', wrote the author of the 1593 *Tell-Trothes New-Yeares Gift*.[171] Orgilus recognises in Ford's *The Broken Heart* (*c.*1629) that Bassanes's fears about his wife's fidelity arise 'out of a self-unworthiness'.[172] Similarly, when the writer William Heale tried to explain men's behaviour, he concluded that 'jealousy is a child conceived of self-unworthiness, and of anothers worth, at whose birth fear made it an abortive in nature, and a monster in love'.[173] Thus Othello, through Iago's scheming, experiences feelings of fear and inadequacy when he compares himself with Cassio. Cassio is a 'proper man' who to Othello appears to have many of the qualities which he lacks. He has verbal ability and social sophistication which Othello cannot parallel. Although Othello can boast of military achievement, he knows he is 'rude' in speech,

> for I am black
> And have not those soft parts of conversation
> That chamberers have,

Cassio's physical appearance also contrasts with Othello's blackness, for Cassio is 'fram'd to make women false'.[174] Ultimately, it is Cassio's qualities which make Othello fear being a cuckold, not those of Desdemona. Desdemona never commits adultery, and the words of the Restoration playwright Wycherley could well apply to Othello: 'cuckolding, like the smallpox, comes with a fear'.[175] Heale believed that it was this fear that led men to 'obtain the full sight and perfect assurance of our own misery', and another contemporary thought that a feature of jealousy was that it 'labours to seek out what it hopes it shall not find'.[176] So men anticipated their worst fears about being cuckolded by picturing or imagining them.

Jealousy is shown to be an emotion which can develop from faint suspicion to a morbid or pathological state. It can manifest itself by a man taking measures which he believes will prevent his wife from committing adultery. Jealousy in this sense became essentially a defensive posture.[177] Playwrights of the period satirised the actions of these jealous husbands. Bassanes in *The Broken Heart* orders the window next to the street to be boarded up because he thinks it 'gives too full a prospect to temptation' for his wife. The suitably named Pinchwife in *The Country Wife* locks his wife in the house and will only let her walk through the town if she puts on men's clothes.[178]

Pathological jealousy occurs when a husband suffers from severe delusions about his wife's behaviour and neurotically seeks evidence to 'prove' what he already 'knows' to be true.[179] Jealousy in early modern texts is shown to be painful until 'proven'; Othello talks of the pain on his forehead as he thinks of the cuckold's horns, and he wishes Iago had not told him of his suspicions as they have set him 'on the rack' and 'torture' him.[180] In one ballad jealousy is said to be worse than the pains of hell, and in another it is compared with 'tormenting Lice, or Fleas'.[181] As Lisa Jardine writes, 'jealousy is the humiliating condition of *doubt* in relation to your own honour and your wife's obedience'.[182] The only way that men can seek an end to this agony is to find the 'truth':

> I'll see before I doubt, when I doubt, prove,
> And on the proof, there is no more but this:
> Away at once with love or jealousy![183]

Mrs Marwood explains to Mrs Fainall in Congreve's *The Way of the World* (1700) that making her husband jealous is 'as bad', and will cause her husband as much pain, as her actually committing adultery. For if she was unfaithful, and 'he should ever discover it, he would know the worst, and be out of his pain', whereas if she made him jealous he would instead forever 'continue upon the rack of fear and jealousy'.[184]

In their bid to escape from the 'rack' of jealousy and their search for proof, men are often overhasty and misled by their suspicions. Both Othello and Leontes misinterpret small signs or gestures as confirmation of their suspicions. Leontes sees Hermione's 'paddling palms . . . pinching fingers . . . and making practis'd smiles' with Polixenes as an indication of her betrayal. 'My life stands in the level of your dreams', says Hermione to her husband. For Othello a missing handkerchief becomes confirmation of Desdemona's guilt, proving as Iago recognises that,

> trifles light as air
> Are to the jealous, confirmations strong
> As proofs of holy writ.[185]

Bassanes and Pinchwife are made to look ridiculous, and the actions of Othello and Leontes are shown to be without reason. A man's behaviour changes with the development of jealousy, and as it does so it becomes more and more destructive to honour. 'Jealousy

. . . is as irksome to bear in a man as a woman, and so much more in a man, because thereby he looseth his honour', thought one treatise writer in 1599.[186] Jealousy could destroy a man's honour because it led to irrational behaviour. The most frequent simile used in conjunction with jealousy is that it is like a disease or madness. Alice accused her 'jealous harebrain' husband of behaving like a 'frantic man' in *Arden of Faversham* (*c.*1591); Falstaff says that Ford has 'the finest mad devil of jealousy in him . . . that ever governed frenzy' in *The Merry Wives of Windsor*; and Paulina says Leontes is mad for accusing Hermione of adultery in *The Winter's Tale*.[187] In a period when reason was regarded as the touchstone of manhood, a man possessed of such an affliction could not be thought honourable. In Ford's *The Broken Heart* Bassanes's jealous behaviour towards his wife is described as 'lunacy' by one witness. Bassanes's jealousy is so excessive that he even accuses Ithocles, his wife's brother, of cuckolding him. Ithocles believes that this can only show that Bassanes's jealousy 'has robbed him of his wits'. Once Bassanes has lost control of reason, Ithocles argues that he is an unfit husband to govern a wife, and promises that he will only return his sister,

> When you shall show good proof that manly wisdom,
> Not overswayed by passion, or opinion,
> Knows how to lead your judgement.[188]

Hence the success of Iago's plan. He can dishonour Othello simply by inspiring him to be jealous; no adultery need take place. Horner explains to Pinchwife when they discuss women that a cuckold and a jealous husband can be subject to the same degree of public dishonour for,

> if she cannot make her husband a cuckold, she'll
> make him jealous, and pass for one, and then 'tis all one.[189]

So, for example, in *The Merry Wives of Windsor*, far from his jealousy preventing his dishonour, Ford's behaviour of attempting to surprise his wife in the act of adultery only renders him a ludicrous figure and a fool who is fit for laughter, and undeserving of social honour. In *The Winter's Tale* Leontes also loses his honour through his jealousy. Paulina says that Leontes's 'weak-hing'd fancy' of jealousy which led him to slander his wife will make him 'ignoble' and 'scandalous to the world'.[190]

If at this point we briefly turn to husbands' statements in marriage separation cases, we find evidence that men were sensitive to accusations of jealousy. These men did not want to be thought of as the Bassanes or Pinchwives of their local community. When Captain Charles Skelton returned from sea and heard reports that his wife had been unfaithful, he claimed that 'he had so good an opinion of her that he could no ways believe the same'. Similarly, Thomas Earl of Stamford argued in 1686 that although he was told that his wife had engaged in 'many lewd embraces . . . yet he had that love and honour for her that he did give no faith or credit to the reports'.[191] Several husbands appeared to be eager to deny that their jealousy had affected their wives' liberty; in 1674 John Turner of Swanwick, Derbyshire, said that he had never confined his wife to her chamber or charged her 'not to stir over the threshold of the said chamber in his absence upon peril of her life'. Thomas Rayner claimed that he only put a bolt of his wife's chamber door during the night because he was afraid that she in her anger would set the house on fire, and said that he only locked her in one day when 'she had threatened to kill a young girl who then lived with them'.[192] After ten years' separation in 1585 Lady Willoughby wrote to her husband to try and negotiate coming back to live with him. She told him of rumours she had heard that on her return he intended to act as a jealous husband;

> that I should take heed and beware how I come to you again, for you had determined and vowed that if ever you took me again, you would keep me shorter than 'ere I was kept, that you [would] lock and pin me up in a chamber, and that I should not go so much as into the garden to take the air, without your leave and license.

Sir Francis Willoughby angrily replied to this letter, arguing that her letter contained much 'that may minister occasion of offence'.[193] The label of jealous husband was clearly damaging to male reputation.

Finally, jealousy can cause just what it is trying to prevent as it is portrayed as driving women to adultery. A jealous husband frequently withdraws his affection from his wife. Hermione feels that Leontes's love is gone but she knows 'not how it went'.[194] Horner in *The Country Wife* declares that,

> a foolish rival and a jealous husband assist their rival's designs; for they are sure to make their women hate them, which is the first step to their love for another man.

The actions of the jealous husband can be so extreme that they provoke his wife to adultery. Pinchwife's attempts to keep his country wife from the temptations of London society only arouse Margery's curiosity, as Alithea warns, 'You suffer none to give her those longings you mean, but yourself.'[195] Similarly, in the ballad 'The Discontented Married Man' maids are warned not to marry jealous men because their restrictions on their wives' behaviour will make the women 'lose both wit and sense' until they commit adultery.[196] Again, in 'The Married Man's Lesson' the chorus line warns men against jealousy, 'for jealousy makes many good women bad'.[197] Jealousy in this context is shown to be an ineffective means of control.

Fictional sources show that ideas of male honour were all-pervading; they were thought to even shape male imagination and fantasy. However, it was not honourable to admit to jealousy or to be subject to extreme or pathological jealousy. It was just as dishonourable to be out of control with jealousy, as it was to be exposed as a cuckold. Observed all the time by friends and neighbours, men walked a tightrope between losing control of their wives, and showing excessive concern for their chastity which could be labelled as jealousy. A man had to be watchful of his wife to defend his honour, but could never admit to being afraid.

Jealousy: A Case Study

Samuel Pepys's diary provides a highly valuable insight to the thinking of one seventeenth-century married man. As historians we are extremely fortunate that Pepys chose to write about his jealousy of his wife in his diary, an emotion, as we shall see, that he was reluctant to confess to his wife, let alone any of his male friends. We know that Samuel was not alone in his jealousy, as he records occasions when his wife, Elizabeth, was also jealous of him. Given Pepys's dalliances with female servants she probably had good cause.[198] One instance of Samuel's jealousy, though, was when his wife took dancing lessons with a Mr Pembleton. Pepys recorded his fears about his wife's relationship with Pembleton throughout much of 1663, eight years after his marriage to Elizabeth Pepys. The words recorded in his diary often echo those of the jealous husbands of Shakespeare, Ford and Wycherley.

Pepys confessed that given his own numerous infidelities – 'upon a small temptation I could be false to her' – he had little right 'to expect more justice from her'. But his jealousy affected him so profoundly that he was able to dwell upon little else. 'Now, so deadly full of jealousy I am, that my heart and head did so cast about and fret, that I could not do any business', he wrote on 15 May 1663. He wrote that the jealousy made him 'ready to chide at everything' and led him to many sleepless nights. As his jealousy grew, the symptoms became worse, and he realised that it made him think and behave without reason. Pepys described it as 'a great disorder', then a 'devilish jealousy [which] makes a very hell in my mind'. Finding his wife and Pembleton alone in the house on 26 May 'made me almost mad' Pepys confessed. A week later his head ached with jealousy, even though a few days earlier he had realised that his jealousy was 'a madness not to be excused'.

Pepys's jealousy, like that described by Heale, and acted out by Othello and Leontes, labours to 'seek out what it hopes it shall not find'.[199] He is twice reduced to 'lying to see whether my wife did wear drawers . . . and other things to raise my suspicion of her': he assumes that if he looks up his wife's skirts and finds that she is properly clothed that he will have no cause to doubt his wife's chastity. He listens to the sounds of his wife and the dancing master moving in the room above his chamber, questions a servant to see whether he is acting as a go-between, and on his return to the house he even goes 'to see whether any of the beds were out of order or no'.

Pepys was troubled to know what action he should take. When he first became suspicious he made excuses to his wife for his bad temper, 'was forced to say that I had bad news from the Duke concerning Tom Hater, as an excuse to my wife'. Nine days later he wrote of the dilemma that faced him, 'being unwilling to speak of it to her for making of any breach and other inconveniences, nor let it pass for fear of her continuing to offend me and the matter grow worse thereby'. Not wanting to make matters worse between himself and his wife by admitting he did not trust her, Pepys was also concerned not to appear a wittol cuckold who took no action and became even more open to mockery.

To some extent, the situation resolved itself when his wife's course in dancing lessons came to an end, but after experiencing some six weeks of intense jealousy, it is hardly surprising that memories of Pembleton periodically haunted Pepys. A month later he imagined seeing Pembleton in a crowd, and the old symptoms of jealousy came once again to the fore: 'Lord, how my blood did rise in my face and I fell into a sweat from my old Jealousy and hate.' Matters were not helped by Pembleton's attendance at the same church as the Pepys. Samuel was suspicious of his wife's intentions whenever she appeared anxious to attend church. On two occasions when he went to church on his own and saw Pembleton enter and leave, he became convinced that it was because Pembleton had plans to visit his wife in his absence, and was forced to hurry home, only to find his fears ill founded. Matters finally improved when on 18 October Elizabeth Pepys introduced her husband to the new wife of Pembleton. It is fascinating how Pepys found Pembleton's marriage reassuring: 'it is strange to see how by use and seeing Pembleton come with his wife thither to church, I begin now to make no great matter of it, which before was so terrible to me'. It appears that Pembleton no longer posed a threat to Pepys once he had domestic concerns of his own. Pembleton's married status meant that he did not fulfil the stereotype of the Restoration rake or gallant, but instead that he shared the concern of all husbands to gain honour by keeping his own wife under control.

Finally, it is interesting to reflect upon Pepys's thoughts at the end of a month of his wife's dancing lessons. 'My wife and I (by my late jealousy, for which I am truly to be blamed) have not that fondness between us which we used and ought to have, and I fear will be lost hereafter if I do not take some course to oblige her and yet preserve my authority.' From this diary entry it is clear that Pepys knew that his jealousy had no basis or reason as he could never prove that Elizabeth had been unfaithful. At this point he also recognised that his jealousy had driven the relationship apart. But despite his concerns, Pepys had retained an awareness of the real issue at stake in his marriage: how he could 'oblige' his wife without lessening his authority or control over her. Defending manhood in a bid to prevent its loss was no easy task.[200]

This chapter has shown that for men of all social groups, loss of sexual reputation had profound and serious consequences. Without the sexual control of his wife, it was thought that all other attempts of a husband to rule his marriage partner would be futile, leaving him to be exposed as the husband of a scold as well as that of an adulteress. A variety of community rituals directed at the couple made it clear that ultimately it was always the man who was at fault for the breakdown in familial order. The cuckold's role and status within the community was made vulnerable by his wife's behaviour. For the upper sorts, who frequently held offices of public and political importance, and whose position continued to depend at least partly on the integrity of their lineage, the damage that loss of sexual reputation could incur must have appeared most acute.

A seventeenth-century proverb aptly described the anxiety of men's position: 'Honour and ease are seldom bedfellows'.[201] The risk of being cuckolded was never far from men's minds, and required them to consider their interaction not only towards their wives, but also with their boyhood friends. Much of the contemporary literature reveals a profound uneasiness and discomfort about how manliness could be affected by emotional experience and expression. Whether passionate love or jealousy, male authors depicted emotion as potentially threatening to manhood, and they portrayed male characters as encountering these emotions in excess to highlight their damaging effects. Reason and emotion are repeatedly posited as opposites, with the consensus that emotional expression can jeopardise manly self-control. Pepys's diary reveals how one man felt unable to air his emotions publicly, yet could draw upon the common words and images about jealousy within his culture to express his feelings in written form. Other men who feared or suspected loss of honourable manhood looked to alternative outlets for release, and as we shall see in the next chapter, these could take on a more destructive and violent form.

Notes

1. See, for example, DDR.V.9. f. 170v; DDR.V.10A. f. 52r; DDR.V.10B. ff. 337, 343; CA, Case 1215 (1665), Eee2, f. 7; CA, Case 9913 (1668), Eee2, f. 806; J. Godolphin, *Reportorium Canonicum* (London, 1678), pp. 516–20; M. Ingram, *Church Courts, Sex and Marriage in England, 1570–1640* (Cambridge, 1987), pp. 309–11; T. Meldrum, 'A women's court in London: defamation at the Bishop of London's consistory court, 1700–1745' *London Journal* 19, 1 (1994), pp. 9–10; L. Gowing, *Domestic Dangers: Women, Words, and Sex in Early Modern London* (Oxford, 1996), pp. 125–32.
2. DDR.V.12. ff. 287v, 290r.
3. W. Shakespeare, *King Lear* (*c.*1605), ed. K. Muir (London, 1990), I.iv.294–6; II.iv.275–6.
4. As cited in S.D. Amussen, *An Ordered Society: Gender and Class in Early Modern England* (Oxford, 1988), p. 123.
5. See, for example, 'Advice to Batchelors', *Roxburghe*, vol. III, pp. 376–9; 'The Patient Husband and the Scolding Wife' (*c.*1673), *Roxburghe*, vol. VII, part I, pp. 182–4; and 'The Invincible Pride of Women' (*c.*1686–88), *Roxburghe*, vol. VII, part I, pp. 20–1.
6. 'The Discontented Married Man', *Roxburghe*, vol. I, pp. 295–9; for a full account of this ballad see E.A. Foyster, 'A laughing matter? Marital discord and gender control in seventeenth-century England' *Rural History* 4, 1 (1993), pp. 16–17.
7. DDR.V.12. f. 140–141r.
8. See, for example, 'The Henpeckt Cuckold' (*c.*1689–91), *Roxburghe*, vol. VII, part II, p. 432; 'My Wife will be my Master' (*c.*1640), *Roxburghe*, vol. VII, part I, p. 188; and 'The Jolly Widdower', *Pepys*, vol. IV, p. 102.

9. 'The Cuckold's Complaint' (*c.*1689–91), *Roxburghe*, vol. VII, part II, p. 431.

10. See, for example, 'The Cuckold's Lamentation of a Bad Wife', *Roxburghe*, vol. III, pp. 635–7; and 'My Wife will be my Master' (*c.*1640), *Roxburghe*, vol. VII, part I, pp. 188–9.

11. CA, Case 6019 (1675), Eee6, ff. 33v–34r.

12. CA, Case 2730 (1688), Ee7, f. 18, Eee7, ff. 60r, 64v, 72v, 75r, 79v, 80v, 82v, 84v, 85v, 90v.

13. CA, Case 4642 (1698), Eee8, f. 615; for a similar story of marriage breakdown from the Chichester court nearly one hundred years earlier see Gowing, *Domestic Dangers*, pp. 196–8.

14. Anon, *Arden of Faversham* (*c.*1591); for a ballad see, for example, 'Mistress Arden of Faversham' (1633), *Roxburghe*, vol. VIII, part I–II, pp. 49–53; see also C. Belsey, 'Alice Arden's crime', in R. Wilson and R. Dutton, eds, *New Historicism and Renaissance Drama* (New York, 1992), pp. 131–44.

15. 'The Lamentation of Master Page's Wife' (1591), *Roxburghe*, vol. I, pp. 555–8; 'The Sorrowful Complaint of Mistress Page', *Shirburn*, no. XXVII, pp. 111–13; Belsey, 'Alice', p. 137.

16. S.D. Amussen, '"Being stirred to much unquietness": violence and domestic violence in early modern England' *Journal of Women's History* 6, 2 (1994), p. 76; F.E. Dolan, *Dangerous Familiars: Representations of Domestic Crime in England 1550–1700* (Ithaca NY, 1994), pp. 89–106; J. Wiltenburg, *Disorderly Women and Female Power in the Street Literature of Early Modern England and Germany* (Charlottesville VI, 1992), pp. 220–3.

17. See, for example, J.A. Sharpe, 'Domestic homicide in early modern England' *Historical Journal* 24, 1 (1981), pp. 36–8.

18. 'The West Country Weaver' (*c.*1685), *Roxburghe*, vol. VII, part I, pp. 22–3; 'Mirth for Citizens' (*c.*1671), *Roxburghe*, vol. VIII, part III, pp. 699–700.

19. L. Gowing, 'Gender and the language of insult in early modern London' *HWJ* 35 (1993), p. 16.

20. Belsey, 'Alice', p. 136; T. Stretton, 'Women and litigation in the Elizabethan Court of Requests' (unpublished Ph.D. thesis, Cambridge University, 1993), pp. 223–4, 236.

21. CA, Case 8209 (1676), Eee5, ff. 440v, 441v; Eee6, ff. 62v, 63v, 64v; CA, Case 4834 (1669), Eee3, ff. 320–1, 326v–328r, 341r; CA, Case 8648 (1686), Ee6, f. 111v.

22. 'A Merry Discourse' (*c.*1603–25), *Roxburghe*, vol. I, pp. 249–53; 'The Cuckold's Lamentation of a Bad Wife', *Roxburghe*, vol. III, pp. 635–7.

23. DDR.V.12. ff. 283v–285r; 288r–288v; also see Ingram, *Church Courts*, p. 183, and Gowing, *Domestic Dangers*, pp. 180, 183, 207, 228–9.

24. DDR.V.11. ff. 409–414r, 428v–432r.

25. CA, Case 4177 (1669); CA, Case 3270 (1675); CA, Case 2402 (1677); CA, Case 2476 (1684), and CA, Case 8736 (1685).

26. CA, Case 3270 (1675) and CA, Case 8736 (1685).

27. Gowing also believes that the degree of female violence against husbands was often exaggerated so that it was always represented as murderous in intent, see *Domestic Dangers*, pp. 228–9.

28. DDR.V.11. f. 70r.

29. Amussen, *An Ordered Society*, p. 131; Ingram, *Church Courts*, p. 254; D.E. Underdown, *Revel, Riot and Rebellion* (Oxford, 1985), pp. 100–1; J.A. Sharpe, *Crime in Seventeenth-Century England* (Cambridge, 1983), p. 62; A. MacFarlane, *Marriage and Love in England* (Oxford, 1986), p. 240; A. Fox, 'Ballads, libels and popular ridicule in Jacobean England', *PP* 145 (1994), p. 62.

30. As cited in Fox, 'Ballads, libels', pp. 74–5.

31. M. Ingram, 'Ridings, rough music and the "reform of popular culture" in early modern England' *PP* 105 (1984), pp. 79–113, and 'Ridings, rough music and mocking rhymes in early modern England', in B. Reay, ed., *Popular Culture in Seventeenth Century England* (London, 1985), pp. 178–88; Fox, 'Ballads, libels', pp. 47–83;

for mocking rhymes directed towards women see L. Gowing, 'Women, status and the popular culture of dishonour' *TRHS* Sixth Series, VI (1996), pp. 225–34.

32. Ingram, 'Ridings' *PP*, p. 101.

33. DDR.V.11. ff. 68–70r, 77v, 78r, 96r; for the practice of literate members of a community recording and reading mocking rhymes for others see Fox, 'Ballads, libels', pp. 58–60.

34. CA, Case 8136 (1669), Eee3, ff. 605r, 606v, 613v, 616v.

35. C. Kahn, *Man's Estate: Masculine Identity in Shakespeare* (Berkeley CA, 1981), p. 122.

36. 'The London Cuckold' (1686), *Roxburghe*, vol. VIII, part III, pp. 603–4; 'All such as lead a jealous life', *Shirburn*, no. LXIV, pp. 263–7.

37. W. Shakespeare, *Othello* (*c.*1604), ed. M.R. Ridley (London, 1986), III.iii.288; W. Wycherley, *The Country Wife* (1675), ed. J. Ogden (London, 1991), IV.iv.74; 'The New Married Couple' (*c.*1675), *Roxburghe*, vol. IV, pp. 17–19.

38. 'The Cuckold's Lamentation of a Bad Wife', *Roxburghe*, vol. III, pp. 635–7; 'The Wheel-Wrights Huy-and-Cry' (1693), *Pepys*, vol. IV, p. 115.

39. 'The Jolly Widdower', *Pepys*, vol. IV, p. 102.

40. As cited in Gowing, *Domestic Dangers*, p. 96.

41. M. Ingram, 'Ridings' *PP*, pp. 79–113.

42. Amussen, *An Ordered Society*, p. 118; K. Newman, *Fashioning Femininity and English Renaissance Drama* (Chicago IL, 1991), p. 35.

43. DDR.V.9. f. 174r; OED; E.P. Thompson, *Customs in Common* (London, 1991), pp. 471–2; Ingram,'Ridings' *PP*, p. 82.

44. M. Ingram, 'Juridical folklore in England illustrated by rough music', in C. Brooks and M. Lobban, eds, *Communities and Courts in Britain 1150–1900* (London, 1997).

45. Newman, *Fashioning*, p. 35; Thompson, *Customs*, p. 488.

46. W. Shakespeare, *The Merry Wives of Windsor* (1597), ed. H.J. Oliver (London, 1993), V.v; A. Parten, 'Falstaff's horns: masculine inadequacy and feminine mirth in *The Merry Wives of Windsor*' *Studies in Philology* 82 (1985), pp. 184–99.

47. J.G. Smith, *Charlton: A Compilation of the Parish and its People*, vol. III (privately printed, 1984), pp. 409–28; H. Adshead, 'Cuckold's Point' *Port of London Authority Monthly* (September 1954), pp. 197–9; Thompson, *Customs*, pp. 483–4; R.W. Malcolmson, *Popular Recreations in English Society 1700–1850* (Cambridge, 1973), pp. 77–8. Charlton still has a Horn Fair Festival, but it is now celebrated in June. There remains a point on the Thames known as 'Cuckold's Point' at Rotherhithe, see *Bartholomew's Reference Atlas of Greater London* (Edinburgh, 1968), p. 76.

48. As cited in Smith, *Charlton*, p. 409.

49. L. Woodbridge, *Women and the English Renaissance: Literature and the Nature of Womankind, 1540–1620* (Urbana IL, 1986), pp. 172–3.

50. B. Capp, *The World of John Taylor the Water Poet 1578–1653* (Oxford, 1994), p. 116, footnote 103.

51. R. Latham and W. Matthews, eds, *The Diary of Samuel Pepys* (London, 1970–83), vol. IV (1663), p. 50.

52. 'Hey for Horn-Fair' (1685), *Roxburghe*, vol. VIII, part III, pp. 665–6; see also 'A New Song On Horn-Fair' (1685), *Roxburghe*, vol. VIII, part III, pp. 667–8; and J. Wardroper, ed., *Lovers, Rakes and Rogues* (London, 1995), pp. 271–3, 353.

53. 'The Dyer's Destiny' (1685–88), *Roxburghe*, vol. IV, pp. 405–7; 'The Scolding Wife's Vindication' (*c.*1689), *Roxburghe*, vol. VII, part I, p. 197; for other references to Horn Fairs see, 'The Catalogue of Contented Cuckolds', *Roxburghe*, vol. III, pp. 481–3; 'The Well-Approved Doctor', *Pepys*, vol. IV, p. 149; Anon, *Bull-Feather Hall* (London, 1664), pp. 11–15; Anon, *The Fifteen Comforts of Cuckoldom* (London, 1706), p. 7.

54. T. Southerne, *The Wives' Excuse* (1692) ed. R. Jordan and H. Love (Oxford, 1988), I.i.125–8.

55. M.P. Tilley, *A Dictionary of Proverbs in England in the Sixteenth and Seventeenth Centuries* (Ann Arbor MI, 1950), C886.

56. Smith, *Charlton*, pp. 412–15.
57. M.P., 'A Banquet for Sovereign Husbands', *Pepysian Garland*, pp. 328–31, much of the third and fourth stanzas were badly damaged; Capp, *The World of John Taylor*, pp. 115–16.
58. M.P., 'Have among you! good Women', *Roxburghe*, vol. I, pp. 435–40.
59. DDR.V.12. f. 71–72r; for other examples see DDR.V.9. f. 182r; DDR.V.11. f. 167–168r; DDR.V.12. f. 141r; for women who were threatened with this punishment in Restoration London see CA, Case 1215 (1665), Eee2, ff. 6–7 and CA, Case 4188 (1668), Ee3, f. 431r; see also D.E. Underdown, 'The taming of the scold: the enforcement of patriarchal authority in early modern England', in A. Fletcher and J. Stevenson, eds, *Order and Disorder in Early Modern England* (Cambridge, 1987), pp. 127–8.
60. DDR.V.9. ff. 249–50, 257r.
61. As cited in Ingram, '"Scolding women cucked or washed": a crisis in gender relations in early modern England?', in J. Kermode and G. Walker, eds, *Women, Crime and the Courts in Early Modern England* (London, 1994), p. 61.
62. Underdown, 'The Taming', pp. 116–36; Ingram, '"Scolding"', pp. 48–80; Thompson, *Customs*, p. 502; W.J. Hardy, ed., *Hertford County Records: Sessions Rolls 1581–1698*, vol. 1 (Hertford, 1905), p. 48, the exact date of this presentment is uncertain.
63. 'The Cucking of a Scold', *Pepysian Garland*, pp. 72–7.
64. Ingram, 'Ridings' *PP*, pp. 82, 98.
65. 'The Cock-pit Cuckold', *Pepys*, vol. IV, p. 141; 'The Merry Cuckold', *Roxburghe*, vol. II, pp. 5–8; 'Household Talk' (1603–25), *Roxburghe*, vol. I, pp. 441–6.
66. CA, Case 1813 (1673), Ee4, f. 120r; CA, Case 8350 (1673), Eee5, f. 70v.
67. Ingram, 'Ridings' *PP*, p. 98.
68. Wiltenburg, *Disorderly Women*, p. 156.
69. As cited in K. Thomas, 'The place of laughter in Tudor and Stuart England' *Times Literary Supplement* (21 January 1977), p. 80.
70. As cited in Ingram, 'Ridings', in Reay, ed., *Popular Culture*, p. 176.
71. As cited in S.C. Sen Gupta, *Shakespearian Comedy* (Oxford, 1950), p. 1.
72. I. Donaldson, *The World Upside-Down:Comedy from Jonson to Fielding* (Oxford, 1970); N.Z. Davis, 'Women on top' in her *Society and Culture in Early Modern France* (London, 1975), pp. 124–51.
73. As cited in E. Tillyard, *Shakespeare's Early Comedies* (London, 1965), p. 14.
74. H. Bergson, *Laughter* (London, 1921), pp. 136, 197.
75. Thomas, 'The place', p. 77.
76. Thompson, *Customs*, p. 489.
77. J.K. Campbell, *Honour, Family and Patronage: A Study of Institutions and Moral Values in a Greek Mountain Community* (Oxford, 1964), p. 313.
78. As cited in R. Cust, 'Honour and politics in early Stuart England: the case of Beaumont *v.* Hastings' *PP* 149 (1995), p. 82.
79. F. Dabhoiwala, 'The construction of honour, reputation and status in late seventeenth- and early eighteenth-century England' *TRHS* Sixth Series, VI (1996), p. 204.
80. As cited in K. Hodgkin, 'Thomas Whythorne and the problems of mastery' *HWJ* 29 (1990), p. 35.
81. Shakespeare, *Othello*, III.iii.363; E. Partridge, *Shakespeare's Bawdy: A Literary and Psychological Essay and A Comprehensive Glossary* (London, 1955), p. 155; M. Hattaway, 'Fleshing his will in the spoil of her honour: desire, misogyny and the perils of chivalry' *Shakespeare Survey* 46 (1994), p. 131.
82. See, for example, J. March, *Actions for Slaunder* (London, 1647), and Godolphin, *Reportorium Canonicum*, ch. 38, 'Of Defamation'.
83. DDR.V.11. ff. 478v–481; DDR.V.12. ff. 4v, 5.
84. Ingram, *Church Courts*, p. 309.
85. CA, Case 8344 (1675), Eee5, f. 519.

86. CA, Case 6234 (1662), Ee1, f. 67r; for other examples see CA, Case 6292 (1669), Ee3, ff. 480v–481r; CA, Case 2730 (1688), Ee7, f. 17.

87. 'The Catalogue of Contented Cuckolds', *Roxburghe*, vol. III, pp. 481–3; 'The discontented Married Man', *Roxburghe*, vol. I, pp. 295–9.

88. CA, Case 8209 (1676), Eee5, ff. 439v–441r; Eee6, ff. 61v–63r.

89. L. Roper, *Oedipus and the Devil: Witchcraft, Sexuality and Religion in Early Modern Europe* (London, 1994), pp. 55–6.

90. A.J. Fletcher, 'Honour, reputation and local officeholding in Elizabethan and Stuart England', in Fletcher and Stevenson, eds, *Order and Disorder*, p. 112.

91. F. Heal, 'Reputation and honour in court and country: Lady Elizabeth Russell and Sir Thomas Hoby' *TRHS* Sixth Series, VI (1996), pp. 169–78; Cust, 'Honour and Politics', pp. 82, 93, and for previous discussion of these cases see Chapter 2 above; for other examples of JPs who faced sexual slander see Fox, 'Ballads, libels', p. 81, n. 64.

92. As cited in S.D. Amussen, 'Gender, family and the social order, 1560–1725', in Fletcher and Stevenson, eds, *Order and Disorder*, p. 205.

93. D. Rollison, 'Property, ideology and popular culture in a Gloucestershire village' *PP* 93 (1981), pp. 70–97.

94. S. Hindle, 'The shaming of Margaret Knowsley: gossip, gender and the experience of authority in early modern England' *CC* 9, 3 (1994), pp. 391–419.

95. D. Turner, '"Nothing is so secret but shall be revealed": the scandalous life of Robert Foulkes', in T. Hitchcock and M. Cohen, eds, *English Masculinities, 1660–1800* (forthcoming from Longman).

96. Latham and Matthews, eds, *The Diary of Samuel Pepys* vol. VIII (1667), p. 596, vol. IX (1668), p. 53.

97. P. Croft, 'The reputation of Robert Cecil: libels, political opinion and popular awareness in the early seventeenth century' *TRHS* Sixth Series, I (1991), pp. 43–69; A. Bellany, '"Raylinge rymes and vaunting verse": libellous politics in early Stuart England, 1603–1628', in K. Sharpe and P. Lake, eds, *Culture and Politics in Early Stuart England* (London, 1994), pp. 285–310; for the link between private morals and political competence later in the century see M. Hunt, *The Middling Sort: Commerce, Gender, and the Family in England, 1680–1780* (Berkeley CA, 1996), pp. 197–8.

98. CA, Case 10141 (1674), Eee5, ff. 462v–463v; three other witnesses then testified to John Harding's good name, see ff. 475v–478v; for a further example of a male witness being discredited on sexual grounds see CA, Case 207 (1675), Eee5, f. 559v; Eee6, ff. 84v–85r.

99. See, for example, Fletcher, 'Honour, reputation', p. 97.

100. P.J. Corfield, 'Dress for deference and dissent: hats and the decline of hat honour' *Costume* 23 (1989), pp. 68, 74.

101. Courtin, *Rules of Civility*; Gailhard *The Compleat Gentleman*; see also A.C. Bryson, 'Concepts of civility in England *c.*1560–1685' (unpublished D.Phil. thesis, Oxford University, 1984), p. 109.

102. Ingram, *Church Courts*, p. 112; R. Gough's *The History of Myddle (1701–1706)*, ed. P. Razzell (Sussex, 1979) was an account of the inhabitants of the Shropshire village which was ordered according to their places in the pews of the parish church.

103. P. Griffiths, *Youth and Authority: Formative Experiences in England 1560–1640* (Oxford, 1996), pp. 105–9.

104. As cited in Underdown, *Revel, Riot*, p. 22, for pew disputes see also pp. 14, 29–33.

105. Amussen, *An Ordered Society*, pp. 212–14.

106. 'The Lamentation of a new married man', *Euing*, pp. 380–1.

107. M. James, *Family, Lineage and Civil Society: A Study of Society, Politics and Mentality in the Durham Region 1500–1640* (Oxford, 1974), pp. 121–3.

108. DDR.Box, no. 414 (1633–34), *Richard Clay* v. *Robert Atchinson.*

109. OED; P. Clark, *The English Alehouse: A Social History 1200–1830* (London, 1983), p. 156.

110. 'Match me this Wedding' (1636–41), *Roxburghe*, vol. II, pp. 178–82; J. Evelyn, *A Character of England* (London, 1659), pp. 36–7; W. Congreve, *The Way of the World* (1700), ed. B. Gibbons (London, 1994), IV.i.238–9.

111. Courtin, *The Rules of Civility*, p. 108.

112. DDR.V.8. f. 155–156r; J. Wright, ed., *The English Dialect Dictionary* (London, 1898); for another dispute arising between men from pledging see S.D. Amussen, 'The gendering of popular culture in early modern England', in T. Harris, ed., *Popular Culture in England,* c.*1500–1850* (London, 1995), pp. 63–4.

113. R. Ashley, *Of Honour* (*c.*1596–1603), ed. V.B. Heltzel (San Marino CA, 1947), p. 36; for the language of 'sorts' see K. Wrightson, 'Estates, degrees, and sorts: changing perceptions of society in Tudor and Stuart England', in P. Corfield, ed., *Language, History and Class* (Oxford, 1991), ch. 2, and '"Sorts of people" in Tudor and Stuart England', in J. Barry and C. Brooks, eds, *The Middling Sort of People: Culture, Society and Politics in England, 1550–1800* (London, 1994), ch. 1.

114. DDR.V.10B. ff. 335–6, 338, 342v–343r.

115. DDR.V.11. f. 225–226r.

116. Fox, 'Ballads, libels', p. 75.

117. DDR.V.11. ff. 397v–399r.

118. 'The Jolly Widdower', *Pepys*, vol. IV, p. 102.

119. 'Children after the rate of 24 in a year' (*c.*1635), *Pepys*, vol. I, pp. 404–5; 'The Country Girl's Policy' (*c.*1765), *Roxburghe*, vol. VII, part II, pp. 286–7.

120. MacFarlane, *Marriage and Love in England*, p. 242.

121. I. Benvenuto, *The Passenger* (London, 1612), as cited in R. Kelso, *Doctrine for the Lady of the Renaissance* (Urbana IL, 1956), p. 99.

122. As cited in Capp, *The World of John Taylor*, p. 116.

123. C. Gibbon, *The Praise of a Good Name* (London, 1594), p. 15; W. Shakespeare, *The Winter's Tale* (*c.*1609), ed. J.H.P. Pafford (London, 1990), III.ii.44.

124. CA, Case 2730 (1688), Ee7, f. 18v.

125. CA, Case 5938 (1697), Eee8, ff. 421–5, 434v, 449r.

126. As cited in P. Crawford, 'The construction and experience of maternity in seventeenth-century England', in V. Fildes, ed., *Women as Mothers in Pre-Industrial England* (London, 1990), p. 10.

127. CA, Case 10406 (1671), Eee4, ff. 512–19; CA, Case 9870 (1669), Eee3, f. 547.

128. As cited in L. Stone, 'Honor, morals, religion, and the law: the action for criminal conversation in England, 1670–1857', in A. Grafton and A. Blair, eds, *The Transmission of Culture in Early Modern Europe* (Philadelphia PA, 1990), p. 282.

129. Shakespeare, *The Winter's Tale*, I.ii.119–46; see also D. Schalkwyk, '"A lady's 'verily' is as potent as a lord's": women, word and witchcraft in *The Winter's Tale*' *English Literary Renaissance* 22, 2 (1992), pp. 242–72.

130. W. Shakespeare, *The Tempest* (*c.*1611), ed. S. Orgel (Oxford, 1987), I.ii.55–7; K.E. Maus, 'Horns of dilemma: jealousy, gender and spectatorship in English Renaissance drama', *English Literary History* 54, 3 (1987), p. 561.

131. M.R. Sommerville, *Sex and Subjection: Attitudes to Women in Early-Modern Society* (London, 1995), p. 120.

132. DDR.V.12. f. 177r.

133. CA, Case 4695 (1671), Eee4, f. 393r; for another example see Gowing, *Domestic Dangers*, p. 89; for discussion of the possible impact on children who were targets of such slander see E. Foyster, 'Silent witnesses? Children and the breakdown of domestic and social order in early modern England', in A. Fletcher and S. Hussey, eds, *Childhood in Question* (forthcoming from Manchester University Press).

134. As cited in Amussen 'The gendering', in Harris, ed., *Popular Culture*, p. 58.

135. As cited in K. Thomas, 'The puritans and adultery: the Act of 1650 reconsidered', in D. Pennington and K. Thomas, eds, *Puritans and Revolutionaries: Essays in Seventeenth-Century History Presented to Christopher Hill* (Oxford, 1978), p. 262.

136. CA, Case 5938 (1697), Eee8, f. 474v.

137. J. Ford, *Love's Sacrifice* (*c.*1632), ed. W. Gifford (London, 1895), II.iii; a choppine was a clog worn under the shoe.

138. A. Bray, 'Homosexuality and the signs of male friendship in Elizabethan England' *HWJ* 29 (1990), pp. 1–19.

139. 'Advice to Batchelors', *Roxburghe*, vol. III, pp. 376–9; see also 'The Batchelor's Delight', *Roxburghe*, vol. III, pp. 423–6; 'The Lamentation of a new married man' (*c.*1630), *Pepys*, vol. I, pp. 380–1; and 'The Batchelor's Triumph', *Roxburghe*, vol. III, pp. 427–9.

140. Shakespeare, *The Winter's Tale*, I.ii.67–9; Shakespeare, *Othello*, I.iii.203.

141. As cited in D. Sherrod, 'The bonds of men: problems and possibilities in close male relationships', in H. Brod, ed., *The Making of Masculinities: The New Men's Studies* (Boston MA, 1987), p. 230.

142. Wycherley, *The Country Wife*, III.ii.205; H. Burke, 'Wycherley's "tendentious joke": the discourse of alterity in *The Country Wife*' *The Eighteenth Century – Theory and Interpretation* 29, 3 (1988), p. 235.

143. Bray, 'Homosexuality', pp. 8–16.

144. See Kahn, *Man's Estate*, pp. 120, 144, 150.

145. Wycherley, *The Country Wife*, III.ii.189–92; III.ii.361–4; I.i.222–5; V.iv.432–3.

146. L.J. Mills, *One Soul in Bodies Twain: Friendship in Tudor Literature and Stuart Drama* (Bloomington IN, 1937); N.A. Gutierrez, 'The irresolution of melodrama: the meaning of adultery in *A Woman Killed with Kindness*' *Exemplaria* 1, 2 (1989), pp. 275–6; P. Erikson, *Patriarchal Structures in Shakespeare's Drama* (London, 1985).

147. Shakespeare, *The Winter's Tale*, I.ii.60–2, 65–6.

148. Shakespeare, *Othello*, III.iii.42–90.

149. Shakespeare, *The Winter's Tale*, I.ii.28–87.

150. T. Heywood, *A Woman Killed with Kindness* (1603), ed. B. Scobie (London, 1991), iv.80–2.

151. Gowing, *Domestic Dangers*, pp. 249–51.

152. CA, Case 1888 (1676), Ee4, f. 467.

153. CA, Case 2730 (1688), Ee7, ff. 35–8.

154. As cited in I.K. Ben-Amos, *Adolescence and Youth in Early Modern England* (New Haven CT, 1994), p. 230.

155. As cited in Griffiths, *Youth and Authority*, p. 141.

156. *No Money, no Friend* (1670), see also *The World turn'd upside down* (1680).

157. A conclusion also made by Woodbridge in *Women and the English Renaissance*, pp. 237–9.

158. H.M. Berry, 'Religion, popular print culture, and the construction of gender in late seventeenth century England', unpublished paper delivered to the Ecclesiastical History Conference, Canterbury, July 1996; I am grateful to Helen Berry for allowing me to read this paper.

159. Men were also unwilling to admit to jealousy in the French courts, see N.Z. Davis, *Fiction in the Archives: Pardon Tales and their Tellers in Sixteenth-Century France* (Cambridge, 1987), p. 83.

160. The term reactive jealousy is defined in P. Van Sommers, *Jealousy* (London, 1988), pp. 80, 86.

161. Wycherley, *The Country Wife*, III.ii.253; II.i.231–2; III.ii.249–50.

162. P.N. Stearns, *Jealousy: The Evolution of an Emotion in American History* (New York, 1989), pp. 14–16; M. Breitenberg, *Anxious Masculinity in Early Modern England* (Cambridge, 1996), pp. 175, 185–6.

163. 'John Tomson and Jakaman his Wife', *Roxburghe*, vol. II, pp. 137–42.

164. See, for example, 'The Henpeckt Cuckold' (*c.*1689–91), *Roxburghe*, vol. VII, part II, p. 432.

165. G. Etherege, *She Would if She Could* (1668), ed. C.M. Taylor (London, 1972), III.iii.57–63.

166. Shakespeare, *Othello*, III.iii.344, 347, 370, 419–32; IV.i.35–6.

167. Shakespeare, *The Winter's Tale*, I.ii.194–8; see also D. Cohen, 'Patriarchy and jealousy in *Othello* and *The Winter's Tale*' *Modern Language Quarterly* 48, 3 (1987), pp. 207–23.

168. Tilley, *A Dictionary*, M465.

169. M.P., 'The Married Man's Lesson', *Roxburghe*, vol. III, pp. 231–6.

170. Shakespeare, *Othello*, III.iv.159–60; V.ii.177–8.

171. As cited in Breitenberg, *Anxious Masculinity*, pp. 186, 188.

172. J. Ford, *The Broken Heart* (*c.*1629), ed. B. Morris (London, 1994), I.i.68.

173. W. Heale, *An Apology for Women* (Oxford, 1609), p. 34.

174. Shakespeare, *Othello*, I.iii.390; I.iii.81; III.iii.267–9; I.iii.396; for the meaning of 'proper man' see Chapter 3 above.

175. Wycherley, *The Country Wife*, IV.iv.74.

176. Heale, *An Apology*, p. 34; A. Niccholes, *A Discourse of Marriage and Wiving* (London, 1620), p. 45.

177. Van Sommers, *Jealousy*, pp. 80, 86.

178. Ford, *The Broken Heart*, II.i.1–8; Wycherley, *The Country Wife*, III.ii.

179. Van Sommers, *Jealousy*, pp. 150, 157.

180. Shakespeare, *Othello*, III.iii.288, 341, 374.

181. 'All such as lead a jealous life', *Shirburn*, no. LXIV, pp. 263–7; 'Household Talk', *Roxburghe*, vol. I, pp. 441–6.

182. L. Jardine,'"Why should he call her whore?" Defamation and Desdemona's case', in M. Tudeau-Clayton and M. Warner, eds, *Addressing Frank Kermode: Essays in Criticism and Interpretation* (Urbana IL, 1991), p. 143, the italics are Jardine's.

183. Shakespeare, *Othello*, III.iii.194–6.

184. Congreve, *The Way of the World*, II.i.47–52.

185. Shakespeare, *The Winter's Tale*, I.ii.115–16; III.ii.81; Shakespeare, *Othello*, III.iii.327–9.

186. As cited in Breitenberg, *Anxious Masculinity*, p. 189.

187. Anon, *Arden of Faversham* (*c.*1591), ed. M. White (London, 1982), xiii.88–105; Shakespeare, *The Merry Wives of Windsor*, V.i.18–19; Shakespeare, *The Winter's Tale*, II.ii.29; III.71.118.

188. Ford, *The Broken Heart*, III.ii.182–4.

189. Wycherley, *The Country Wife*, I.i.434–5.

190. Shakespeare, *The Winter's Tale*, II.iii.118–20.

191. CA, Case 8350 (1673), Ee4, f. 302v; CA, Case 8648 (1686), Ee6, f. 110v.

192. CA, Case 9344 (1674), Ee4, ff. 256–83; CA, Case 7550 (1688), Ee6, ff. 182v–183r.

193. As cited in A.T. Friedman, 'Portrait of a marriage: the Willoughby letters of 1585–1586', *Signs* 11 (1986), pp. 551–2; I am grateful to Jenny Kermode for bringing my attention to this article.

194. Shakespeare, *The Winter's Tale*, III.ii.95–6.

195. Wycherley, *The Country Wife*, III.ii.58–61; III.i.16–17.

196. 'The Discontented Married Man', *Roxburghe*, vol. I, pp. 295–9.

197. M.P., 'The Married Man's Lesson', *Roxburghe*, vol. III, pp. 231–6.

198. For a good account of the Pepys' marriage, and details of some of Samuel Pepys's extra-marital affairs see A. Fletcher, *Gender, Sex and Subordination in England 1500–1800* (London, 1995), pp. 168–72.

199. Heale, *An Apology*, p. 34.

200. Latham and Matthews, eds, *The Diary of Samuel Pepys*, vol. IV (1663), pp. 140–205, 229, 277–8, 291, 300, 318, 337–8, 347; Pepys's jealousy of his wife reoccured in 1665–66 when he became suspicious of the intentions of her painting-master, see vol. VI (1665), p. 246, and vol. VII (1666), pp. 115–17.

201. Tilley, *A Dictionary*, H568.

CHAPTER FIVE

Restoring Manhood

One important distinction between male and female honour was that men, unlike women, had the possibility fully to restore their honour after it had been lost. A woman's sexual reputation was arguably the sole component of her honour, so that as Ruth Kelso has recognised in her study of Renaissance texts for women, 'let a woman have chastity, she has all. Let her lack chastity and she has nothing.' Loss of sexual honour for a woman was equivalent to death; Hero in *Much Ado about Nothing* (1598) is presumed dead when she falls faint after hearing her chastity questioned on her wedding day. Barnabe Rich believed in 1613 that if a woman's honour was tainted, 'she must rub off the skin to wipe out the spot'. Martin Ingram writes of how when a Yorkshire woman in this period heard another being defamed she commented 'they might as well take her life as her good name from her'.[1] Thus women who fought defamation cases in the church courts were seeking to defend rather than restore their sexual honour by arguing that it had never been lost. For unmarried women, if their virginity had been taken the situation was irredeemable. For men, however, whose honour rested more clearly upon a wider basis of concerns than simply sexual reputation, and whose sexual reputation did not rest on the existence of a physical phenomenon such as the hymen, honour was recoverable. 'Ages and sexes have their distinct laws', Fulke Greville wrote in the 1630s, 'our reputations not easily shaken, and many ways repaired; theirs [women's], like glass, by and by broken and impossible to be healed.'[2] Furthermore, husbands were expected to respond and take action if their wives shamed them by committing adultery; it was seen as 'primarily a matter of household discipline', whereas women were advised to be passive and patient even if their partners were unfaithful.[3] The main condition for the recovery of male honour was that its restoration be witnessed by others. Men needed their contemporaries to recognise their attempts to restore honour, informally in front of neighbours and servants, or formally in the courtroom. This chapter explores the relative effectiveness of the legal and extra-legal options open to men who wished to respond to dishonour.

Legal Action and Defamation

If men had greater opportunity to restore their damaged honour than women, then the most obvious question which immediately arises is why was it women rather than men who flocked to the church courts to fight defamation suits in the seventeenth century? For example, 140 of 225 defamation cases heard in the Durham consistory court between 1604 and 1665 were brought by women, and 163 out of the 192 defamation cases brought to the court of Arches in the years 1661–1700 had female plaintiffs. Historians who have studied the church court records of Wiltshire, York, Ely, Norfolk, London and Chichester have all found that the proportion of defamation suits brought by women, particularly those concerned with sexual reputation, increased throughout the seventeenth century. The insult which was used with most frequency against these women was 'whore'.[4] If sexual reputation was so important to men, then why do we find so few records of defamation suits initiated by men? Were church consistory courts increasingly 'women's courts' only discussing 'women's' issues or concerns? Chapter 3 showed that the double sexual standard does not provide us with a satisfactory answer for the predominance of female plaintiffs. Susan Amussen's initial suggestion that women were more likely to face sexual defamation than men because their 'limited roles in their families' prevented them from exposure to more wide-ranging non-sexual insults has been largely dismissed. We know now that although authors of prescriptive literature may have advised women to stay indoors and only have domestic concerns, the reality of most women's lives necessitated their entry into the public sphere. Many women were slandered outside the home whilst fulfilling an economic or social role such as going to the market, milking cows, or serving as midwives.[5] What was in fact more important in determining the likelihood of a woman facing both sexual defamation and then going to court to defend herself against that slander was her marital status. In theory, every time a woman spoke in the church courts the court clerk should have noted her marital status (single, married, or widowed) next to her name. Unfortunately, at least in the Durham church courts and the court of Arches, this was not always carried out with 100 per cent consistency so that precise figures comparing marital status are not possible.[6] But the overall impression we are left with is that the majority of female plaintiffs were married women. For example, in the Durham church courts between 1604 and 1665, we know for certain (because a husband's name was noted by the clerk at the start of a deposition, or because a witness referred to the plaintiff as a married woman during their statement) that at least 83 (close to 60 per cent) of the 140 female plaintiffs were married. From the court of Arches records of 1661–1700 at least 103 (63 per cent) of the 163 female plaintiffs who brought defamation cases were married. Ingram has estimated that about 70 per cent of female plaintiffs who complained of sexual slander in the church courts of late sixteenth- and early seventeenth-century Wiltshire, York and Ely were married. Laura Gowing has noted that both female plaintiffs and defendants in the London church courts between 1570 and 1640 were mostly married. Using a smaller sample of cases from the cause papers of 1690s York, and concentrating just on those which involved sexual slander, Jim Sharpe found that a staggering 79 per cent of female plaintiffs were married women.[7] So not only were the church courts increasingly dealing with the business of female plaintiffs, but as the seventeenth century progressed they were also concerned with hearing the cases of married women. The full significance of the marital status of these women has been too readily overlooked. If we turn our attention to a close examination of the contexts in which these married women were slandered, then we may gain some answers to the question of why they so frequently became plaintiffs in the church courts, as well as a clearer picture of the nature of male and female reputation.

CIRCUMSTANCES OF DEFAMATION

There were a wide range of different circumstances in which men and women could be sexually slandered. Historians who have studied church court records have observed that suits brought after sexual slander were often concerned with issues which were in fact not sexual, but were rather the culmination of long-term 'neighbourhood' disputes. Arguments over debt repayment or property disputes could often culminate in sexual slander. When houses were closely packed together in urban areas, many quarrels also broke out over household noise, leaking drains and broken fences and walls.[8] But married women were particularly vulnerable to sexual slander in this context because they were so often slandered by 'association' with their husbands. That is, women found themselves facing the insults of those who were angry with their husbands. For example, in March 1618 when Mary Dobson fell arguing with Anthony Garnett over some flax they were weighing together she accused him of 'connycatching' (cheating) her and then turned on Jane Garnett, Anthony's wife, and called her 'connecatch quean drunken bitch, and said she thought the devil was in her, she the said Jane being then great with child'.[9] In 1624 Anne Swalwell was slandered as an 'old bawd' and a 'whore' by Grace Rutlidge because Grace believed that Anne's husband had caused her husband to get into trouble with the local authorities.[10] When Cuthbert Jackson started arguing about some pigs owned by John Chamber which Cuthbert claimed had strayed on to his ground in Gateside, a witness observed how the dispute passed 'from less to more' when Cuthbert then proceeded to call John's wife a whore and cheat.[11] Edith Cratchley was prosecuted as a whore on the basis of slander in Wiltshire in 1619. As Ingram has recognised, she was in fact a 'victim of local hostility against her husband', who was suspected amongst other crimes of fathering a bastard and sheep stealing.[12] Another example is that of Margaret Postgate, who in May 1620 was called whore by Elizabeth Wales after her husband Thomas Postgate went to collect debts from Elizabeth in Chester le Street, Durham. Ann and Roger Howard were so angry at Richard Delves's attempt to collect a subscription for the Fruiters' Company in 1664 that they slandered Richard's wife, who was absent from the scene, as a proud and drunken whore.[13] None of these arguments had started over sex, but each of these women had become victims of sexual slander because others had been disgruntled with their husbands' business dealings.

There are other cases in which women are caught in the crossfire of an argument between men and are slandered. For example, the Durham consistory court heard in March 1634 how Alice Coleman had sat between Amor Patterson and Robert Dawson at a wedding dinner at Newbiggin. When the two men, who had been drinking, started to quarrel, Alice intervened 'and laboured to pacify them'. Amor then turned to Alice and called her a 'scurvy base idle queane'. When Amor's wife later scolded her husband for treating Alice in this way he was reported to have said 'what care I for her', and repeated the slander.[14] Similarly, when William Chapman and Roger

Harper started to fight in the doorway of John Fletcher's house in South Shields, and Isabell Chapman appeared and tried to help her husband, she was called 'arrant whore' by Roger, thrown to the ground, and accused of being 'drunk with his means'.[15] A fight broke out in the street at Bedlington when the constable, William Watson, tried to put William Skipsey in the stocks. Jane Skipsey rushed to the scene and pulled Watson by the jerkin to try and prevent him from doing her husband any further harm. Watson then turned on Jane and called her an 'arrant pockie whore'.[16] When Christopher Simpson and George Craggs started quarrelling in Gilesgate at Durham and Edeth, wife of Christopher, asked George 'what reason he had to use her husband so', she was also called a whore.[17] Ann Bath asked a similar question to Walter Lewis in a London victualling house in 1663, when she found him striking her husband and arguing over debts. She also ended up being called a whore, and the child who was with her, a bastard.[18] It is women who are the plaintiffs in all of the defamation suits which followed, but the circumstances in which they were slandered reveal little about female sexual reputation, and much about male behaviour if not reputation. It is often when women intervene in male quarrels or try to defend their husbands' reputations that they are slandered. There is a sense in which women are the easy victims of slander, of a society in which men could let their anger out upon women because they believed that women did not have the strength of words or fists to fight back. Perhaps slandering a man's wife was an easier option than facing up to the man himself. Of course, these women were not powerless, they could, and often did, take the men who insulted them to court. But suits such as those of Isabell Chapman, Jane Skipsey, Edeth Simpson and Ann Bath did not just serve these women's interests. Arguably, by bringing the cases to court they were also gaining a wider audience for the original quarrel involving their husbands.

A crucial factor which determined whether a married woman went to court after she was called whore was if her husband was present when she was slandered, or if he later heard through gossip that she was labelled whore. For calling a wife whore was an effective insult because it represented a two-pronged attack aimed at the wife and the husband: if a married woman was a whore then her husband was a cuckold. The insult 'whore' told a husband that he had lost sexual control over his wife. Hence men were very sensitive to gossip about their wives' behaviour. Durham consistory court heard in November 1604 how George Cuthbert of Usworth suspected that Elizabeth Philipe had been gossiping about his wife's relationship with one Robert White. He angrily confronted Elizabeth's husband in the street. An argument broke out between the two men. It was Winifred Cuthbert who had been called whore, and Elizabeth Philipe who had spread the gossip, but it appears that it was their husbands who found these facts most disturbing. George clearly believed that the gossip that Robert White 'occupieth' his wife 'up the house and down' was affecting his reputation. By attacking the husband of the gossiper he was implying that Elizabeth's husband should have been able to control his wife's talk. Elizabeth's husband rose to the challenge of the argument by ordering his wife to come before them. Perhaps unsurprisingly Elizabeth tried to avoid the charge of gossipmonger by blaming the spread of gossip upon her cousin. George Cuthbert found that he was unable to stop the flow of gossip informally, so his wife Winifred subsequently brought a defamation suit against Elizabeth, an action which must have served to abate the worry and anger of her husband, as well as defend her good name.[19]

That slanderers intended the insult of 'whore' to have the dual purpose of affecting both husband and wife is shown by the fact that the slander of 'whore' was sometimes deliberately addressed to, or directed at, the husband. His cuckoldry was often the wounding point at issue. For example, just before Christmas 1616 John Casson told William Taler that his wife Jane Taler was 'an abominable whore'; in around 1619 at Chester le Street Roger Colson told John Sander that Isabell Sander 'had nothing to do when her husband was at London but go up and down a whoring'; and Ralph Eglesfield was told in May 1629 that his wife 'had laid six weeks together with another wife's husband'. In all three cases the wives of the husbands mentioned became plaintiffs in the defamation suits which followed.[20] There are many more examples of defamation cases from across the period which were brought by women and which tell us that husbands were present when their wives were called whores.[21] Sometimes the slanderer even called for the husband's attention. One night in Newcastle between Michaelmas and Martinmas 1627 Elizabeth Bateman was so angered by her neighbour Katherine Bindlosse's intrusion into her house that she went to the door of the Bindlosse's house and called for George Bindlosse before shouting to him 'thou art an honest man but thy wife . . . is both a thief and a whore'.[22] In Shoreditch around Easter 1676 Sarah Hill twice came to the door of Frances Taylor and started accusing her of accepting gifts to have sex in bawdy houses with one William Hitchman. Then, 'directing her speeches to the said producent's [Frances's] husband', and in front of their two sons, Sarah first told Frances's husband that William had bought Frances oysters 'on purpose to make your wife lusty for him', and the next day warned him 'you were best took care that you do not get pox of your wife'.[23] Slanderers such as Elizabeth Bateman and Sarah Hill deliberately drew the husband's notice to the insult because they knew that male sexual reputation rested on female chastity.

CONSEQUENCES OF DEFAMATION

Elizabeth Bateman contrasted the honesty of George Bindlosse with the dishonesty of his wife ('thou art an honest man but thy wife . . . is both a thief and a whore') as a deliberate ploy to cause discord between the couple. Elizabeth implied that George had been 'honest' in the sense that he had been innocent of Katherine's behaviour, not that his own honesty or reputation would remain unaffected by his wife's behaviour. There is ample evidence from other cases that once a husband heard that his wife had been called a whore discord usually followed. Jane Romwhate caused much trouble between several wives and their husbands by her gossip in Heighington at the start of the seventeenth century. She provoked 'much discontent' between Janet Morecock and her husband when she told John Morecock that his wife did 'fully love another man besides her husband'. When Jane had words with Ralph Wren she 'used such speeches' that she caused Ralph to beat his wife, 'moved great anger between them', and 'caused them to part for a time'. Finally, when she called Helen Heighington a 'frantic bedliner and barsot gentlewoman' at a churching dinner at Lammas 1609 she caused 'much disagreement' between Helen and her husband. It was Helen who brought the defamation case against Jane in which four female witnesses told the court of her disruptive behaviour.[24] Jane was known to be an 'angry woman' and a 'very turbulent and troublesome neighbour' who had so abused her own husband that her next neighbour was 'carried upon a stang about the town'. Riding the stang, as Chapter 4 explained, was a northern custom or variant of charivari in which a man was mounted astride a pole borne on the shoulders of two men, and carried through the streets for derision. Jane's behaviour had become so objectionable and such a public nuisance that it had been singled out for this punishment. Her own mother was 'so ashamed and grieved at her ill using therein as that she is loth to come in her company'. Despite this common knowledge about Jane, the husbands of Heighington still reacted angrily against their wives when Jane questioned their honesty, and her unscrupulous use of insult resulted in the disruption of a whole community. The 'truth' of her talk does not seem to have concerned these husbands. What mattered was that her words called into question their reputations as well as their wives'. It is clear from their response that the insult 'whore' affected men as well as women.

If a married woman was called whore it demanded a response, even if the slanderer was, like Jane Romwhate, of dubious reputation so that her words should have held little credit. Mary Goodall, and interestingly the man who was accused of being her lover, Charles Thornehill, launched separate defamation suits against Sara Glover in 1664 after she accused them of having an adulterous affair together. They felt that Sara's words should be taken seriously, even though, like Jane Romwhate, Sara 'having beaten her husband' had caused 'a riding about the same' in the Whitechapel community where they all lived. Sara was a well-known troublemaker, she had called one of the witnesses whore on an earlier occasion, and at another time Sara's husband was forced to come and carry her away 'in his arms' whilst she was angrily slandering Mary Goodall and Charles Thornehill.[25]

A case which raises similar issues was heard in the court of Arches in 1672. On 2 September John Francis went to the Three Tunns in the parish of St Sepulchre, London, to try and fetch his apprentice whom he suspected of drinking and gambling in the alehouse. Not finding his apprentice, he angrily accosted the alewife, Susan Almond, and accused her of encouraging his apprentice to waste his time and money, of being 'an old whore', and of swindling money even from her own husband, 'in so much that he could not appear in Smithfields or elsewhere to buy goods'. After such provocation, John should perhaps have predicted that Susan would respond strongly. She 'replied by slandering his wife', who was initially absent from the scene, by saying that Elizabeth Francis was 'a whore a Tallow faced Brazen faced whore, and was in bed with two men at one time in Fogwell Court in Charterhouse Lane', repeating the slander once Elizabeth entered the room. Once again, a married woman was slandered after her husband had been involved in a quarrel that initially had little to do with her sexual reputation. Angry at John Francis's accusations, Susan Almond had drawn upon the worst insults she could think of for a married man. By using the language of whoredom she could powerfully insult him. According to Sarah Randall, a neighbour to the Almonds, and a witness to the dispute, Susan Almond was 'a person of a slanderous tongue and hath abused this deponent [witness] and her husband, and she doth others'. But despite the circumstances of the quarrel which led up to the slander, and the neighbourhood reputation of Susan Almond, it was still John's wife, Elizabeth Francis, who ended up initiating legal proceedings in the defamation suit which followed.[26]

If a married woman was called whore, or her husband a cuckold, it appears that marital discord frequently followed. Sometimes the damage which had occurred to a marriage as a result of slander was spelled out to the court. For example, when Gregory Hutchinson spread rumours in Durham city that Isabelle Moore was committing adultery with James Noble, her husband became 'much discontented with her', so that Gregory had to make a public apology to Isabelle in 1605.[27] On Easter Tuesday 1619 Agnes Hall told her neighbours how Barbara Archbald had 'got a new gown and a petticoat for lying one night with Mr Sanderson'. The result of this slander was that it 'bred great dissension betwixt her the said Barbara and her husband'.[28] After Richard Widdowes called Francis Frissell 'Cuckold, Cuckoldly Knave and Cuckoldly Curr' in Lesbury, Northumberland, in August 1607, it was noted by two witnesses that an 'evil argument [had] thereby grown betwixt him and his wife'.[29] In the court of Arches, in addition to some cases in which witnesses gave general statements about marital discord, the discontent which sexual slander caused between couples was often also described in more detail. Some husbands, such as Alice Starky's in 1666, were reported to refuse to sleep with their wives after they had been slandered as whores.[30] Other wives, like Joan Lomax in 1675, were turned 'out of doors', or like Ann Whitacre of St Martin-in-the-Fields, Middlesex, were deserted by their husbands when they were called whore and their husband cuckold.[31] Those who witnessed an incident of slander lamented the consequences which they predicted would follow, and sometimes even intervened in a quarrel in the hope that they could avert marital discord. When Elizabeth Masters saw Elizabeth Staunton scolding Elizabeth Newbury as she sat next to her husband under a window of her house in Stepney, Masters approached Staunton and 'prayed her to be sparing in her words for that the said Mistress Newbury's husband would in likelihood take offence against his wife', but Staunton carried on regardless.[32]

In this context, it is easy to see how going to court to fight a defamation suit would have been regarded as one way that a wife might hope to appease her husband. Women were accustomed to the notion that if their sexual reputations were questioned, then the reputations of the men who were intended to govern them would also be affected. We have seen in Chapter 3 above that single women as servants or daughters could end up in court fighting defamation suits if their masters or fathers believed that their honour had been impugned. In some marriages, a husband made the launching of a defamation suit after slander the condition of the restoration of their relationship. Mary Weaver heard Bridget Clarke's husband tell Bridget 'twice or thrice' in early 1674 that he 'would never again bed with her unless she would vindicate herself' of the slander of whore. Elizabeth Jones's husband of St Giles-in-the-Fields threatened 'to turn her out of doors till she had cleared herself, and under that danger she is at present', a witness warned.[33] Andrew Reynolds deserted his wife in March 1667 after she was called whore, and he a cuckold, and was reported to have said on his departure, 'that he would never dwell with her again until she had cleared herself'.[34] Of course, witnesses may have included such stories of marital discord in their statements to ensure that the words and actions of the defendant were seen in the worst possible light, and to give the court the impression that the fate of a marriage as well as the reputation of an individual depended on its judgement. To justify the appeal of a defamation case to the court of Arches, witnesses who spoke in this court may also have felt more need to draw attention to the disruptive consequences of the slander. But stories of marital discord were by no means standard in cases in which a wife had been sexually slandered, so that we are left with the impression that when witnesses did give details of marital disharmony, they may have done so for reasons other than just legal expediency. The pressure on a wife to go to court after sexual slander could be intense, and could stem from neighbourly as well as spousal expectations. Helen Stephens reported that after Giles Roberts had been called a cuckold, neighbours in Hampton, Middlesex, 'have harboured some ill thoughts' of Giles's wife, Elizabeth, 'saying that had she not been guilty she would have cleared herself'. To be free of any aspersions of guilt, Elizabeth began a defamation suit against her husband's slanderer.[35]

There are still further cases to be explained in which married women are plaintiffs in the church courts when the original sexual slander had been directed against their husbands. When John Marley fell arguing with Timothy Burrell on the Sandhill in Newcastle in 1622, and Timothy called John a 'cuckoldly fellow', even though there is no indication that John's wife was present at the time of the quarrel, she and her husband launched a joint defamation suit against Timothy.[36] The Restoration court of Arches heard three joint husband and wife actions after the husband had been called cuckold.[37] But rather than joint actions, when legal action followed after the insult of cuckold, it was more likely to be brought by the wife alone. In the Durham church court there were three cases in this period in which a man was called cuckold but his wife acted as the plaintiff in the defamation case that followed.[38] In the court of Arches, on fifteen occasions married women were the sole plaintiffs after their husbands had been called cuckolds. Sometimes they had also been called whores, but on other occasions they had not even been present when the insult of cuckold had been uttered. For example, there is no indication that Lady Sarah Garrard was present when her husband, Sir Thomas, argued with George Humble in the churchyard of West Ham, Essex, in the autumn of 1676. The quarrel had broken out when Sir Thomas had asked George for some money which he owed, and resulted in George calling Thomas a 'Cuckoldy Dog', and claiming that he had repaid Thomas the money he owed 'by half a crown at a Time', implying that Thomas acted as a pimp for his wife. The insults had all been directed to shame Sir Thomas, yet his wife was the plaintiff in the defamation suit which followed.[39]

Work of other historians for later periods indicates that this pattern of women acting as plaintiffs after their husbands had been called cuckolds continued. Tim Meldrum's survey of the London consistory court in the early eighteenth century has shown that in all cases when the slander of cuckold was used 'it was the wives of those abused as cuckolds who stood as producents', and Polly Morris's survey of the Somerset church courts 1733–1850 also found that men who faced the slander of cuckold 'invariably sent their wives into court to clear their reputations'.[40] Of course, the insult of cuckold implied that a wife had been adulterous and so these female plaintiffs were seeking to clear their reputations of such a charge. But as earlier chapters have argued, the slander of cuckold was a powerful one to direct against a man because it was an explicit accusation of failure in manliness. Only a man who could not govern his own wife could become a cuckold. In this context, by ensuring that his wife subsequently appeared as a plaintiff in the church court after sexual slander, a man could send a clear message to his neighbourhood that he had reassumed control over his household.

FUNDING LEGAL ACTION

Although Lady Sarah Garrard was the plaintiff in the defamation case described above, one witness testified that 'Sir Thomas pays the charges of this suit'.[41] If we are fully to understand the role that defamation cases played in the personal and neighbourhood conflicts of the period, important evidence about the cost of cases in the church courts also needs to be examined. If a person brought a suit fees had to be paid to various court personnel: the judge, registrar and apparitor. We know that the cost of initiating a case was low. Durham statutes in 1573 suggest that the cost of issuing a citation was 6d. To put this cost into perspective, Ingram has suggested that the daily wage of a labourer was less than a shilling, and R.A. Marchant estimates that a North Riding carpenter before the civil war would have earned a similar daily wage.[42] Wages of those working in the Durham area are difficult to estimate, but it seems reasonable to expect that they were on a par with other regions.[43] But at each stage of a suit the cost of a case mounted, so for example in Durham in 1573 the cost of the examination of principal parties was 12d.[44] The duration and the complexity of the case increased its cost, and if a case proceeded to sentence, costs relative to average earnings could be high. Thus Ingram has found that in Wiltshire 'an unusually simple' defamation case in 1615 cost £2 10s, and a more complex suit in the same year cost £4 13s.[45]

In 1597 Archbishop Whitgift issued a standard table of fees, and evidence suggests that many church courts kept their fees roughly in line with this standard, so that regional variation in fees was slight. In addition, there is some evidence that fees could be waived for very poor defendants, and that the real cost of a suit did not rise through the period.[46] Thus a table of fees due in Durham consistory court in 1708 shows that the cost of a citation had only risen by 1d since 1573.[47] Since this was a period of inflation, the cost of business in the church courts was becoming cheaper as time went on, and the Puritan criticism that the church courts charged exorbitant fees was therefore largely unjustified.[48] Many cases were resolved before they reached the most costly stage of a sentence. However, the loser of a suit had to pay the other party's costs as well as his own, and witnesses expected to be reimbursed for any expenses or loss of earnings they had incurred whilst appearing to give evidence.[49] Hence Gowing estimates that the cost of litigation in the London church courts could have been between £1 and £10 in early seventeenth-century London, and Sharpe believes that by the end of the seventeenth century to fight a defamation suit to its conclusion could have cost as much as £8.[50] Pursuing a case to the Restoration court of Arches as an appeal obviously increased costs. Five bills of costs which survive from the defamation cases studied in this court show total costs varying from about £8 to over £14.[51] It has been calculated that building craftsmen in southern England earned 18d–20d a day between 1687 and 1701. Legal costs may well explain why the majority of litigants in the court of Arches were from the middling sorts or above.[52]

But if a married woman brought a defamation case against another wife, who was responsible for the payment of court fees? The answer must lie in who held the strings to the household purse during marriage. Amy Erickson has shown how in practice within many marriages the doctrine of coverture, whereby women lost all their personal property and control of their real property to their husbands, was modified to allow wives separate estate and pin money.[53] So it is conceivable that some married women would have had sufficient money of their own to meet the expenses of fighting a defamation suit.

However, within Durham church court records there is one very important case which may shed some light on who was normally expected to foot the bill for defamation suits. In the early 1630s Elinor Rawlyn, wife of Robert, brought a defamation case against one Cecilie Smith of Denton. After the suit had commenced the curate of Denton tried to effect a reconciliation between the two parties. Significantly, rather than directly approaching Elinor, he first approached her husband and asked him if 'he the said Robert was content' if Cecilie Smith paid his wife 20s 'for her satisfaction touching the said cause and the charges of the Court'. Robert was happy with the sum suggested and Cecilie agreed to the payment. Then Robert, not Elinor, gave an order 'for staying the further prosecution of the said cause'. The parties met in a friend's house in Denton one day in Martinmas 1632, drank a pledge to one another, and Cecilie agreed once more to give Elinor the 20s. However, by the time a bill of charges from the court case had been procured, Cecilie had married one Richard Oswald. Richard Oswald went to visit Robert Rawlyn and, with the curate as his witness, offered 'to pay such charges as should be reasonably required', but claimed that a bill of 20s was 'very excessive', and refused to pay the same. The curate notes in his witness statement that despite her husband's refusal, Cecilie 'always was and yet is very willing to pay such reasonable charges as was to that time expended in that cause'. With no settlement reached, in November 1633 Cecilie Smith launched a defamation suit against Elinor Rawlyn, presumably after Elinor claimed that Cecilie could or would not pay what she was owed, and witnesses related to the court the history of their disagreement.[54]

Whilst it appears that if the charges were paid the actual transfer of money would have been from wife to wife, the husbands of both women were the key movers in the negotiations which took place. At times the wives seem to take little part in the decisions which are made: the curate approaches Elinor's husband to see if he finds a monetary settlement satisfactory; it is Robert Rawlyn who calls a halt to the legal proceedings which his wife had initiated; and when Cecilie marries it is the two husbands who meet to discuss terms. It is clear from the curate's actions that men as the managers of household budgets and debt collectors were expected to play key roles in financing the legal actions of their wives. In this case it seems that the management of an action brought by a married woman was in the hands of her husband.

Witnesses in the church courts were expected to declare their interest in the suit, and their relationship with the parties involved, so that they could avoid charges of accepting bribes and being open to deceit. It is within these statements that the role of some husbands in other sexual slander suits becomes clearest. When Richard Lee, of Washington, Sussex, called Eleanor Butcher whore in her own house, three witnesses stated in 1604 before the Chichester consistory court that they had come at the request and charges of Richard Butcher, her husband. Thomas Page in the same year told the court that 'he came at the instance, request and charge of Edward Legate husband of the said Mary Legate', after she had been slandered by Julian Legate. The experience of Agnes, wife of Richard Danniel, in 1603 shares similarities with that of Elinor Rawlyn and Cecilie Smith described above. After she had been slandered by Robert Bishoppe of Selsey, Sussex, and a defamation case begun, she, her husband and Robert agreed on a reconciliation. But when she queried her husband about who would pay the court fees, he replied 'I pray thee wife, hold thyself contented, Goodman Bishoppe and I are agreed for the charges.' Once again, negotiations about a defamation case had been agreed between men without the participation of its female plaintiff.[55]

The records of the court of Arches show that the involvement of some husbands in defamation suits in which their wives are plaintiffs continued after the Restoration. Mary Blanchet had been slandered as a whore in Southampton in November 1690. When she brought a defamation suit to the court of Arches in the following June, one of her witnesses declared that he came to court 'at the desire of her husband', John Blanchet, and that 'this cause is carried on at the charge of John Blanchet'. John's concern with the suit was such that between a month and six weeks before it reached the Arches he had written to the same witness, 'desiring this respondent [witness] to mind this matter for the love of God and when he should have occasion for more money he would send it to him and thanking him for his Friendship'. Mary is never mentioned in this pre-court correspondence.[56] Other husbands were less generous in their promises or gifts to witnesses, but their interest in their wives' cases is still apparent. Three female witnesses who spoke for Mistress Hickman in a sexual defamation suit against Mistress Lucke in 1667 told the court that they had 'a glass of wine at the charge of the husband of Mistress Hickman'. Three other witnesses for the defendant Mistress Lucke admitted that they had come to the court at the request of Lucke's husband.[57] After Ann Piper, of Croydon, Surrey, was called a whore, her husband promised to bear the charges of Henry Messenger, a witness in her suit, and to pay him for his day's work and loss of time. He also promised to reimburse a master for the loss of a day's service from an apprentice who acted as witness.[58]

At times the management of these defamation suits appears to be totally out of the wife's control and pursued in her name only. Joan Martin was the named plaintiff in a defamation suit against Jason Cardron after he had called her husband Charles 'cuckoldly fool' in a dispute over church repair funds to which Jason had refused to contribute. But one of the witnesses declared that he 'hath heard the said [Charles] Martin say that if the said Cardron would come and acknowledge before half a dozen of the Best of the parish that he had abused the producent [Joan] by the foresaid words, and would pay the charges that he had been at *he* the said [Charles] Martin would relinquish *his* suite commenced by *him* against Cardron'.[59] The apology would be to Joan, but all the indications are that this would be orchestrated by her husband, and only he would decide if the defamation suit would be dropped.

The extent of Charles Martin's involvement in his wife's suit may have been unusual, but there are signs that in such cases husbands continued to show interest. Polly Morris, in her study of defamation cases in Somerset 1733–1850, found evidence 'in later years' that even when the plaintiff was named as a married woman 'proxies continued to bear a good many husbands' signatures, testifying to the fact that proctors were frequently hired by the married couple and not simply by the wife'.[60] Richard Burn, who wrote the most important handbook on ecclesiastical law in the eighteenth century, wrote that although it should not be in a husband's power to hinder or restrain a wife's legal proceedings, if a married woman 'sue in the spiritual court, and recover costs, if the husband release them, the wife is barred. For since the husband is liable to the charges of the suit expended by the wife, he shall have the costs in recompence; besides that, the wife cannot have a chattel interest exclusive of her husband.' The woman's marital and legal status as a 'feme covert', in other words, excluded her both from the payment and reward of legal costs.[61]

In summary, we must look more carefully at what motivated so many married women to fight sexual defamation suits in this period. It has been argued by Sharpe that the 'initiation of a suit for defamation might be interpreted as the first step towards bringing neighbourly tensions to a close'. Gowing has taken this theme of neighbourly dispute in another direction, arguing that women used sexual insults to their own ends in the streets and houses of their neighbourhoods, and then in the courtroom, often to further rather than settle disputes.[62] But both historians miss what was the primary reason behind the initial decision by many married women to take legal action: the desire to end marital discord. The importance of the insult of whore for a husband's sexual reputation, as well as a wife's, has previously been underestimated, leaving us with a distorted picture of how honour systems in this society operated. Women may have adopted and adapted the language of whoredom to suit their own ends. But the core meaning of these words was one that had been originally created by men to fit a male political agenda designed to restrict and confine women's behaviour. It was men who desired to make women their property and who had first defined what it meant to be chaste, and what to be a whore. The insult of 'whore' would always take on additional meanings when it was directed against a married woman because it also labelled her husband a cuckold. The insult charged the wife with challenging a gender hierarchy based on notions of patriarchy, and her husband with failure to uphold that hierarchy by sexual control. The dependency of men on their wives' chastity meant that those who wished ill upon a married man need only insult his wife sexually to devastate his reputation. The power of the insult was such that the credit or reputation of the slanderer mattered little to its victims. The anger of men whose wives were called whore could be predicted by those who witnessed the slander, because it was popularly acknowledged that these men would also be wounded by the insult. According to contemporary prescriptive literature, women were meant to be chaste in talk and behaviour. Standing up in court and discussing sexual reputation was in itself inconsistent with these ideas of female chastity and honour.[63] But this study has shown how it was sometimes necessary for women to act in this way, because women's sexual reputation was of such great importance for husbands, as well as the women themselves. In some cases sheer anger of a husband may have been sufficient to persuade wives to bring cases.

The issue of church court fees provides further evidence to support the theory that husbands were often behind their wives' legal actions. Initiating a defamation suit was inexpensive, but to be confident of the ability to pursue a case to its close could require quite considerable financial investment. The existence of the rules of coverture would have made it very difficult for a wife to bring an action of which her husband strongly disapproved, because the law gave him theoretical control over the household purse strings. For these reasons it seems likely that wives who launched defamation suits must have consulted, or even sought permission from their husbands before initiating procedures. It also seems logical that the financial backing of husbands was more likely to have been provided when the husbands themselves had an interest in the suit. Cases which reveal details of the involvement of husbands in their funding and organisation show that some husbands believed that enabling their wives to fight defamation cases on their behalf was an effective way of reasserting male honour which had been open to question. In their anxiety hastily to reassert their own reputations, the concerns of their wives could be overlooked, and whilst most men wielded control over household expenditure on legal affairs, some women could find themselves used as pawns in legal disputes managed by their husbands.

Outside the courtroom married women who faced sexual insult rarely reacted as helpless victims. They often gave their slanderers as good as they got, and sometimes their insults turned into blows and punches. Once in the courtroom, women were far from being simply 'the dupes of patriarchal machinations', whose words in the courtroom can today only be regarded by historians as the product of 'patriarchal ventriloquism'.[64] There is little doubt from the evidence of the large numbers of married women, in addition to significant numbers of unmarried and widowed women, fighting cases across the country, and throughout this period, that many women took advantage of the unique legal rights offered to them in the church courts. But for married women there was another, preliminary stage to this legal process, in which the interests of their husbands played a crucial part. The initial decision to go to law was often inspired by a desire to defend their husbands' good name as well as their own. Once in court, for many wives settling neighbourhood grievances must have been of secondary importance to restoring marital harmony.

In this context, the fate of married women who were prepared to pursue cases when they did not have the support of their husbands is telling. Isabelle, wife of Isaac Murdocke, sued Francis Sharpe for defamation in 1668 after he called her whore during an argument between Isaac and Francis. The matter had been put to arbitration and neighbours had tried to bring the parties to an out of court settlement. But according to one witness Isabelle had refused to have anything to do with these negotiations, and insisted on the continuation of the suit at law, 'although her husband was inclined to making an end thereof'. This independence of mind appears to have won disapproval rather than admiration from her male neighbours. One declared that he believed Isabelle 'was and is a woman of a High Spirit, impatient of injuries, and that it is against her nature to pass by abuses that touch her good name'. Without the backing of her husband, a married female plaintiff ran the risk of being represented as an unnecessarily litigious and troublesome woman. Indeed, it could be argued that the involvement of husbands in the sexual defamation cases of their wives had become so conventional that without his support a married woman defending simply her own reputation was regarded by contemporaries as out of place, and extraordinary.[65]

Legal Action and Adultery

In 1673 Captain Charles Skelton returned from sea to hear reports that in his absence his wife, Dorothy, had committed adultery with Charles Brooks, a servant to Baron Brouncker. Charles Brooks swore that Dorothy had given him the pox, and when Charles Skelton visited Brooks he found him to be a dying man. Charles Skelton's mother advised her son 'of the great dishonour done to her family' by his wife. Skelton was to tell the court of Arches in the same year that 'knowing he can neither with safety nor credit continue with her [he] doth endeavour to procure a divorce or separation'.[66]

The remainder of this chapter will examine the options open to men when evidence of wife adultery became so convincing to them that they were certain that their sexual honour had been lost. It will explore what psychologists have labelled as 'reactive jealousy': behaviour of husbands who had become certain that their wives had been unfaithful and they had been cuckolded.[67] For the many husbands who did not catch their wives *in flagrante delicto*, the point at which rumours and defamatory talk became 'evidence' of wife adultery varied, and could depend on how far they were already inclined to be jealous or suspicious of their wives. Faced with stories of his wife's adultery from a number of different sources, Charles Skelton chose to take legal action, a decision which would have met with approval from many contemporary moralists. They argued that men should always go to the law to seek redress for dishonour, rather than take matters into their own hands. Thomas Heywood, writing under the name T.H. Gent, wrote in 1657 that it was only 'inhumane rashness' which led cuckolded men 'to be their own justifiers', by which they 'mingled the pollution of their beds, with the blood of the delinquents'. Jean Gailhard also appealed to men's reason when he argued that 'all rational men' would agree that 'it is not fit a man should be judge or executioner in his own case'.[68]

But the choice between legal and non-legal methods of responding to dishonour caused by a wife's adultery was not as straightforward as these writers might seem to suggest. If a man's wife had played the whore, and he had consequently lost his sexual reputation, going to court to defend his name could have acted further to expose his shame. Hence when stories of wife adultery were only gossip and rumour, as we have seen, the strategy of men sending their wives to the church courts to plead on their behalf in defamation suits may have been appealing. But if husbands believed or discovered that these stories could not be so readily dismissed, they could then take action against their wives and sue for marital separation. This entailed a husband and his witnesses talking openly in the courtroom about the details of his failed marriage. This may have been an unattractive course of action especially when, in the late seventeenth and early eighteenth centuries, newspapers began to print some of the more sensational details of marriage separation cases, thereby drawing even more humiliating attention to the cuckold. One husband complained in 1733 that anyone who appealed a matrimonial case to the court of Arches 'must expect to have as much filth as a scavenger's cart will hold emptied upon him'.[69] Even if a husband could convince the church courts that his wife had committed adultery, the most he could hope for was separation from bed and board since most men could not gain full divorce until 1857. Separation could prove to be a lengthy and costly legal process, as a husband was bound to maintain his wife whilst the case was being heard, and to pay for her legal costs as well as his own.[70] 'The last Remedy they have is to try the Law', joked the author of one contemporary jest book when he described the 'ass cuckold'. 'There they find ease by Lopping their Horns', he continued, 'and for a great deal of Money, and Disgrace, purchase the Salve of Separation, to anoint their Forehead, to drive away the Head-ache.'[71]

Husbands in Restoration drama complained that the church courts operated a marriage separation system which always penalised the male party. Sir John Brute in *The Provoked Wife* (1697) wishes his wife could be proved unfaithful: 'Pox on her virtue! If I cou'd but catch her Adulterating, I might be Divorc'd from her by law', to which Heartfree replies, 'And so pay her a yearly pension, to be a distinguished cuckold.' Meanwhile Sir John's wife, who is also dissatisfied with the marriage, has already admitted to her niece that 'these are good times; a woman may have a gallant and a separate maintenance too'.[72] In fact, if a wife was found guilty of committing adultery with a gallant, unless she was protected by a private deed of separation, she could be left penniless. Her husband could seize all her private property and savings, and she was unable to enter into any legal contract or credit agreement.[73] Why dramatists chose to portray the husband's position in this way is not clear, but it may be because they wanted to reflect popular male sentiment which persistently held that the legal system was prejudiced against cuckolds, despite much evidence to the contrary.[74]

Women could be awarded alimony if they successfully sued their husbands for separation on grounds of cruelty, but it is clear that many men felt anger and resentment that they should have to maintain their wives in this way. Sir John Cremor was advised by a friend to 'use' Ursula Cremor 'like his wife, or else that he would allow her a Competent maintenance and that she might live apart from him'. He angrily replied that he would continue to treat her as he pleased for 'I know the Court of Arches hath no power but to commit me to prison and there will I remain as long as I live rather than she shall have a penny of my Estate.'[75] As Elizabeth Harbin fled from her violent husband in Yeovil, Somerset, in 1669 he cried after her 'Go and the devil go with you, get what maintenance you can.'[76] John Bradley showed a similar disdain for the power of the law when he accused his wife Cecily of trying to get a separate maintenance, claiming 'I am not afraid of the Law'.[77]

The small number of marriage separation cases which reached the church courts may reflect the unpopularity of this legal remedy for dishonour. In Durham consistory court, for example, there were only four cases for marriage separation between 1604 and 1631, and historians who have studied other consistory court records have also noted the comparative rarity of these cases.[78] It is only by looking at the records of an appeal court such as the court of Arches which attracted cases from a wider geographical area that we can find greater numbers of separation cases. Parliamentary divorce was too expensive for most, and before 1700 only two private acts for divorce were introduced.[79] It is hard to know how far divorce or separation affected a man's honour since after the parties left the courts the details of their lives tend to disappear from the historical record. We rely on clues from witness statements such as that made by William Rouse, an apothecary from St Clements Danes, Middlesex, who believed that the Bound couple should be encouraged to stay together, for the 'peace of their own minds', and to prevent 'the disreputation to their Family, which otherwise [would] necessarily follow'.[80]

Evidence suggests that husbands who did decide to take legal action and sue their wives for adultery in the church courts employed special pleading strategies to try and win sympathy and support for their cases. When a man used the slander of cuckold against another it was easy for him to mock the husband who by his poor sexual performance had been a cuckold of his own making. However, it was an entirely different matter when a man himself found he had been cuckolded. His wife's inconstancy questioned his sexual prowess, but we can hardly expect many men to admit that they were at fault. It was far easier to project the image of the 'self-made' cuckold on to others, than to swallow the bitter pill oneself. Thus for the cuckold the attribution of blame shifted from him to his wife. Adulterous women in the courtroom became scapegoats for male fears about their own sexuality. In the courtroom husbands and the witnesses who acted for them constructed narratives which applied the stereotype of 'whore' to the women who were suspected of committing adultery. A whore was a woman whom no man could satisfy, hence when John Charnock was convinced that his wife was committing adultery, he expected it to assist his case when he related how he had spoken to the relatives of his wife's previous husband, and was told by them that she had 'abused' him 'in the like manner, and is not to be satisfied with one man'.[81] Even the lovers of adulterous women are portrayed as fearing that they will be unable to match the desires of whores: 'I think I shall not be sufficient to supply thy wants', Elizabeth Northmore's lover pitifully pleaded when she asked 'will you have again?' Elizabeth is shown as demanding never-ending sex since she was heard by Thomas Carter, who worked in the same household, to have boasted to her lover 'if you could hold out I could afford you in my body every hour'.[82]

Women were not only shown as insatiable once aroused, they were seen as seductive by nature. Lovers such as the apprentice Tarrant Reeves who found themselves discovered felt able to try to convince the courts that they had been seduced rather than been the seducers: 'his Mistress instigated him thereto', Tarrant said.[83] Wives who were accused of adultery such as Mary Hockmore not only refused to be controlled by their husbands but were also shown to continue this reversal of gender roles by acting the dominant partner with their lovers. When Mary deserted her husband in Devon to come to London with midshipman Charles Manley in 1698, a fellow lodger witnessed a fight between the pair. When Charles pushed Mary from him she angrily exclaimed, 'how now you pitiful Rascal I would not take this from my husband much less from you that am my servant'.[84] The world is turned upside down in this adulterous relationship, for it appears that the woman gains the dominant position, and her lover is relegated to servile status.

Similar portrayals of adulterous wives as powerful and insatiable whores who gain extraordinary enjoyment from sex have been found in the Elizabethan court of Requests and in London church court records.[85] It would appear that women who questioned husbands' potency by their words or actions could find themselves exposed to public male censorship. David Lindley has provided us with new and important insights into the history of Frances Howard, who in 1613 sought an annulment from her first husband Robert Devereux, third Earl of Essex, on the grounds of his impotence, and was later accused of murdering Sir Thomas Overbury for his opposition to her remarriage to the Earl of Somerset, Robert Carr. In the trial that followed, Frances found that the pursuit of the annulment suit had 'exposed herself to attack because of the threat her suit offered to male potency', and that by this same action she 'rendered herself vulnerable to another charge. In declaring her husband impotent she was inevitably characterised as expressing a longing for sex', and for having the insatiability of a whore.[86] The prosecution against Frances, as well as husbands who sued their wives for adultery, were supported by a wealth of misogynist literature which portrayed women as creatures of lust. 'Most women have small waists the world throughout', *The Revenger's Tragedy* (1607) taught, 'But their desires are thousand miles about'.[87] A satirical pamphlet published in the 1640s argued that women should have at least two husbands because monogamy left too many wives dissatisfied sexually.[88] Another example is that of Thomas D'Urfey's 1699 collection of ballads which contained a song entitled 'The Wife Hater'. This told the audience that no matter what type of woman a man married, he was sure to be cuckolded. For weaker vessels may,

> Spring leak or split against a rock,
> And when your fame's wrapped in a smock,
> 'Tis easily cast away.[89]

Whores cast male fame away because they had no shame or guilt about the consequences of their actions for their husbands' reputations. Husbands and the witnesses who acted for them in adultery suits in the court of Arches appear to be anxious to show how adulterous wives lacked shame. When Thomas Carter related stories of Elizabeth Northmore's adultery he emphasised that she was 'not abashed' at his entering the kitchen when her lover 'had his hands under [her] clothes so high that he could see her knees'. On another occasion Thomas was in the larder when Elizabeth and her lover were making love in the adjoining kitchen. After sex Thomas related how he saw Elizabeth take her lover's 'yard and rolled it on her knee and wiped it with her shift', and then turning to Thomas 'asked him whether he was going to sup and told him that if he had not there was some victuals in the Cupboard'. That Elizabeth was so openly committing adultery in the kitchen, and was with apparent ease able to turn her attention from sex to the feeding of her household, was intended, we may assume, to show the shamelessness of whoredom.[90] Similarly, Francis Francklin, the cousin of Philip Litchfeild who brought an adultery suit against his wife in 1670, noted the complacency of Elizabeth Litchfeild when she was caught committing adultery. As the wife of an alehouse keeper Francis believed Elizabeth 'with too much willingness' permitted her customers to be 'familiar' with her. One day when Francis visited the house to pay a debt he found Elizabeth upstairs 'with all her coats up', and a bricklayer upon her 'having his breeches down'. When Francis 'blamed her for such her crime' he found that 'she did not in the least deny' the adultery. There was no doubt in Francis's mind that Elizabeth had been caught in the act, but her denial would have represented a sense of ignominy and an unawareness that what she had done was harmful to her own reputation and that of her husband. Instead all she was concerned about was her own safety, asking Francis 'by no means to tell her husband'. Elizabeth's lewd behaviour led her to be reprimanded and labelled as a whore by Francis's friend, Richard Charnock. Richard had never even met Elizabeth's husband, but when he discovered Elizabeth committing adultery in November 1669 he cried 'pox on you for a whore', and went to her and 'gave her a slap with his hand'.[91]

Richard's anger and response to Elizabeth's adultery is set in context when we understand that whores were regarded as dangerous women who were capable of offending many, 'Yet she must die, else she'll betray more men' Othello resolved as he entered Desdemona's chamber.[92] Even though many married women who committed adultery may have had only one lover, and until the eighteenth century the word 'whore' was rarely used to imply prostitute, in the male imagination once a woman had initially transgressed she would repeat the sin over and over again,

> for if a woman
> Fly from one point, from him she makes a husband,
> She spreads and mounts then like arithmetic,
> One, ten, a hundred, a thousand, ten thousand,
> Proves in time sutler to an army royal.[93]

Thus in defamation cases the most frequently chosen adjectives used in conjunction with whore were 'common whore' and 'arrant whore'.[94] When Thomas Somerly tried to persuade Ann Cripps to return to her husband after she had taken to living with one William Cheeseman in 1677, she refused saying she would never renounce her lover. But Thomas declared to Ann that as an adulterous woman he believed that she must have more lovers than just William, for 'she that would be a whore to one would be so to more', an accusation which Ann strongly denied.[95] Ann, and other women who were accused of adultery, had to fight against the weight of popular tradition which labelled them as whores. In the popular imagination whores shared common characteristics of being powerful, insatiable women with no regard for their own honour, or that of others. In the courtroom some cuckolded husbands were able to use these stereotypes to condemn their wives and detract attention away from their part in marriage breakdown.

As a response to male sexual dishonour, the sanctions of secular jurisdiction may have had greater appeal for the lower sorts, who often probably could not afford the costs of suing for separation in the church courts. Adultery was a breach against the peace and as such offenders could be examined by JPs and punished by carting, whipping or imprisonment.[96] These punishments were designed to shame the adulterer and as such some husbands may have viewed them as suited to the offence. Familiarity with these punishments is shown by slanderers who called women 'carted whore'. For example, when Elizabeth Stevenson and Mary Chambers fell arguing in Windlestone, Durham, in 1609, Mary called Elizabeth a 'common carted whore and cried for a whip and a cart for her'.[97] Husbands were willing to take this action against their wives; on St Bartholomew's Day 1661 John Johnson had a JP issue a warrant against his wife Susan and two female servants who were then living at Mile End in London. The justice examined the women about the adulterous behaviour of Susan, and then sent Susan to prison 'where she stayed for two nights and two days'.[98] It is questionable how effective this action was, especially as it must have been seen to some extent as an admission by the husband that he could no longer control his own affairs. When John Johnson sought the aid of the secular authorities, it represented a transferral of control and a resignation of authority which he never regained. After being released from prison Susan refused to return to her husband, she argued for fear of him again sending her to prison.

Angry and suspicious husbands could always threaten to imprison their wives; in 1668 John Ward beat his wife in her kinsman's house in Holborn 'calling her whore and saying he would fetch a constable', and witnesses reported in 1669 that James Whiston of St Andrews, Undershaft, London, would often call his wife whore, 'and threatened to put her in prison', where she would 'starve and rot'.[99] But for a man to actually carry out these threats was probably seen as a sign of weakness indicative of marriage breakdown, and as such was not a response which would have regained honour. That witnesses who acted for the wives of John Ward and James Whiston in their cases for separation on grounds of cruelty chose to tell the courts of the husbands' threats of imprisonment, may show that this behaviour would not have been regarded as manly or honourable.

Unlike women, who were ready to slander their husbands' whores, men very infrequently directed verbal abuse or legal action against their wives' lovers. As will be argued throughout this chapter, it was men's wives rather than their male rivals who were most often the targets of their anger. Thus one case which merits our detailed attention because of its rarity is that in which Thomas Rawdon brought Christopher Dickon to the Durham consistory court in January 1637 for committing adultery with Isabell his wife. Before coming to court Rawdon had already confronted Dickon outside his home at Burdon 'telling him that a whore and a harlot were best together and so threatened to put his wife out of doors with him the said Dickon'. When Dickon had the audacity to declare that Rawdon 'should be welcome to lie of any bed in his house', Rawdon replied that 'if he lay of any of his beds he would not go to make a whore of his wife'. Rawdon saw male infidelity as tolerable as long as it did not threaten another man's property. Furthermore, in Rawdon's eyes it was men who made women whores. This latter argument was developed in the remarks made by the two witnesses who acted for Rawdon, who presented Dickon as the person who deceived and betrayed Rawdon. We are told how Dickon on one occasion sent Rawdon to fetch a horse which was half a mile from Rawdon's home. Dickon 'made show as though he would have gone home to his own house', but once Rawdon was out of sight he turned back to visit Rawdon's wife. Dickon also took the opportunity to cuckold Rawdon in his absence when Rawdon was away in Durham city. One witness, who stood beneath the chamber window after Dickon had gone into Rawdon's house, heard Dickon boast to Isabell 'that he then occupied her better than her husband had done for a year before, as he well durst say'. We cannot know for certain why Rawdon made the unusual decision to take his wife's lover to court. Dickon's arrogance may have made Rawdon realise that 'angry words' would have no effect. But going to court made him a public cuckold, a humiliation which perhaps could only be borne if Dickon was presented as a man who had no respect for other men's property, and thus was a threat, not only to the Rawdon household, but to the wider social order.[100]

As has been shown above, when cuckolds went to the courts, whether it was to fight for separation against their wives, or to prosecute their wives' lovers, their witnesses needed to present their stories in such a way as to point the finger of blame away from the husband. Adulterous wives needed to be proved uncontrollable whores, their lovers agents of familial and social disorder. Given the risk that witnesses' stories would not prove convincing, it is little wonder that many husbands sought other means to restore their honour, and only saw legal redress as a last resort.

Reconciliation

Within early modern society there were many informal mechanisms for reconciliation between parties who had by whatever means damaged reputation. Parish ministers, JPs, local gentry, or other friends of the parties often acted as arbitrators in disputes.[101] Their aim was to reconcile the parties and restore reputation without necessitating legal action. For example, in 1605 Durham consistory court heard how Gregory Hutchinson had a special meeting with Isabelle Moore in St Margaret's church in Durham city. In front of the curate 'and some other of their Neighbours' Gregory begged Isabelle's forgiveness for spreading gossip that she was an adulteress.[102]

In this context pledging could play a useful social role as parties could mark agreement with a drink. Historians of church court records have found evidence of pledging serving this function across the country.[103] The practice can be seen from the defamation case of Peter Forster against Robert Huntley. In June 1606 they had an argument over a game of bowls about some 7d 'in question betwixt them'. This resulted in Robert Huntley calling Peter Forster a 'scurvy pocky knave'. A few months later the two were together at William Mallabar's house in Newcastle for supper. A 'motion', or suggestion, directed towards Robert Huntley and Peter Forster was made by one of those present, 'that the matter in controversy might be ended betwixt them and a kindness made', or expressed in another way by a different witness, 'that the said parties should be friends'. To this, recalled John Chaytor, 'the said Robert did drink to the said Peter and he . . . pledged him'. Peter Forster hesitated before returning the pledge, but eventually at the persuasion of his friends he agreed that 'he would pledge the said Huntley in kindness, but he would not for any entreaty put up those words that the said Huntley had spoken against him, for it stood upon his credit to clear himself thereof'. For Peter Forster that Robert Huntley was willing to pledge him in front of friends was not enough. He felt the need for his 'credit' to be recognised amongst the wider community, and he believed that the only way to do this was by going to court.[104] It appears that as there were degrees of shame to which a man could be subjected, there was a point at which forms of informal settlement such as pledging were no longer regarded as adequate responses.

Our problem is that since there were usually no records made of arbitration or out of court settlements, except when they failed and the dispute came to the courts, we shall probably never know how often men did find informal arbitration a satisfactory remedy to damaged honour. It is similarly difficult to estimate how many husbands reacted as those who heard sexual slander against wives often predicted, and carried out their threats to put their wives 'out of doors'; in other words, did not attempt to continue their marriages once they had been cuckolded. It is probable that the occasion of adultery could provoke marriage breakdown in this way. It may have led some couples to separate informally, or for one partner to desert the other without the sanction of the church courts. Risk of detection and prosecution for this offence was low; Ingram has found that fewer than two cases for unlawful separation per year were recorded in the three main Wiltshire jurisdictions between 1615 and 1629.[105] Details of this response to male dishonour were only recorded when one of the partners later decided formally to separate and bring a marriage separation case to the church courts. When in 1575 Henry Bland, a sailor from King's Lynn, returned from sea to find his wife pregnant, she was 'put away'. It was five years later that Henry brought a separation suit to the courts.[106] Men such as James Leech of Cripplegate, London, quite literally attempted to distance their reputations from those of their adulterous wives. James's wife complained in 1661 that more than seven years previously her husband had refused to let her back into the house when upon 'groundless' suspicion he became convinced that she had been unfaithful. Thomas Middleton's attempts to rid himself of his wife were less successful. He told the court of Arches in 1662 that his wife's persistent adulterous and disobedient behaviour forced him to 'put her out of his house' because he could no longer 'endure the same'. But his wife continued to walk by his door with 'loose and suspicious persons', and so that 'she should not walk abroad to disgrace him', Thomas had to offer her a private room in his house with 'all necessaries fit for her'.[107]

Men who were forced to keep adulterous wives within their households could still disassociate themselves from their wives by refusing any further sexual contact. Once a partner had broken the marriage contract by committing adultery, moralists agreed that the injured spouse no longer owed any conjugal debt to his partner.[108] This belief finds expression in popular literature, for example in Richard Braithwait's *Ar't asleep Husband?*, a collection of 'witty jests' and 'merry Tales'. In one tale when a husband finds his wife committing adultery his response is to 'divorce' her from his bed.[109] There is some evidence that this action was taken in reality. When

Anne Fanne was called whore by Margaret Smith in London, the consistory court heard in 1610 that Anne's husband had been so offended that he refused to let her lie with him. A similar fate awaited Alice Starky when she was called whore by Margaret Slade in the summer of 1666.[110]

It was noted in the previous chapter that one consequence of a wife's adultery could be that a husband was driven into debt. One practical response to this was for the husband to announce that he would no longer be responsible for any debts that his wife might incur. Edmund Clarke divorced his credit from his wife's when he 'caused it to be cried in Winchester and two other places that she was not to be trusted'. Similarly, in 1669 John Milner of St Clement Danes, Middlesex, 'fearing that she might run him into debt', had papers or bills set upon posts in the city of London forbidding any person to trust his wife.[111] All these husbands had been deserted by their wives and their actions sometimes could go a step further when they claimed that their wives had taken household goods and other property with them as they departed. The anger of husbands in these cases must have been at least partly directed at their wives' lovers who, having stolen a marriage partner, could also appear to be benefiting financially from the liaison. Ann Cripps had only been married to John of Shadwell, Middlesex, for seven months when she left him to live with William Cheeseman. John complained to his friend that his wife had 'robbed him of his goods', and, together with a constable, they went to where Ann and William lodged. They told Ann that William 'might be hanged for running away with another man's wife who had broke open her husband's Trunks'. Ann boldly defended her lover and replied that 'he did not steal her, but she stole him, and that she would be hanged rather than he should be hanged'.[112] According to witnesses who spoke for Cecily Bradley in 1663, John Bradley was a violent man who kept suspicious company with a widow Anne Cooke. Despite his own adulterous behaviour, when John beat his wife he would accuse her of being unfaithful. When he was imprisoned in the Tower for suspected treason, Cecily removed some of the goods from their house, arguing that it was to keep them safe. When John was suddenly released, however, he called his wife a 'Barbados whore' and accused her and her friends of stealing his goods. Enraged, he went to a JP who told him 'that he could not commit her upon the account of felony she being his wife'. So John tried another tactic, and persuaded his brother-in-law, Thomas Fenton, to claim that some of the stolen goods were his. Cecily and her friends were brought to the Old Bailey and charged with felony, a charge which could have cost them their lives, but were acquitted when Thomas's story was proved false. John Bradley was unable to produce a single witness to prove that his wife had been unfaithful in the separation case for cruelty which followed. His behaviour appears to have been provoked by hatred and anger, and fuelled by a desire for revenge.[113]

It is likely that some other husbands attempted to reach a financial settlement with their wives' lovers. In Erpingham, Norfolk, in 1614 John Friend's neighbours believed that he must have been 'corrupted with money' to accept his wife's adultery with William Fuller. When a tailor from Lichfield in 1701 found a man in bed with his wife he bargained with his wife's lover for compensation 'for injury he received', starting with a demand for £10, and finally settling for £5.[114] Husbands could also seek monetary compensation in a more formal manner by suing the lover for damages in actions of criminal conversation ('crim. con.') within the common law courts. This new form of legal action was introduced in the late seventeenth century and may have developed from the more informal compensation agreements. Crim. con. actions were only slowly adopted as a course of action for cuckolded husbands; there is only one mention of a case within the statements of parties in the seventeenth-century court of Arches.[115] Lawrence Stone has found only fourteen cases between 1692 and 1730. The reasons why the action for criminal conversation was introduced remain obscure, but Stone's generalised explanation that there was a 'a shift from an honour and shame society to a commercial society' seems unconvincing.[116] As we shall see, violence was to remain a popular response to loss of male honour, whatever innovatory alternatives the law courts were to offer. If the rise of crim. con. actions is evidence of shifting attitudes, then it is certainly only reflective of change amongst the upper sorts. The high cost of bringing these cases restricted this way of responding to dishonour to the wealthy. As with other legal action, bringing a crim. con. case could also expose the cuckolded husband to embarrassing publicity, and this may partly explain why such actions remained relatively rare. Newspapers such as the *London Daily Advertiser* and *The London Times*, as well as the law reports gave details of these cases in the eighteenth century.[117] Yet the financial potential of crim. con. actions is revealed in Alexander Denton's separation case against his wife in 1688, in which witnesses stated that he had successfully won £5,000 in damages from her lover Thomas Smith. How far even large sums of money helped to alleviate feelings of shame and loss, however, remains unclear.[118]

Whilst there is evidence of one-off payments between husbands and their wives' lovers, this response to dishonour was probably not readily or frequently accepted. In a society which laid so much emphasis on men maintaining exclusive sexual ownership of their wives, it seems unlikely that as G.R. Quaife suggests 'many private whores were encouraged by their husbands'.[119] The idea that a man could make a living by accepting regular payments from his wife's whoredom was sufficiently alien to seventeenth-century definitions of honourable manhood that it could be employed as an insult to damage male reputation. Your wife 'hath been a whore from her Cradle', Mary Lawly railed against Edward Clarke in his victualling house in the winter of 1669, and 'you . . . are a pimp', she declared.[120] Popular literature also mocked men who made money in this way. Ballads such as 'The Rich and Flourishing Cuckold well Satisfied' (1675), in which a cuckold so profits from his wife's adultery that he always has rich dinners, a cellar full of wine, fine clothes, and so much gold that it runs out of his horns, were clearly intended to be comical. The idea that a wife should have a trade that maintained her husband, as 'The Merry Cuckold' suggests, represented an inversion of traditional roles that was fit only for laughter. But whilst these ballads may have exaggerated the degree to which cuckolded husbands were able to make a living from their partners' adultery, the fact that many feature husbands accepting money from their wives' lovers may reflect that one-off payments were a feature of lower-class society.[121] Although the exchange of money may have actually helped to settle many village disputes, this did not, of course, prevent ballad writers such as Martin Parker toeing the moral line on the issue. His story of 'The Cooper of Norfolk' told how the cooper gained access to the brewer's silver and gold after he discovered their adultery. The ballad ends, however, with a verse warning other couples against this response to dishonour,

> Let no marry'd couple, that hear this tale told,
> Be of the opinion this couple did hold,
> (To sell reputation for silver or gold)
> For credit and honesty should not be sold.[122]

Violence against Men

Within a culture which associated manhood with physical strength, being able to defend one's honour with one's fists was important.

Refusal to fight could render a man open to mockery and insult. Hugh Porrye 'in most unseemly mann[er]' called William Goodwin 'coward and boy', and 'with a loud voice affirmed that he kept better men . . . to wipe his boots and shoes', when William declined to fight with him in Jacobean London.[123] The alehouse and its immediate environs was a favourite location for righting wrongs with violence. As an important centre for male conviviality, the alehouse offered a public forum for the testing of manhood, and the drink consumed may have made arguments more heated, with blows more likely to result. Thomas Brennan has found that sexual insults directed at men were a common source of trouble in Parisian taverns, and Peter Clark has argued that the English alehouse 'provided an important place for the settling of local conflicts'.[124] The pattern of insult followed by a brawl was a common one; 'about a year ago an attorney of this place gave me ill language in a tavern and I boxed his ears', wrote Samual Carter to Sir George Treby in 1683. 'About a month since the very same man in the very same place gave me much the same vile language', Carter continued, adding that this second insult was followed by more boxing, and with the attorney responding by throwing a bottle at Carter, and Carter then hitting his opponent with some candlesticks.[125] Sharpe has found from his survey of homicide records from the Essex assizes that the combination of a meeting in an alehouse and 'falling out over a bill or a game of cards, or the imagining of a new insult or the remembering of an old one' could be fatal.[126] John Beattie has found similar evidence of men fighting each other after insults in his survey of the Surrey assizes of the late seventeenth century. Boxing matches were regarded as the 'popular duel' and were 'controlled and apparently well-ordered contests that would result in a settlement that both would accept with honor'.[127]

The records of brawls found in the quarter sessions and assizes can, however, be frustrating for the historian because they so rarely tell us what words had been used in the original insult to provoke the fight. However, there are indications that men often found fighting an effective response to insult, presumably because it provided immediate satisfaction, and an opportunity to reassert manhood publicly. It is noticeable from the behaviour of men once a fight had been won, how immediately it was assumed by both parties that their disagreement had been conclusively resolved, and that therefore previous differences should be forgotten. John Spayne and Thomas Bryant met and fought over Judith Symon's hand in marriage at a sluice between Dymchurch and Romney in Kent on

2 May 1598. According to Thomas, 'after which their fighting [he] and Spayne went together to St Mary's-in-the-marsh unto a victualling house there where they drank together and were good friends'.[128] When Thomas Pouncey insulted Richard Paty in an alehouse in Dorchester in 1637 they went outside and fought with their fists, afterwards returning to the alehouse to drink, 'all bloody with fighting'.[129]

The comparatively ordered nature of these fights contrasts with the ballad depictions of frenzied violent attacks of husbands who caught their wives and their lovers *in flagrante delicto*. Some ballads portray husbands threatening to castrate their wives' lovers. 'The Lancashire Cuckold' says he will whip out the 'nutmegs' of the man he finds in his bed unless he is offered sufficient monetary compensation, 'The Country Cuckold' pulls out his knife to deprive his adulterous neighbour of his talent, forcing his victim to plead 'spare the Tools, and take this Money', and one contented cuckold relates to his friends that until his wife's lover provided him with 'rich sparkling wine' he 'liquor'd his hide'.[130] We cannot quantify the extent of this kind of violence in reality, but it certainly occurred. A wife from East Coker, Somerset, confessed that when her husband found her in bed with her lover he 'drew his knife and ran after him to have killed him'.[131] The courts were likely to view this type of violence by husbands sympathetically. When a corkcutter in London in the mid-eighteenth century found his wife and her lover in bed, and killed the man in a rage, the judge convicted him of manslaughter, saying he was to be burnt 'gently' in the hand 'because there could be no greater provocation'.[132] However, as will be shown below, violence of this sort was more likely to be directed at a wife than at her lover.

The ritual of the duel was distinctive among the gentry as a means of defending and restoring honourable manhood. In 1576 the first fencing school was established by Blackfriars and soon a large number of books were published on the art of duelling. Stone notes that the number of duels recorded in newsletters and correspondence rose from five in the 1580s, to thirty-three in the decade from 1610 to 1619.[133] Duels were featured or mentioned in many of the plays performed throughout the period by playwrights from Shakespeare to Vanbrugh.[134] Despite legal condemnation and periodic prosecution against those who engaged in duelling, the practice continued to thrive throughout the seventeenth century. This was a form of violence which was highly ritualised and codified. Insults were formalised into the 'giving of the lie' and were followed by letters of challenge, which often reveal the motivation behind the duels which then ensued. In the seventeenth century Henry Knight of Tythegston, Wales, challenged a rival as a fool and a liar, 'which I am ready to make good as a gentleman ought'.[135] Duels were fought in response to a number of insults, of which a small number included the sexual. Samuel Gibson acted as a witness when Thomas Duffet sued for separation on grounds of adultery in 1676, and revealed that Thomas had fought a duel concerning his wife Lucy with her alleged lover Nicholas Throgmorton.[136] A duel which achieved wider notoriety was that fought between George Villiers, the second Duke of Buckingham, and the Earl of Shrewsbury in 1668. Buckingham had been accused of adultery with the Countess of Shrewsbury, and in the duel which followed he inflicted serious wounds on the Earl, from which he later died.

Criticisms of this type of response to dishonour varied in their sophistication of argument. Samuel Pepys clearly did not regard the Countess of Shrewsbury as a woman worth fighting over. On hearing about the duel he noted with some sarcasm, 'this will make the world think that the King hath good councillors about him, when the Duke of Buckingham, the greatest man about him, is a fellow of no more sobriety than to fight about a whore'.[137] Ballads which told of combats which had occurred emphasised the tragedy of the loss of young noble lives. When two of the King's favourites, Sir James Steward and Sir George Wharton, killed each other in a duel after an argument over a game of cards, a ballad writer concluded his story of events by

> wishing that quarrels all may cease
> And that we still may live in love, in prosperous state, in joy and peace.[138]

Puritan writers saw the duel and the honour code it embraced as in direct conflict with Christian values.[139] The author of *The Office of Christian Parents* (1616) urged his readers to teach their sons 'meekness of spirit' so they did not engage in the 'abhomoninable wickedness' that was duelling. The desire for revenge, which so often provoked duelling, 'hath thrust out reason, and possesseth the rule of the soul', which the author thought 'doth altogether carry away the man, and suffereth him not to be any more a man'. Anger expelled a man's reason so that a duel fought under these circumstances could only serve to diminish rather than enhance claims to manhood.[140]

Many argued that a man should seek satisfaction for injury in the courts; when Sir Francis Bacon was Attorney General he described duelling as an affront to the law which was based on a false code of honour, 'a kind of satanical illusion and apparition of honour'.[141] Speaking in the Star Chamber in 1615 Sir Francis believed that duelling would only decline in popularity once it lost its social exclusivity; 'I should think, my lords, that men of birth and quality will leave the practice when it begins to be vilified, and come so low as to barber-surgeons and butchers, and such base mechanical persons.'[142] But it was because legal remedies were seen as inadequate, illustrated by the limited success of the Earl Marshal's court in the early seventeenth century in attracting business, that men from the social elite continued to respond to dishonour using the sword.[143] As Adam Smith wrote in 1753, 'affronts in company are most atrocious crimes; the trifling sum of five or ten pounds is by no means an adequate compensation for them'.[144] The practice of duelling was to continue well into the eighteenth century, even though it attracted criticism in periodicals such as *The Gentleman's Magazine*, and attention amongst the debating circles of London.[145] As Donna Andrews has explained, it was not until new notions of honourable manhood based on 'reasonableness, Christianity, and commerce' were posited by the middle classes as alternatives to those which had been the basis of aristocratic privilege, that duelling became an outmoded form of male behaviour.[146]

Violence against Women

Rather than fight their male rivals, many men who thought they had been cuckolded instead chose to target their anger against their wives. Usually physically weaker than any real or imagined male rival, women could easily become the victims of this type of male anger. But men showed their anger to their wives in a whole range of different ways, and their violence could range and develop from verbal to physical abuse. As will be argued, however, there was a point at which violence by husbands directed against women did not aid in the restoration of honourable manhood, but instead served to cause further damage and shame.[147]

By degrading their partners by calling them whore, some husbands may have hoped to elevate their own position; it may have been, as Coppélia Kahn has argued, a means for a husband to 'regain a measure of dignity'.[148] For others it may have been a way of 'jumping the gun', of anticipating the worst and labelling your wife as a whore before others did, and so avoiding the accusation of ignorance or being a wittol cuckold. The large number of witnesses who related to the church courts how men called their wives whores shows how readily this insult came to the lips of angry husbands. Ann Fox of Barking, Essex, lived with Rachael and John Norcott in the mid-1650s and often heard John call his wife 'Damn'd Whore and damn'd Jade'; Ann Boteler complained in 1672 that her husband often called her 'vile and base woman and whore'; and Hester Denton of Hillesden, Buckinghamshire, told the court of Arches that she was forced to leave her husband for he would call her 'Bitch and whore, and the like and said [she] . . . might go where she pleased like a whore or a Jade as she was'.[149] Lady Cockwood in Etherege's *She Would if She Could* (1668) lamented that men responded to their own failures in this way: 'This is the usual revenge of such base men as thou art. When they cannot compass their ends, with their venomous tongues to blast the honour of a lady.'[150]

Other husbands threatened to mark their wives as whores. Angry wives who warned that they would slit the noses of their husbands' whores have already been discussed in Chapter 3, and it seems that this was also a punishment that husbands threatened for unfaithful wives. When John Norcott called his wife whore he also said 'he would give her a whore's mark', and after Grace Hubbard left her husband he declared that if he met her again 'he would slit her nose'.[151] In 1669 James Whiston made his intentions quite clear when he said he would give his wife a whore's mark for he 'would put his fingers into his nose and wrest it to show how he would use her'. Some men were even prepared to carry out these threats. Joseph Pattison of the city of Durham said in 1631 that he had seen Robert Peacock 'pull his said wife . . . by her nose till blood gushed out by reason of her absence from her house when he came home'.[152] Why a slit nose had become the symbol of a whore is not entirely clear. As Valentin Groebner has pointed out, using evidence from fifteenth- and early sixteenth-century Nuremberg court records, a cut nose could be a visible symbol for lost female honour, and a mutilated face a fitting punishment for a woman who may have used her appearance to seduce her lover into their betrayal of her husband.[153] In Restoration England, when Humphrey Mildmay of Somerset said he would slit his wife's nose, he said that it would mark her 'for an ugly beast'.[154] So just as with husbands who called their wives whore, slitting a nose could have been regarded as a signal that a husband was no fool for he recognised his wife for what she was and was prepared to take action. Gowing argues that noses were phallic symbols so this revenge was a type of castration.[155] A more probable explanation is that along with the vagina and mouth, the nose was seen as another outlet of the female body which could become polluted with sex and sin. Just as scolds, as we shall see, had their tongues cut and bled, so whores could have their noses cut to cleanse and purify the whole body.[156]

Wives certainly expected that if they were discovered to be unfaithful they would be subject to physical violence by their husbands. When Anne is discovered committing adultery in Heywood's *A Woman Killed with Kindness* (1603) she pleads with her husband,

> mark not my face
> Nor hack me with your sword, but let me go
> Perfect and undeformed to my tomb.[157]

When Abigail Lea became pregnant whilst her husband was away in Virginia she took steps to give birth to the child in secret, for she told her lodger 'that she feared that if it should come to the ears of her husband that she had a child in his absence he would kill her'.[158] When the Earl of Macclesfield endeavoured to see his wife who he believed was sheltering at her sister's house in November 1696, he had to give assurances that even if he found that she was pregnant with another man's child 'no violence, or ill usage should be done to the said Countess'.[159]

From marriage separation suits it appears that suspected wife adultery was a common cause of marital violence. When Christopher Evans returned home to hear rumours that Humfrey Pritchard had been in his wife's bed, witnesses told the London consistory court in 1613 that he pulled her out of bed and kicked her with his feet.[160] Records from the Restoration period tell similar stories. Thomas Middleton admitted in 1662 that he struck his wife, but this was only after she continued to keep lewd company despite his desire and requests for her to do otherwise.[161] In July 1668 Barbara Ward went to visit her kinsman Captain Hinson at his house at St Mary le Savoy, Middlesex. About two weeks later Ward's husband burst angrily into the house, beat her and pulled her handkerchief so tightly round her neck that she feared she would choke to death. As he beat her he called her bitch and whore, and when Captain Hinson's wife later searched for a meaning for this violence she recalled how at Easter time Ward's husband had told her that 'his wife was a whore, and that he was very well satisfied that she was a whore, and that he would have nothing to do with her'.[162] John Charnock argued in 1673 that his wife's 'abuses of him have been such that would have provoked any person' to anger. She openly committed adultery and told her husband that his lack of sexual prowess meant that he deserved such treatment. She continually scolded and brawled at him, dressed in clothes that would 'disgrace' him, and provided inadequate food for him and his guests. In this context John's admission that he once hit her 'over the mouth with the back of his hand without doing her any hurt, nor was there any blood caused thereby' could be presented as a mild response.[163] The merchant Richard Goodall presented the story of his violence to his adulterous wife in a similar way. After forbidding her from keeping 'suspicious' company, he twice found her in bed with different men. When she reviled him after he questioned her behaviour on the first discovery, he gave her 'a little light tap upon her head with his hand which as he believes would not have hurt a child of two years old'. On the second occasion he struck her 'softly upon the head with his slipper'.[164] A final example is that of Edmund Clarke who told the court of Arches in 1676 of the debauched lifestyle of his wife Martha who had driven him into debt by her 'entertainment' of troops in his house, and who had become 'so shameless' that 'she did go hand in hand with some of them into the cathedral church of Winchester'. When finding his plate missing he questioned her and she replied in a 'scornful manner', pushing him away. Given all this provocation Edmund declared that in response he only 'gently pushed his hand, and no more'.[165]

It was not until 1891 that the right of husbands to punish or correct their wives using physical means was finally legally rejected. Until that time, even if husbands killed their adulterous wives they could expect the courts to be lenient, for whilst they would be technically guilty of manslaughter, in practice most courts would have regarded adultery as severe provocation.[166] So why did husbands such as John Charnock, Richard Goodall and Edmund Clarke feel they had to defend their actions when their wives had betrayed them, and why did they describe their correction of their wives to the court as mild, even gentle? If we look at the views expressed in seventeenth-century popular culture and Puritan moral treatises we may find some answers.

The right of husbands to maintain household control by violence was the subject of much contemporary debate and concern. Many writers contested the proverb which taught that 'a woman, a spaniel, and a walnut tree, the more they're beaten the better they be'.[167] In the Martin Parker ballad 'Well met, Neighbour', wife beating is described as behaviour to which only cowardly men resort,

For those that will beat their wives,
They dare not, with swords and staves,
Meet men in the field for their lives.

Whilst manhood may have rested on physical strength, ballads show wife beating as strength which is misdirected. The wife in another ballad by Martin Parker, 'Hold your Hands, Honest Men!', proudly describes the physical agility and strength which her husband can display when wrestling, leaping, running and vaulting. But all is not well because he cannot 'rule his hands', and when angry or drunk he beats her. The message of this ballad is simple,

if you desire to be held men complete,
What ever you do, your wives do not beat.[168]

A man who beats his wife invites social comment, a shameful consequence since the household is meant to be under his sole jurisdiction. In a further ballad written by Martin Parker in the 1630s, a wife is married to 'A He-Devil' who beats her, treats her like a slave, and spends her portion. She describes how,

Heele with his girdle lace my skin,
though all the neighbours blame him.[169]

In both the ballad and the play Alice Arden tells her neighbour Master Greene stories of how her husband has beaten her to win his sympathy and support for her cause against her husband. In the play Alice says that,

When he is at home, then have I froward looks,
Hard words, and blows to mend the match withal.

Greene is 'grieved' that 'so fair a creature should be so abused', and resolves that he will be the man who 'shall set you free from all this discontent'. Similarly, in the ballad version, Alice relates to Greene how her husband,

When he comes home he beats me, sides and head,
That I do wish that one of us were dead,

at which Greene becomes 'incensed' with anger. Alice shows herself to be a 'skilful manipulator of effect', for by playing the part of the abused wife she knows that she can win the support of her neighbours.[170]

Disapproval of wife beating is shown in other plays from across the period. Sparkish in *The Country Wife* (1675) is horrified when he finds the jealous Pinchwife threatening his wife with a sword.[171] Vanbrugh's *The Provoked Wife* (1697) shows that beating is ineffective as a corrective and may even provoke a wife to worse behaviour. When Lady Brute talks to her niece about her husband she says, 'he has used me so barbarously of late that I could almost resolve to play the downright wife – and cuckold him'. Constant considers his chances of adultery with Lady Brute are higher because she is beaten by her husband. After he has seen her beaten by Sir John he declares that,

> a husband is scarce to be borne upon any terms, much less when he fights with his wife. Methinks she should e'en have cuckolded him upon the very spot, to show that after the battle she was master of the field.

Finally, Lady Brute's niece Bellinda makes it quite clear that honourable men do not beat their wives when she announces that, 'if a man has the least spark of either honour or good nature, he can never use a woman ill that loves him and makes his fortune both'.[172]

Wife beating could be viewed as dishonourable because when men were angry they risked losing their control over an important component of their manhood: their reason. When Othello strikes Desdemona after he has been tricked into believing that she has accepted the sexual advances of Cassio, the statesman Lodovico cannot believe his eyes. He asks,

> Is this the noble Moor, whom our full senate
> Call all in all sufficient? This is the noble nature,
> Whom passion could not shake? whose solid virtue
> The shot of accident, nor the dart of chance,
> Could neither graze, nor pierce?

He concludes that Othello has changed from a man who was so in control that 'passion could not shake' to one who may be 'light of brain', whose 'wits' may not be safe.[173]

Many of the conduct book writers who condemned wife beating did so because they believed it led men to lose their reason. One of the first objections that William Heale raised in his tract against wife beating was that since men, unlike other beasts, had reason, they should behave in a manner superior to beasts. He advised husbands that 'wives are to be persuaded by reason, not compelled by authority'. William Gouge instructed husbands never to 'rebuke their wives when they are in a passion'. For passion raised 'a dark mist before the eyes of reason; which, while it remaineth, keepeth reason from giving any good direction'.[174] The author of *The Lawes Resolution of Women's Rights* argued in 1631 that a husband could only exercise 'reasonable correction' of his wife.[175] William Whateley wrote that it was wisdom and prudence, synonyms for reason, which should ensure that a man's authority was 'free from excess, and free from defect'. When men became passionate with anger, Whateley warned, then they forget 'the use of thy reason'. Whateley was unusual amongst conduct book writers, for he believed that a husband could beat his wife, but only when faced with 'the utmost extremities of unwifelike carriage'. In other words, extreme disobedience or defiance could call for extreme measures.[176] Without reason such behaviour could be regarded as madness. In marriage a man and woman became one flesh, so who 'but a frantic, furious, desperate wretch will beat himself' asked Gouge.[177] Henry Smith resolved that 'these mad men which beat themselves should be sent to Bedlam till their madness be gone'.[178] The Homily on marriage, recited in many churches, also taught that a man who beat his wife was like a madman.[179] If a man did beat his wife, the consequence for his honour was made clear by John Dod and Robert Cleaver: 'he which woundeth her, woundeth his own honour'.[180] 'God forbid that! For that is the greatest shame that can be, not so much to her that is beaten, but to him that doth the deed', taught another homily.[181] In 1711 Richard Steele in *The Spectator* condemned wife beating when he wrote: '[C]an there be any thing more base, or serve to sink a Man so much below his own distinguishing Characteristic (I mean Reason)... as that of treating an helpless Creature with Unkindness, who has ... deliver[ed] her Happiness in this World to his Care and Protection?'[182]

Whilst we know from court records that many men did not follow the instructions of Gouge, Smith, Heale, Dod and Cleaver, and Steele to never beat their wives, it is also apparent that there were stages at which a husband's violence would be condemned by other members of the household and the wider community. Discovering the levels or degrees of violence which were acceptable is very difficult given the inevitable variation in toleration levels between couples and within communities. But it is significant that wives were able to bring cruelty cases against their husbands and gather witnesses to support them when they could prove that violence had been in response to wifely behaviour which did not threaten a husband's reputation as a worthy or honourable man. Servants and friends were appalled when husbands responded to relatively minor misdemeanours with severe violence. In the 1660s a witness for Cecily Bradley told the court of Arches how Cecily was beaten when she failed to prepare her husband's dinner on time.[183] A witness for Rachael Norcott told how Rachael's husband had been so dissatisfied with the butter on his pudding that he threw a stool at her with such force that she fell into a swoon.[184] Thomas Stoddard of Eltham, Kent, admitted his wife was chaste, but had provoked him to violence in 1684 because she was a poor cook who allowed 'Lamb and other good victuals' to spoil.[185] Finally, a servant of the Hubbards, who were wigmakers in St Clement Danes, Middlesex, recalled how the couple had two main arguments which led to violence. One of these had been caused when Grace Hubbard had not made her husband's shirts 'as he would have them'. It may have been after this occasion that another witness saw that Grace's mouth and lips had been so badly swollen by the beating that she could not even 'get ale into her mouth'.[186] Witnesses in these cases were not willing to interpret this violence as lawful 'reasonable correction'. For these were not beatings of a kind which restored household order by reminding subordinates of the importance of obedience. Instead, this marital violence was so excessive that it destroyed order, and with it a husband's honour. This violence did not demonstrate a man's control of his wife, but by its unreasonableness his lack of self-control. An honourable man did not maintain household control with unreasoned and excessive violence.

It is within this cultural context that husbands who chose to defend their violence in the church courts found it most expedient to present their behaviour as a response to adultery, an example of extreme wifely disobedience which many would agree required a severe response. If they also argued that they exercised restraint when disciplining their wives, by hitting 'gently', not drawing any blood and so on, husbands could endeavour to show that they had used reason in their use of strength, and avoid any accusations of lack of control or madness.

However, when we turn to look at the statements of witnesses who spoke in cases where husbands presented this type of defence, we find that their words often portray an uneasiness and uncertainty that adultery had taken place, and a fear that the beatings had therefore been unjustified. Thomas Crosfeild spoke for Martha Clarke and denied that she had played the whore with the troops in Winchester, instead arguing that she had always carried herself with 'conjugal respect and obedience to her said husband'. He remembered how after about six months of marriage Edmund Clarke had spoken of his wife and 'commended her . . . and said he believed she was very virtuous'. Instead of deserved beatings in response to adultery, Thomas partly attributed Edmund's violence to drink.[187] Henry Loades, who acted as a witness for Ellen, wife of John Charnock in 1673, said that 'he never heard unless it was from the said John or his brother that the said Ellen was of a loose life'.[188] Witnesses for Rachael Norcott, whose husband often called her whore when he was violent, could find no reason why he should have thought his wife unfaithful. One male witness wondered how Rachael could bear her husband's cruelty with such patience, she 'never giving him any occasion for such madness or distraction she being most obedient'.[189]

The madness which this witness described was that associated with jealousy. One of the reasons why Heale thought the courts rather than husbands should deal with a wife's adultery was because the law could recognise 'the jealousy of husbands touching their wives' incontinence', and distinguish 'actual proof' from 'the brain-sick fancies of their fond husbands'.[190] Those who witnessed husbands beating their wives were also anxious to make this distinction, and to establish that beatings had a cause, and were not just triggered by jealous imagination. Frequently witnesses depose that they asked the husband the reason for their violence. Sarah Dobson asked Rachael's husband, John Norcott, 'why he abused his wife'; Edward Trussell asked John Hooper in June 1673 'whether he was not ashamed to use his said wife as it appeared he had'; and when one witness questioned John Bradley about why he beat his wife, he later recalled that John did not offer any reason but 'laughed and did not deny the said cruelty'.[191] Witnesses questioned the motives behind Sir Oliver Boteler's cruelty to his wife, one asking him 'why he used his lady so ill, when . . . she loved him so dearly', another asking why he was violent when she was known to be virtuous. It is noticeable that social status did not deter witnesses to domestic violence asking questions; both of the latter witnesses were servants in the Boteler household.[192] Finally, it is important to remember that those wives who brought cruelty suits against their husbands were all seeking to establish recognition that, as Desdemona says as she is beaten, 'I have not deserv'd this.'[193]

When witnesses could see no reason for wife beating and were convinced that a wife was virtuous, they were ready to label the husband's actions as dishonourable. Several witnesses who saw Robert Peacock thrust his pregnant wife out into the street in Durham city after he had beaten her 'told him it was a shame for him to abuse his wife after that manner'.[194] When Richard Greene of Downton, Wiltshire, continued to abuse his wife in 1623, 'all the street cried shame at him'.[195] Some took more active steps to help or rescue the wife. This was even at the risk of also becoming subject to violence, for example Ann Pease was a neighbour to John and Cecily Bradley in Haymarket, and several times went upstairs 'to pacify the said John' when he was beating his wife, 'who hath sometimes struck her for her pains'. When John started to strip his wife of her clothes in an alehouse because he claimed she had been a whore, the wider community became involved. Customers gathered around and some cried 'shame upon him', so that John was forced to 'run away as fast as he could run, and many after him, crying stop him he hath killed his wife'. When Ellenor Younger's husband beat her on the belly when she was pregnant, and called her whore in the streets of Cheapside in 1670, her neighbours came out of their shops and sent for constables.[196]

Occasionally action was taken to exclude a known wife-beater from 'honourable' male company. The elders of Broadmead Baptist church in Bristol reproved Thomas Jacob for his mistreatment of his wife and other ill behaviour. When they learnt in March 1678 that he had been 'very much in Drink, and very rude, fighting in the street, and that he had given his wife some blows', they expelled him from their congregation.[197] Other witnesses to marital violence went as far as to declare that a husband's very claim to manhood was jeopardised by his violence. Edward Trussell of St Martin-in-the-Fields claimed in 1673 that Elizabeth Hooper was 'commonly pitied by her Neighbours and persons of quality for her sufferings and the unmanly Actions wherewith . . . the said John [her husband] hath treated her'.[198] Humphrey Mildmay of Queen Camel, Somerset, defended himself in court in 1672 by denying that he had ever struck his wife, saying he did 'account it a very unmanly unworthy thing for any gentleman so to do'. One of Humphrey's servants supported his master by claiming that he had never seen Humphrey behave in any 'unmanly' way towards his wife.[199] Elizabeth Spinkes brought a cruelty case against her husband to the London consistory court between the years 1711 and 1713. It was claimed during the case that Elizabeth had attempted to 'scandalise [her husband's] good name and reputation', by telling others of how he beat her. It was clearly thought that the good name of a man could be damaged if he was known as a wife-beater.[200]

A remarkable expression of public disapproval against wife beating occurred in Bristol in 1667. One witness stated that the cruelty of William Bullocke against his wife was so notorious that it was of common report in Bristol and Bath 'and many miles about'. His treatment of Posthuma, his wife, was thought to be 'cruel and inhumane' so that he was 'much cried shame of'. He was so hated that he was forced to employ a constable 'to guard him from the fury of the people and especially the women who knew him to be a base fellow and his said wife to be a good and virtuous Gentlewoman'. Few dared to be seen with William, and men boasted that even if they were paid £40 they would not 'walk the streets with him'. Posthuma took up separate lodgings from her husband, no doubt for her own safety. But anger with William erupted in February 1667 when he decided to walk through Bristol to the house where his wife was living and attempt a reconciliation. A crowd of people gathered around William and followed him, calling him 'base names telling him his wife was too good for him'. They showed their disapproval by throwing dirt at him, and appeared so menacing that William was forced to take shelter in a house 'to avoid the fury of the people'.[201] William Bullocke's behaviour towards his wife led him to be socially ostracised from his community, and to become the victim of a loud mocking demonstration characteristic of charivari. E.P. Thompson found that it was not until the nineteenth century that the majority of charivaris were triggered by wife-beaters rather than husband-beaters, so the action against William was probably unusual in this period.[202] But the anger of Bullocke's local community was fuelled by the fact that Posthuma was a 'good and virtuous Gentlewoman' who did not deserve such vicious treatment from her husband, who was a 'base fellow' and a 'rogue'.

Much of this book has shown that in this period marrying, and subsequently maintaining exclusive sexual control of a woman, could hold great importance for a man's personal sense of worth as well as his social prestige. But it is suggested here that in their anxiety to be seen to be in control, some men became overly jealous, suspicious and hasty in calling their wives whore. The danger was that some men then treated their wives as whores, threatening or actually subjecting them to verbal, physical or sexual violence.[203] A case study of the Boteler marriage shows how the codes of ideal manhood in the early modern period could engender domestic violence. Ann Boteler brought a suit for separation to the court of Arches in 1672. Over sixteen years of marriage, according to Ann and the twenty-two witnesses who spoke for her, Oliver had repeatedly called her whore and other abusive names, beaten her and threatened to 'beat out' her brains, thrown chamber pots and a chair at her, kicked her out of the house in the middle of the night, boasted of his sexual inconstancy and infected her with the pox. He was alleged to have whipped and beaten three of their children in front of her, dangling the eight-year-old Elizabeth over three flights of stairs, threatening to drop her if anybody interfered with him. In his need to control his wife Oliver demanded from her total obedience, and he tested and inflated his sense of authority by commanding Ann to perform demeaning and nonsensical tasks. When he went to bed he commanded her to stand by his bed and watch over him all night, even though on one occasion she was pregnant and was only permitted to wear a smock. On another occasion one witness recalled how Oliver 'made her kneel down by his bedside' and 'forced her to bow and incline herself with her face to the floor', telling her 'I will have or will make you as submissive as my spaniel'. He tried to force her to drink a glass of wine when she abstained from alcohol, and made her take off her shoes and stockings even when there were servants in the room, saying that she was 'not worthy to wipe his shoes'. His insistence on obedience even extended to his attempt to force her to yield sexually to him in front of the servants, pulling her clothes off, and then beating her when she refused to oblige him. His violent anger could break out whenever he became suspicious that his wife was disobedient, and could be triggered by his irritation at minute details of her behaviour. On one occasion he became angry and violent when he saw her wear a hood and handkerchief around her neck, saying that he had forbidden her to wear the same, pulling them off her and throwing them into the fire.[204]

Sir Oliver's behaviour was exceptional in its scale and brutality. The combined physical, sexual and mental cruelty which Lady Ann suffered, and Sir Oliver's abuse of both his wife and children, was relatively unusual in this period. It is impossible to accept Stone's assertion that there is 'nothing uncommon about the cruelty' in this case.[205] What the case provides for us is an example of the extremes to which patriarchal power could be taken, and the lengths to which some men would go to gain control over their wives. Servants and neighbours could continue to condemn the violent behaviour of men such as Sir Oliver, or even label it as madness; one servant described how he had 'fantastic fits' before beating Lady Ann, another witness said Sir Oliver was 'like a mad man' who frightened his wife and servants when he was in a rage.[206] But whilst honourable manhood depended so heavily on the sexual control of women, incidents of unwarranted violence against wives would reoccur. Sir Oliver took his theoretical rights to their most extreme conclusion. In this sense, he was a product, albeit a dysfunctional one, of his age.

Taming the Scold

In popular thinking a woman who was an adulteress was also likely to be a scold. The community response to scolds by ducking or cucking has already been discussed in Chapters 3 and 4, but within ballad literature there were also a number of stories which gave husbands clues as to how to regain control and restore reputation without requiring outside intervention. One category of these cures for scolds advised husbands of ways that they could deprive their wives of their power and force them once more to be reliant on their husbands' good will. The husband in 'My Wife will be my Master' realises that his wife has become a scold because she controls the household budget, so he vows that if he is ever a widower and decides to remarry, 'I mean to keep her poor and the purse I mean to carry.'[207] When a ploughman marries and his scolding wife refuses to help him by working, he finds 'An Easy Way to tame a Shrew' by giving her nothing to eat until she starts earning her keep by spinning. This 'taming a Shrew by gentle means' is similar to the way that Petruchio tames Kate by depriving her of food and sleep in Shakespeare's *The Taming of the Shrew* (*c.*1591).[208]

A far more severe approach was suggested by John Taylor in his *Divers Crab-tree Lectures* (1639), in which one husband says he tamed his wife with violence, sleep-deprivation, hard work and a diet of bread and water.[209] Some ballads tell similarly violent tales. One man threatens to tie up his wife's tongue to make her wish that she had 'never used it, / With such ill-be-fitting terms and so abusing it.' His threatened punishment closely resembles the official punishment of the scold's bridle.[210] A doctor in 'A Caution for Scolds' ties the scolding wife to a bed and shaves her head, letting her blood. He tells her that he will then,

> cut her tongue, and when a gallon you have bled,
> 'Twill cure that violent noise in your head.[211]

The idea of bleeding the scold may have been drawn from popular medical opinion at this time, which held that such methods could restore the crucial balance of body fluids or humours. The practice of actually bleeding the offending organ also has parallels with that used by contemporaries to put a stop to the harmful activities of witches. Just as it was believed that if a witch was scratched or bled she would lose her magical powers, so it follows that if a wife lost blood from her tongue she could lose her ability to scold.[212] The doctor in 'A Caution for Scolds' succeeds, we are told, because he exercises 'sharp usage' and keeps her 'low'. This approach of demeaning and humiliating the scold is also practised in the Restoration ballad 'The Scolding Wife'. The husband and his friends in this ballad make the wife look as if she had been born in Bedlam by tying and wringing her arms until they bleed, tearing her clothes, and fastening an iron chain around one of her legs. He humiliates her in public as she has humiliated him by dragging her through the streets, crying for all his neighbours to see how she has gone mad and is now utterly dependent upon him. In another ballad of the same title dated 1689, a husband blinds his wife with mercury and leads her through the streets with a dog and bell to achieve the same effect.[213]

The stories told in these ballads were designed to be sensationalist and shocking, as well as blatantly misogynist. There was clearly a market for stories about men who gained total control by inflicting violence on women. The power of the ideas and ideals of male domination over women in this society was such that it could shape the male imaginary world. But the stories of the ballads described above were ones which pandered to fantasies of male deviance. For their advocation of violence in marriage goes against the grain of the mass of seventeenth-century discourses which condemned such behaviour. Men may have fantasised about gaining domination in this way, but in reality it was widely acknowledged that such methods were unacceptable, and could jeopardise rather than gain claims to reputable manhood. Popular theories about how to tame scolds which shared similarities with the stories of ballads certainly circulated in this society. Gowing has found an excellent example of this in her study of the London church courts. Thomas Rogers told the consistory court in 1613 that he once 'had heard of a man that had a wife given much to talking and he persuaded her to be let blood in the tongue and thereby made her to talk more mildly', so that the next time Rogers's wife took to scolding him, he 'willed her to hold her peace and said that if she would not he would pull out her tongue'.[214] There is also some evidence that some husbands threatened, or actually did commit their wives to Bedlam or some other madhouse in an attempt to 'cure' them of their disobedience.[215] But there is nothing to suggest that the degree of violence described in the ballads – blinding, wringing of limbs or worse – would have been tolerated in reality.

Good sex was an alternative cure for scolds proffered by the ballads. 'Simple Simon' was so desperate with misery at his scolding wife that he even tried to poison himself. His wife's scolding only ceased when he managed to 'please' his wife in bed. Simon's neighbours knew that he achieved this aim when after one night he so 'well pleased his Wife' that 'ever since that time he / hath liv'd a quiet Life'.[216] This was a cure that struck at the root of the cause of scolding, for it was popularly believed that if a man could gain sexual control over his wife all other obedience would follow. This was recognised by the unfortunate 'Henpeckt Cuckold' who warns other men to establish sexual control from the start of a marriage,

> Let him that a Widow woes, or courts a Maid to his Froe,
> Take her down in her Wedding-Shoes: Else 'tis a Word and a Blow.[217]

Contented and Wittol Cuckolds

In many popular ballads of the seventeenth century men decide not to respond to their wives' infidelity, but instead accept their fate and join with other cuckolded men for good fellowship and a 'contented' life. In 'The Catalogue of Contented Cuckolds' 'ten honest tradesmen' meet in a tavern and exchange stories of how they were made cuckolds. They resolve to be contented, 'and never repine', and some even make money out of their wives' whoredom. In 'Household Talk' one friend tells the other that he should not be afraid of being cuckolded since 'a cuckold is a good man's fellow'. These men banish all jealous thoughts, so instead of their horns causing them pain and suffering, theirs are called 'Bull's Feathers', which are worn with pride at meetings in the Bull-Feather Hall. They laugh at 'that which so much troubles others', and share jokes about the impossibility of controlling women's desires. Women's insatiability, a doctor tells his friends, has meant that ever since Eve men have been unable to dominate: 'the best of us all / Cannot be our wives' keepers, they are subject to fall'.[218] Whilst sexual jealousy causes rivalry and competitiveness between men, these ballads argue that as cuckolds are from all trades they should join together as 'good fellows'.[219] 'The Glory of all Cuckolds' urges cuckolds to unite for,

> Diana was a Virgin pure,
> Among the rest Chaste and Demure,
> But you know well that I am sure,
> What Acteon did endure.
> If Men have Horns from such as she,
> I pray then let us all agree.[220]

'The Merry Cuckold' teaches others to,

> Learn, as I do, to bear with your wives;
> All you that do so, shall live merry lives.[221]

Given the value attached to keeping wives constant, the idea that in reality men would have happily admitted to their friends that they were cuckolds is ludicrous. What was more likely was that some husbands who did know they were being cuckolded took no action, hoping their shame would never be known by their neighbours, and that their wives would eventually tire of their lovers. 'The London Cuckold' realises that

> Prating like a Fool is fulsome, silence cures the horned pate.
> Should I blow my trumpet out, I should raise the Rabble rout,
> Have the boys about my ears, and endure their flouts and jeers.

Another husband hopes that his wife will be discreet when she commits adultery, for he would not 'care greatly' if his neighbours 'knew it not'.[222] One ballad advises that if husbands do 'cast off' their care and show patience, their wives will leave their vices and lead a new life.[223] Such patience will have its rewards, a mother promises her son-in-law in 'The Discontented Married Man', for in time his wife's beauty will wear off and her gallants will abandon her.[224] A similar message of patience was the subject of one jest in Braithwait's *Ar't asleep Husband?*, in which a wife tells her husband,

> 'For your horns, Sir, it is far better for you to shroud them, than to blow them: Cover these, and my continence of life hereafter shall amply redeem my honor.' With which promise, Her Husband (good man) became so well contented, as his patience begot in his wife a love to goodness: So as, the comic conclusion of their life closed with much happiness.[225]

The Elizabethan musician Thomas Whythorne wrote in his autobiography that husbands who discovered their wives' infidelity should 'tell her what is said of her, and thereupon to persuade her and to counsel her to a better life . . . so peradventure, she will ever after beware of her fault, or else she will work so closely therein, as it shall not be so much seen'.[226] If a husband followed Whythorne's advice, although after his wife's adultery he might lose his self-respect, he did not risk losing his sexual reputation in the eyes of others.

But if discovered, a contented or quietly patient husband could be mocked and insulted. 'Go, you cuckold, go . . . your horns hang in your light, [that] you cannot see', cried William Beaver to Thomas East in the autumn of 1669, suggesting that Thomas's previous lethargy and apparent contentment at his cuckolded status had allowed his horns to grow so big that he could no longer see how his wife was continuing to cuckold him.[227] 'There goes a contented cuckold', said Elizabeth Cooper as she pointed to Christopher Beaumont in a street near the waterside in Queenhithe, London. According to Elizabeth, Christopher's lack of response to his wife's adultery was also leading to the growth of troublesome horns. Elizabeth had asked Christopher's wife 'where is that contented cuckold your husband . . . he must have a care how he goes to Brainford again, for if he goes to Brainford again he will have a pair of horns so big that he will hardly come in at the high gate'.[228] On other occasions these contented cuckolds could also be subject to the more specific insult of 'wittol'.[229] As Whythorne explained, 'if he be known to know that his wife is a strumpet, and yet doth keep her still, he shall be reputed to be not only a cuckold but also a witwold'.[230] These men were mocked for their stupidity and lack of jealousy in the face of dishonour, 'they believe so well, that they make it an ill conscience to mistrust any ill though they see an other and their wife in bed together'.[231]

Church court records show that wittol was an insult directed against these men; in 1628 in Semington, Wiltshire, Walter Longe declared to William Burges, 'thou art a wittol and canst not pull on a hose of thy head for the bigness . . . of thy horns'.[232] In the same year, Elizabeth Mobbs in Bishopsgate, London, cried to her neighbour, 'get thee in, thou wittol, thou cuckold, and put on thy horns', blowing a horn to attract others to the scene.[233] Just the prospect of being called wittol fills Ford with horror in *The Merry Wives of Windsor* (1597), 'cuckold? Wittol? Cuckold! The devil himself hath / not such a name.' Because Ford does not want to be a wittol, 'a secure ass' who 'will not be jealous', he embarks on elaborate schemes to catch his wife in adultery.[234]

Men were expected to respond when their manliness was questioned by their wives' behaviour, for failure to do so opened them to the further dishonour of being labelled wittols. Gaining honour required a man actively to assert and demonstrate his manhood, so it was assumed that cuckoldry could only be the result of inactivity or passivity. Faced with a wife who was thought to be adulterous, there were a wide range of different actions which husbands could pursue both within the law courts and outside them to restore their reputation. But judging from the relatively small numbers of men who took their marriage business to the church and secular courts, the legal courses of action do not appear to have been popular. By seeking marital separation, pursuing crim. con. actions, or by presenting their wives to JPs for breaching the peace, men were allowing others to take over the reigns of household government. In contrast, by allowing their wives to fight sexual defamation suits, and by pursuing the alternatives to law – seeking informal reconciliation, financial settlement or by directing physical force against male rivals or adulterous wives – men could remain in control of household affairs. Each of these latter options gave husbands the opportunity to send clear messages to the wider community and their wives that they were capable of responding immediately and decisively to any slur on their manhood. Our sources to do not allow us to quantify the number of men who responded to dishonour in these different ways. But whilst the extra-legal options were not dependent on financial means (save duelling which remained an activity confined to the social elite), it is clear that their employment did not always lead to a straightforward restoration of honourable manhood. Honourable manhood depended on the opinions of others, and neighbourhood consensus that the choice and level of a man's response to dishonour was appropriate in relation to the damage he had suffered was vital.

Notes

1. R. Kelso, *Doctrine for the Lady of the Renaissance* (Urbana IL, 1956), p. 24; B. Rich, *The Excellency of Good Women* (London, 1613), pp. 15–16; M. Ingram, *Church Courts, Sex and Marriage in England, 1570–1640* (Cambridge, 1987), p. 165.

2. As cited in C. Herrup, '"To pluck bright honour from the pale-faced moon": gender and honour in the Castlehaven story' *TRHS* Sixth Series, VI (1996), p. 155, for the fate of the Countess of Castlehaven after her sexual honour had been questioned in the public arena of a courtroom see also pp. 155–8.

3. Ingram, *Church Courts*, p. 253; A. Fletcher, 'The Protestant idea of marriage', in A. Fletcher and P. Roberts, eds, *Religion, Culture and Society in Early Modern Britain: Essays in Honour of Patrick Collinson* (Cambridge, 1994), p. 171; K.M. Davies, 'Continuity and change in literary advice on marriage', in R.B. Outhwaite, ed., *Marriage and Society* (London, 1981), p. 61; L. Jardine, *Still Harping on Daughters: Women and Drama in the Age of Shakespeare* (London, 1983), pp. 182–93.

4. Ingram, *Church Courts*, p. 301; S.D. Amussen, *An Ordered Society: Gender and Class in Early Modern England* (Oxford, 1988), pp. 101–3; J.A. Sharpe, *Defamation and Sexual Slander in Early Modern England: The Church Courts at York*, Borthwick Papers 58 (York, 1980), pp. 15, 27–8; and L. Gowing, *Domestic Dangers: Women, Words, and Sex in Early Modern London* (Oxford, 1996), pp. 32–5.

5. See, for example, DDR.V.10A. f. 155v; DDR.V.11. f. 362; DDR.V.8. f. 188; and CA, Case 5138 (1668), Eee3, ff. 249r–250v, 475r–476r, 498v–499v; Amussen, *An Ordered Society*, p. 103.

6. P. Morris in her studies of Somerset church court records also found that the marital status of female plaintiffs was not always recorded, see 'Defamation and sexual reputation in Somerset, 1733–1850' (unpublished Ph.D. thesis, Warwick University, 1985), p. 282.

7. Ingram, *Church Courts*, p. 302; Gowing, *Domestic Dangers*, p. 61; and Sharpe, *Defamation*, p. 27.

8. Ingram, *Church Courts*, pp. 315–16; Sharpe, *Defamation*, pp. 22–3; Gowing, *Domestic Dangers*, pp. 22, 117–19; for examples from the Durham church courts of defamation cases which arose from these types of disputes see DDR.V.8. ff. 122v, 123; DDR.V.9. f. 165v; and DDR.V.10A. f. 88.

9. DDR.V.10B. ff. 372v, 373; Anthony and his wife brought separate suits against Mary Dobson.

10. DDR.V.11. ff. 238v, 239r.

11. DDR.V.11. f. 116.

12. Ingram, *Church Courts*, p. 256.

13. DDR.V.11. ff. 68, 100; CA, Case 2710 (1664), Eee1, ff. 500r–503v, 510, 644r–647r.

14. DDR.Box, no. 414, (1633–34), *Alice Coleman* v. *Amor Patterson.*

15. DDR.Box, no. 414, (1636–37), *Isabell Chapman* v. *Roger Harper.*

16. DDR.V.11. f. 66–67r.

17. DDR.V.11. ff. 425v, 426, 427; for other suits between the Craggs and the Simpsons which followed see DDR.V.11. ff. 435–438r, 446v–447r.

18. CA, Case 598 (1664), Eee1, ff. 68v–71r; for other similar examples see CA, Case 6513 (1668), Eee2, ff. 715r–717r, Eee3, ff. 144v–147r; and CA, Case 4706 (1674), Eee5, ff. 138r–140v.

19. DDR.V.8. f. 5r; for other examples of men confronting the women who they believe to be spreading gossip about themselves or their wives see CA, Case 5422 (1666), Eee2, ff. 80r–84r; CA, Case 5907 (1672), Eee4, ff. 697v–701r.

20. DDR.V.10B. f. 261; DDR.V.11. ff. 162, 170; DDR.V.12. ff. 163v, 164r.

21. See, for example, DDR.V.9. f. 234; DDR.V.10A. ff. 65v, 66a, 67r; DDR.V.11. ff. 57v, 58; DDR.V.11. ff. 66, 67r; DDR.V.12. ff. 72v, 73r, 75; and CA, Case 2710 (1664), Eee1, ff. 500r–510v, 644r–647r.

22. DDR.V.12. ff. 87v, 88, 89r.

23. CA, Case 8986 (1676), Eee6, ff. 44v–48r; for other examples of the slander of whore being directed to the wife's husband see CA, Case 4768 (1667), Eee2, ff. 540v–541r; and CA, Case 5145 (1678), Eee6, ff. 306r–307r.

24. DDR.V.9. ff. 174, 190; bedliner was probably an insult derived from Bedlam and was used to indicate madness; barsot is presumably a derivation of sot to mean drunk.

25. CA, Case 3788 (1664), Eee1, ff. 291r–294v; CA, Case 9126 (1664), Eee1, ff. 295r–299r.

26. CA, Case 3463 (1672), Eee4, ff. 637r–644r.

27. DDR.V.8. f. 77v.

28. DDR.V.10B. ff. 440, 441r, DDR.V.11. ff. 50r, 80, 81r, 89; in volume 11 from f. 80 Agnes is spelt as Ann.

29. DDR.V.9. f. 47; a curr is another word for a dog, OED.

30. CA, Case 8684 (1666), Eee2, f. 218v.

31. CA, Case 207 (1675), Eee5, f. 586v; CA, Case 9873 (1665), Eee1, ff. 778v–779v; for temporary desertion by a husband see also CA, Case 10179 (1674), Eee5, f. 163r.

32. CA, Case 6590 (1670), Eee4, f. 89.

33. CA, Case 1877 (1674), Eee5, f. 304r; CA, Case 5206 (1675), Eee5, f. 464v.

34. CA, Case 7622 (1667), Eee2, ff. 437–440r.

35. CA, Case 7727 (1668), Eee2, ff. 808v–811r.

36. DDR.V.11. f. 207v–208r.

37. CA, Case 5417 (1665); CA, Case 3227 (1669); CA, Case 2979 (1670).

38. DDR.V.8. f. 79v; DDR.V.9. f. 11r; DDR.V.11. f. 58.

39. CA, Case 3605 (1677), Eee6, ff. 145r–146v, 155r–156v, 166r–172v.

40. T. Meldrum. 'A women's court in London: defamation at the Bishop of London's consistory court, 1700–1745' *London Journal* 19, 1 (1994), p. 10; Morris, 'Defamation', p. 284.

41. CA, Case 3605 (1677), Eee6, f. 156v.

42. DDR. vol. XVIII/2 'Statutes of the Consistory Court of the Bishop of Durham, 1573'; Ingram, *Church Courts*, p. 58; R.A. Marchant, *The Church Under the Law: Justice, Administration and Discipline in the Diocese of York 1560–1640* (Cambridge, 1969), p. 145.

43. For estimates of the wages of common labourers in county Durham in the 1670s see D. Levine and K. Wrightson, *The Making of an Industrial Society: Whickham 1560–1765* (Oxford, 1991), p. 188; Levine and Wrightson note on pp. 187–8 that the wages of miners, agricultural workers and wage-workers of Newcastle and the surrounding area for earlier in the century are 'matters almost entirely hidden from us in the available sources'.

44. DDR. vol. XVIII/2; for comparison with the fees charged by the Norwich consistory court in the early seventeenth century see Marchant, *The Church Under the Law*, pp. 18–19.

45. Ingram, *Church Courts*, p. 57; R. Houlbrooke, *Church Courts and the People During the English Reformation* (Oxford, 1979), pp. 50–1.

46. Marchant, *The Church*, pp. 141–6; Ingram, *Church Courts*, pp. 55–8; Meldrum, 'A women's court', p. 3.

47. Chap. Consist.P.Box 1 'The Fees due in the Consistory Court at Durham'.

48. C. Hill, *Society and Puritanism in Pre-Revolutionary England* (London, 1964), pp. 307–9; Marchant, *The Church Under the Law*, p. 235; M. Ingram, 'Puritans and the church courts, 1560–1640', in C. Durston and J. Eales, eds, *The Culture of English Puritanism, 1560–1700* (London, 1996), p. 63.

49. Ingram, *Church Courts*, p. 55; R. Wunderli, *London Church Courts and Society* (Cambridge MA, 1981), p. 54.

50. Gowing, *Domestic Dangers*, pp. 48, 136; J.A. Sharpe, '"Such disagreement betwyx neighbours": litigation and human relations in early modern England', in J. Bossy, ed., *Disputes and Settlements: Law and Human Relations in the West* (Cambridge, 1983), p. 173.

51. CA, Case 9913 (1668), J1/3; CA, Case 2979 (1670), J1/10,12; CA, Case 4349 (1691), J3/9; CA, Case 2452 (1692), J2/36; CA, Case 1921 (1696), J4/31,34.

52. E.A. Wrigley and R.S. Schofield comment upon these figures in *The Population History of England 1541–1871: A Reconstruction* (Cambridge, 1989), pp. 638–41.

53. A.L. Erickson, *Women and Property in Early Modern England* (London, 1993), especially pp. 3–6, 24–6, 100–3, 225–7.

54. DDR.Box, no. 414, (1633–34), *Cecilie Smith* v. *Elinor Rawlyn*; Rawlyn is also spelt Rawlinge.

55. Chichester consistory court, depositions, Ep. 1/11/10, ff. 108–109v, 119; Ep. 1/11/10, ff. 105v–6; Ep. 1/11/9, ff. 257–8; for further examples in this court of

witnesses who said that they came at the request and charge of the husband of the female plaintiff, see Ep. 1/11/9, ff. 156–7; Ep. 1/11/9, ff. 219–21; and Ep. 1/11/10, f. 169v; I am very grateful to Bernard Capp for all these references.

56. CA, Case 950 (1691), Eee7, f. 294.

57. CA, Case 5892 (1667), Eee3, ff. 111v–127r; for another case in which a husband says that he came at the request of the plaintiff's husband see CA, Case 173 (1674), Eee5, f. 159r.

58. CA, Case 7233 (1677), Eee6, ff. 202r–205r.

59. CA, Case 6040 (1665), Eee1, ff. 648r–649v; the italics are my own.

60. Morris, 'Defamation', p. 305.

61. R. Burn, *Ecclesiastical Law* (London, 1763), vol. I, p. 483.

62. Sharpe, '"Such disagreement"', p. 178; Gowing, *Domestic Dangers*, pp. 33–7, 117–19, 133–7, 263–4.

63. L. Gowing, 'Language, power and the law: women's sexual slander litigation in early modern London', in Kermode and Walker, eds, *Women, Crime and the Courts*, p. 40; hence for reasons of modesty the Countess of Castlehaven during the trial of her husband did not give her version of events in the public courtroom, see Herrup, '"To pluck bright honour"', pp. 142, 152; and Frances Howard, who challenged the notion of female silence, found herself open to public censure, see D. Lindley, *The Trials of Frances Howard: Fact and Fiction at the Court of King James* (London, 1993), especially pp. 89, 93, 115.

64. D. Purkiss, 'Women's stories of witchcraft in early modern England: the house, the body, the child' *GH* 7 (1995), pp. 408–9; see also L. Roper, *Oedipus and the Devil: Witchcraft, Sexuality and Religion in Early Modern Europe* (London, 1994), p. 53.

65. CA, Case 6513 (1668), Eee2, ff. 715–717r, Eee3, ff. 144v–147r.

66. CA, Case 8350 (1673), Ee4, ff. 299–303r.

67. P. Van Sommers, *Jealousy* (London, 1988), pp. 80, 86.

68. T.H. Gent, *The Generall History of Women* (London, 1657), p. 248; J. Gailhard, *The Compleat Gentleman* (London, 1678), p. 127.

69. As cited in L. Stone, *Road to Divorce: England 1530–1987* (Oxford, 1990), p. 186.

70. Stone, *Road to Divorce*, pp. 187–90.

71. Anon, *The Lively Character of a Contented and Discontented Cuckold* (London, 1700), p. 2.

72. J. Vanbrugh, *The Provoked Wife* (1697), ed. J.L. Smith (London, 1993), III.i.103–6; see also G.S. Alleman, *Matrimonial Law and the Materials of Restoration Comedy* (Philadelphia PA, 1942), pp. 115–23.

73. Stone, *Road to Divorce*, pp. 4–5.

74. Francis Osborne was another example of a writer who complained bitterly that English law was composed too far 'in favour of wives', even when they were adulterous and bore illegitimate children, see his *Advice to a Son* (1656) in L.B. Wright, ed., *Advice to a Son: Precepts of Lord Burghley, Sir Walter Raleigh, and Francis Osborne* (Ithaca NY, 1962), p. 65.

75. CA, Case 2391 (1667), Eee2, f. 297r; I have found nothing to suggest that the court of Arches had the power to imprison a husband who did not pay alimony.

76. CA, Case 4163 (1669), Eee4, f. 79r.

77. CA, Case 1128 (1675), Eee5, f. 663v.

78. Ingram, *Church Courts*, pp. 181–2; Gowing, *Domestic Dangers*, pp. 183–4; for the relative lack of legal sanctions against adultery in England see A. MacFarlane, *Marriage and Love in England* (Oxford, 1986), pp. 240–4.

79. R. Phillips, *Untying the Knot: A Short History of Divorce* (Cambridge, 1991), p. 65.

80. CA, Case 1055 (1693), Eee7, f. 662; other glimpses into the fate of separated couples have so far told us more about separated women than men, see M. Slater, 'The weightiest business: marriage in an upper-gentry family in seventeenth-century England' *PP* 72 (1976), pp. 43–6; A.T. Friedman, 'Portrait of a marriage: the Willoughby letters of 1585–1586' *Signs* 11 (1986), pp. 542–55.

81. CA, Case 1813 (1673), Ee4, f. 122r; for previous discussion of this case see above, Chapter 3.

82. CA, Case 6692 (1676), Eee6, f. 124v.

83. CA, Case 8136 (1669), Eee3, f. 614r.

84. CA, Case 4642 (1698), Eee8, f. 621.

85. T. Stretton, 'Women and litigation in the Elizabethan court of requests' (unpublished Ph.D. thesis, Cambridge University, 1993), particularly pp. 231–2; and Gowing, *Domestic Dangers*, pp. 192, 198, 200–1, 206.

86. Lindley, *The Trials of Francis Howard*, p. 102.

87. As cited in B.J. Gibbons, 'Gender in British Behmenist thought' (unpublished Ph.D. thesis, Durham University, 1993), pp. 45–6.

88. As cited in J. Wiltenburg, *Disorderly Women and Female Power in the Street Literature of Early Modern England and Germany* (Charlottesville VA, 1992), p. 151.

89. T. D'Urfey, *Wit and Mirth* (London, 1699), p. 128.

90. CA, Case 6692 (1676), Eee6, f. 124r; for further discussion of this case see E. Foyster, 'Marrying the experienced widow in early modern England: the male perspective', in S. Cavallo and L. Warner, eds, *Widowhood in Medieval and Early Modern Europe* (forthcoming from Longman).

91. CA, Case 5720 (1669), Eee4, ff. 205–9.

92. W. Shakespeare, *Othello* (*c.*1604), ed. M.R. Ridley (London, 1986), V.ii.6.

93. T. Middleton and W. Rowley, *The Changeling* (1622), ed. B. Loughrey and N. Taylor (London, 1988), II.ii.60–4; Gowing, *Domestic Dangers*, pp. 59, 66; for the emerging distinction of usage between 'whore' and 'prostitute' see F.N. Dabhoiwala, 'Prostitution and police in London, *c.*1660–*c.*1760' (unpublished D.Phil. thesis, Oxford University, 1995), pp. 17, 61–2.

94. See for example, DDR.V.8. f. 40v; DDR.V.10A. f. 66a/r; DDR.V.11. f. 66; and DDR.V.12. f. 2r.

95. CA, Case 2402 (1677), Eee6, f. 290v.

96. J. Godolphin, *Reportorium Canonicum* (London, 1678), p. 474; K. Thomas, 'The puritans and adultery: the act of 1650 reconsidered', in D. Pennington and K. Thomas, eds, *Puritans and Revolutionaries: Essays in Seventeenth-Century History Presented to Christopher Hill* (Oxford, 1978), pp. 265–6.

97. DDR.V.9. f. 182r; for other examples see DDR.V.11. f. 167–168r; DDR.V.12. f. 71; DDR.V.12. f. 141r; CA, Case 1215 (1665), Eee2, ff. 6–7; CA, Case 4188 (1668), Ee3, f. 431r; Gowing, *Domestic Dangers*, pp. 104–5.

98. CA, Case 5127 (1661), Ee1, ff. 14, 36v–37v.

99. CA, Case 9607 (1668), Eee3, f. 674v; CA, Case 9870 (1669), Eee3, f. 548r.

100. DDR.Box, no. 414 (1636–37), *Thomas Rawdon* v. *Christopher Dickon.*

101. Ingram, *Church Courts*, pp. 34, 111, 207, 318; Sharpe, '"Such disagreement"', pp. 173–7; A. Fletcher, *Reform in the Provinces: The Government of Stuart England* (London, 1986), pp. 66–8, 79–81.

102. DDR.V.8. ff. 77v, 78r, 84a.

103. Sharpe, '"Such disagreement"', pp. 173–7, 182–5; M. Ingram, 'Law and disorder in early seventeenth century Wiltshire', in J.S. Cockburn, ed., *Crime in England 1500–1800* (London, 1977), pp. 125–7; Fletcher, *Reform in the Provinces*, pp. 66–7; Gowing, *Domestic Dangers*, p. 136.

104. DDR.V.8. ff. 178, 197, 200v, 201r, 204v, 205r; for another example of pledging from the Durham consistory court see, DDR.Box, no. 414 (1633–34), *Cecilie Smith* v. *Elinor Rawlyn*; for a later example from the court of Arches see CA, Case 5907 (1672), Eee4, ff. 698v–699r.

105. Ingram, *Church Courts*, pp. 185–6.

106. Amussen, *An Ordered Society*, p. 127.

107. CA, Case 5551 (1661), Ee1, ff. 59, 61v–67r; CA, Case 6234 (1662), Ee1, ff. 118v–122r.

108. T.N. Tentler, *Sin and Confession on the Eve of the Reformation* (Princeton NJ, 1977), p. 219.

109. R. Braithwait, *Ar't asleep Husband?* (London, 1640), p. 50.

110. Gowing, *Domestic Dangers*, p. 127; CA, Case 8684 (1666), Eee2, f. 218v.

111. CA, Case 1888 (1676), Ee4, f. 501r; CA, Case 6292 (1669), Ee3, ff. 482v–485v; for other examples see CA, Case 9388 (1666), Eee2, f. 113v; CA, Case 4177 (1669), Ee3, f. 574r; and CA, Case 10406 (1671), Eee4, f. 513r.

112. CA, Case 2402 (1677), Eee6, f. 288.

113. CA, Case 1127 (1663), Ee1, ff. 483–485, 612–617r; Eee1, ff. 56v–64v, 76v–87v.

114. Amussen, *An Ordered Society*, p. 97; Stone, *Road to Divorce*, p. 244.

115. CA, Case 2730 (1688), Ee7, f. 44r; Eee7, f. 88r.

116. Stone, *Road to Divorce*, pp. 231–51; L. Stone, 'Honor, morals, religion, and the law: the action for criminal conversation in England, 1670–1857', in A. Grafton and A. Blair, eds, *The Transmission of Culture in Early Modern Europe* (Philadelphia PA, 1990), pp. 280–2.

117. S. Staves, 'Money for honor: damages for criminal conversation' *Studies in Eighteenth-Century Culture* 11 (1982), pp. 279–97.

118. CA, Case 2730 (1688), Ee7, f. 44r; Eee7, f. 88r.

119. G.R. Quaife, *Wanton Wenches and Wayward Wives: Peasants and Illicit Sex in Early Seventeenth Century England* (London, 1979), p. 151.

120. CA, Case 1915 (1670), Eee4, f. 215r; for earlier examples see also Gowing, *Domestic Dangers*, pp. 91, 94–5.

121. 'The Rich and Flourishing Cuckold well Satisfied' (1675), *Roxburghe*, vol. VIII, part III, pp. clxiv–clxv; 'The Merry Cuckold', *Roxburghe*, vol. II, pp. 5–8. For other examples of ballads in which husbands accept money after their wives' adultery see 'The Lancashire Cuckold', *Euing*, p. 320; 'The Country Cuckold', *Pepys*, vol. IV, p. 139; 'The Catalogue of Contented Cuckolds', *Roxburghe*, vol. III, pp. 481–3; 'The Dyer's Destiny' (1685–88), *Roxburghe*, vol. IV, pp. 405–7.

122. 'The Cooper of Norfolk', *Roxburghe*, vol. I, pp. 99–104.

123. As cited in P. Griffiths, *Youth and Authority: Formative Experiences in England 1560–1640* (Oxford, 1996), p. 102.

124. T. Brennan, *Public Drinking and Popular Culture in Eighteenth-Century Paris* (Princeton NJ, 1988), pp. 8, 25–6, 52–3, 55, 60–3; P. Clark, *The English Alehouse: A Social History 1200–1830* (London, 1983), p. 153.

125. As cited in S.D. Amussen, 'Punishment, discipline, and power: the social meanings of violence in early modern England' *Journal of British Studies* 34 (1995), p. 24.

126. J.A. Sharpe, *Crime in Seventeenth-Century England* (Cambridge, 1983), p. 131.

127. J.M. Beattie, *Crime and the Courts in England 1660–1800* (Princeton NJ, 1986), pp. 91–4.

128. As cited in D. O'Hara, 'Sixteenth-century courtship in the diocese of Canterbury' (unpublished Ph.D. thesis, Kent University, 1995), p. 156.

129. As cited in D.Underdown, *Fire From Heaven: The Life of an English Town in the Seventeenth Century* (London, 1992), pp. 163–4.

130. 'The Lancashire Cuckold', *Euing*, p. 320; 'The Country Cuckold', *Pepys*, vol. IV, p. 139; 'The Catalogue of Contented Cuckolds', *Roxburghe*, vol. III, pp. 481–3.

131. As cited in Quaife, *Wanton Wenches*, p. 138.

132. As cited in Beattie, *Crime*, p. 95.

133. L. Stone, *The Crisis of the Aristocracy* (Oxford, 1965), pp. 244–5.

134. See, for example, Shakespeare, *Romeo and Juliet* (*c*.1595), ed. B. Gibbons (London, 1980), III.i; *Much Ado about Nothing* (1598), ed. F.H. Mares (Cambridge, 1988), V.i; T. Heywood, *A Woman Killed with Kindness* (1603), ed. B. Scobie (London, 1991), iii; W. Wycherley, *The Country Wife* (1675), ed. J. Ogden (London, 1991), II.i; T. Southerne, *The Wives' Excuse* (1692), ed. R. Jordan and H. Love (Oxford, 1988), I.iii.21–41; Vanbrugh, *The Provoked Wife* (1697), V.ii.

135. As cited in P. Jenkins, *The Making of a Ruling Class: The Glamorgan Gentry 1640–1790* (Cambridge, 1983), p. 200; see also Stone, *Crisis*, p. 244.

136. CA, Case 2891 (1676), Eee6, ff. 93v–94r.

137. R. Latham and W. Matthews, eds, *The Diary of Samuel Pepys* (London, 1970–83), vol. IX (1668), p. 27.

138. 'The Combat of Stewart and Wharton', *Roxburghe*, vol. VII, pp. 595–8; for another example of a ballad about duelling see 'Combat between Armstrong and Musgrave' (*c.*1674–80), *Roxburghe*, vol. VII, pp. 606–8.

139. C.B. Watson, *Shakespeare and the Renaissance Concept of Honour* (Princeton NJ, 1960), pp. 127–35; D.T. Andrew, 'The code of honour and its critics: the opposition to duelling in England, 1700–1850' *Social History* 5, 3 (1980), pp. 416–17.

140. Anon, *The Office of Christian Parents* (Cambridge, 1616), pp. 178–92; see also T. Comber, *A Discourse of Duels* (London, 1687); fears about the dangers of anger to manhood continued, see E. Foyster, 'Boys will be boys? Manhood and aggression 1660–1800', in T. Hitchcock and M. Cohen, eds, *English Masculinities, 1660–1800*, (forthcoming from Longman).

141. As cited in G.M. Walker, 'Crime, gender and social order in early modern Cheshire' (unpublished Ph.D. thesis, Liverpool University, 1994), p. 132.

142. As cited in Amussen, 'Punishment', p. 23, footnote 73.

143. Stone, *Crisis*, pp. 248–9.

144. As cited in Andrew, 'The code', p. 419.

145. For *The Gentleman's Magazine* see, for example, vol. 20 (1750), pp. 219–20, and vol. 25 (1755), pp. 112–14; for debates see D.T. Andrew, *London Debating Societies, 1776–1799* (London, 1994).

146. Andrew, 'The code', passim.

147. My article, 'Male honour, social control and wife beating in late Stuart England' *TRHS* Sixth Series, VI (1996), pp. 215–24, also discusses these themes.

148. C. Kahn, 'Whores and wives in Jacobean drama', in D. Kehler and S. Baker, eds, *In Another Country: Feminist Perspectives on Renaissance Drama* (London, 1991), p. 252.

149. CA, Case 6659 (1666), Eee2, f. 96v; CA, Case 1041 (1672), Ee3, f. 739v; CA, Case 2730 (1688), Ee7, ff. 13v–14r; for other examples see CA, Case 9607 (1668), Eee3, ff. 674v, 688; CA, Case 9870 (1669), Eee3, ff. 547v–555v.

150. G. Etherege, *She Would if She Could* (1668), ed. C.M. Taylor (London, 1972), V.i.137–9.

151. CA, Case 6659 (1666), Eee2, f. 96v; CA, Case 4834 (1669), Eee3, f. 46v.

152. CA, Case 9870 (1669), Eee3, ff. 548r, 550r, 555r; DDR.V.12. f. 288r.

153. V. Groebner, 'Losing face, saving face: noses and honour in the late medieval town' *HWJ* 40 (1995), pp. 1–15.

154. CA, Case 6244 (1672), Ee4, f. 54v.

155. Gowing, 'Language, power and the law', pp. 32, 46, n. 29.

156. P. Stallybrass, 'Patriarchal territories: the body enclosed', in M.W. Ferguson, M. Quilligan and N.J. Vickers, eds, *Rewriting the Renaissance: The Discourses of Sexual Difference in Early Modern Europe* (Chicago IL, 1987), pp. 123–42.

157. Heywood, *A Woman Killed with Kindness*, xiii.99–101.

158. CA, Case 5585 (1667), Eee2, ff. 780–2.

159. CA, Case 5938 (1697), Eee8, ff. 421–2, 424r.

160. As cited in Gowing, *Domestic Dangers*, p. 212.

161. CA, Case 6234 (1662), Ee1, ff. 119v–120r.

162. CA, Case 9607 (1668), Eee3, ff. 673v–674v, 687v–688v.

163. CA, Case 1813 (1673), Ee4, ff. 118v–129r.

164. CA, Case 3789 (1662), Ee1, ff. 195–6.

165. CA, Case 1888 (1676), Ee4, ff. 484–501r.

166. F. Pollock and F.W. Maitland, *The History of English Law* (Cambridge, 1952), pp. 484–5; Thomas, 'The puritans and adultery', pp. 268–9; R. Phillips, *Putting Asunder: A History of Divorce in Western Society* (Cambridge, 1988), pp. 324–5, 331; M.R. Sommerville, *Sex and Subjection: Attitudes to Women in Early-Modern Society* (London, 1995), p. 90.

167. M.P. Tilley, *A Dictionary of Proverbs in England in the Sixteenth and Seventeenth Centuries* (Ann Arbor MI, 1950), W644.

168. M.P., 'Well met, Neighbour', *Roxburghe*, vol. III, pp. 98–103; M.P., 'Hold your Hands, Honest Men!', *Roxburghe*, vol. III, pp. 243–8.

169. M.P., 'A He-Devil', *Pepysian Garland*, pp. 332–6; Wiltenburg, *Disorderly Women*, pp. 93–5.

170. Anon, *Arden of Faversham* (*c.*1591), ed. M. White (London, 1982), I.494–5, 506–12; 'Arden of Faversham' (1633), *Roxburghe*, vol. VIII, part I–II, pp. 49–53; F.E. Dolan, 'Home-rebels and house-traitors: murderous wives in early modern England' *Yale Journal of Law and the Humanities* 4, 1 (1992), pp. 25–7.

171. Wycherley, *The Country Wife*, IV.iv.48–9.

172. Vanbrugh, *The Provoked Wife*, I.i.89–91; IV.ii.27–30; V.ii.129–31.

173. Shakespeare, *Othello*, IV.i.235–78.

174. W. Heale, *An Apology for Women* (Oxford, 1609), pp. 4, 25; W. Gouge, *Of Domesticall Duties*, 3rd edn (London, 1634), p. 389.

175. As cited in S.D. Amussen, '"Being stirred to much unquietness": violence and domestic violence in early modern England' *Journal of Women's History* 6, 2 (1994), p. 71.

176. W. Whateley, *A Bride Bush* (London, 1623), pp. 123, 128–9, 171; Fletcher, 'The Protestant idea of marriage', pp. 172–3.

177. Gouge, *Of Domesticall Duties*, p. 395.

178. H. Smith, *A Preparative to Marriage* (London, 1591), p. 73.

179. M. MacDonald, *Mystical Bedlam: Madness, Anxiety and Healing in Seventeenth Century England* (Cambridge, 1981), p. 102.

180. J. Dod and R. Cleaver, *A Godly Forme of Householde Governement* (London, 1612), sig. G2.

181. As cited in Ingram, *Church Courts*, p. 144.

182. As cited in M. Hunt, 'Wife beating, domesticity and women's independence in eighteenth-century London' *GH* 4, 1 (1992), p. 10.

183. CA, Case 1127 (1663), Eee1, f. 83.

184. CA, Case 6659 (1666), Eee2, f. 101.

185. CA, Case 8770 (1684), Ee6, f. 11.

186. CA, Case 4834 (1669), Eee3, ff. 247v, 299r.

187. CA, Case 1888 (1676), Eee6, f. 278v.

188. CA, Case 1813 (1673), Eee5, f. 23v.

189. CA, Case 6659 (1666), Eee2, f. 124r.

190. Heale, *An Apology*, p. 33.

191. CA, Case 6659 (1666), Eee2, f. 95r; CA, Case 4747 (1673), Eee5, f. 251v; CA, Case 1128 (1675), Eee5, f. 681r; for another example see CA, Case 1813 (1673), Eee5, f. 20v.

192. CA, Case 1041 (1672), Eee4, ff. 856r, 868v.

193. Shakespeare, *Othello*, IV.i.236; for other examples of witnesses to marital violence who tried to determine whether a wife 'deserved' such treatment see Amussen, 'Punishment', p. 13.

194. DDR.V.12. f. 284v.

195. As cited in Ingram, *Church Courts*, p. 180.

196. CA, Case 1127 (1663), Eee1, ff. 62r, 63v; CA, Case 10406 (1671), Eee4, f. 512v.

197. As cited in Amussen, 'Punishment, discipline, and power', p. 14.

198. CA, Case 4747 (1673), Eee5, ff. 250v–251r.

199. CA, Case 6244 (1672), Ee4, f. 51v; Eee4, f. 767r.

200. As cited in Hunt, 'Wife beating', p. 22; a transcription of this case is found in M.R. Hunt, '"The great danger she had reason to believe she was in": wife-beating in the eighteenth-century', in V. Frith, ed., *Women and History: Voices in Early Modern England* (Toronto, 1995), pp. 89–102.

201. CA, Case 1432 (1667), Eee2, ff. 538–40.

202. E.P. Thompson, *Customs in Common* (London, 1991), p. 505.

203. For sexual violence see the Boteler case below; for a husband who threatens to chain his wife to the bed post and have sex with his whores in front of her see CA, Case 1128, (1675), Eee5, f. 670r; for a husband who is possibly answering accusations of marital rape see CA, Case 3603 (1664), Ee2, f. 208r; see also A. Clark, *Women's Silence, Men's Violence: Sexual Assault in England 1770–1845* (London, 1987); and Herrup, '"To pluck bright honour"', passim.

204. CA, Case 1041 (1672), Ee3, ff. 738–741r; 745r–746v; Eee4, ff. 613v–615v, 807–8, 815–818r, 821v–822; 850v–883r; Eee5, ff. 24v–25r.

205. L. Stone, *Broken Lives* (Oxford, 1993), p. 37.

206. CA, Case 1041 (1672), Eee4, ff. 874r, 876r.

207. 'My Wife will be my Master' (*c.*1640), *Roxburghe*, vol. VII, part I, pp. 188–9.

208. 'An Easy Way to Tame a Shrew' (1672), *Roxburghe*, vol. VIII, part III, pp. lxxxii–lxxxiii.

209. B. Capp, *The World of John Taylor the Water Poet 1578–1653* (Oxford, 1994), p. 118.

210. 'A pleasant new Ballad, both merry and witty, / That sheweth the humours of the wives in the City' (*c.*1630), *Pepys*, vol. I, pp. 376–7.

211. 'A Caution for Scolds' (1685–88), *Roxburghe*, vol. III, pp. 508–10.

212. R. Porter, *Disease, Medicine and Society in England 1550–1860* (London, 1987), p. 15; K. Thomas, *Religion and the Decline of Magic: Studies in Popular Beliefs in Sixteenth and Seventeenth Century England* (Harmondsworth, 1971), pp. 633–4.

213. 'The Scolding Wife', *Roxburghe*, vol. VII, part I, pp. 191–3; 'The Scolding Wife' (1689), *Pepys* (1689), vol. IV, p. 136.

214. As cited in Gowing, *Domestic Dangers*, p. 223.

215. For one husband who threatens this see CA, Case 14 (1671), Eee4, f. 333r; for a husband who actually carries out this threat see, Hunt, 'The great danger', pp. 90–1.

216. 'Dead and Alive', *Pepys*, vol. IV, p. 118.

217. 'The Henpeckt Cuckold' (*c.*1689–91), *Roxburghe*, vol. VII, part II, p. 432.

218. 'The Catalogue of Contented Cuckolds', *Roxburghe*, vol. III, pp. 481–3; 'Household Talk', *Roxburghe*, vol. I, pp. 441–6; 'The Bull's Feather', *Roxburghe*, vol. III, pp. 418–20; Anon, *Bull-Feather Hall* (London, 1664), p. 6.

219. See, for example, 'The Cuckoo's Commendation'(*c.*1625), *Pepys*, vol. I, pp. 406–7; 'Cuckold's Haven', *Roxburghe*, vol. I, pp. 148–53; 'The Well-Approved Doctor', *Pepys*, vol. IV, p. 149; D'Urfey, *Wit and Mirth*, pp. 77–8, 108–9.

220. D'Urfey, *Wit and Mirth*, pp. 84–5.

221. 'The Merry Cuckold', *Roxburghe*, vol. II, pp. 5–8.

222. 'The London Cuckold' (1686), *Roxburghe*, vol. VIII, part III, pp. 603–4; 'The Old Man's Complaint' (*c.*1650), *Roxburghe*, vol. VIII, part I–II, p. 197.

223. M.P., 'The Married Man's Lesson', *Roxburghe*, vol. III, pp. 231–6.

224. 'The Discontented Married Man', *Roxburghe*, vol. I, pp. 295–9.

225. Braithwait, *Ar't asleep Husband?*, p. 51.

226. As cited in K. Hodgkin, 'Thomas Whythorne and the problems of mastery' *HWJ* 29 (1990), p. 36.

227. CA, Case 2979 (1670), Eee4, f. 244v.

228. CA, Case 693 (1673), Eee5, ff. 232v–233v.

229. Also spelt wittal, wittold, witwold, see OED.

230. As cited in Hodgkin, 'Thomas Whythorne', p. 36.

231. Anon, *The Court of Good Counsell* (London, 1607), sig. D.

232. As cited in Ingram, *Church Courts*, p. 309.

233. As cited in B. Capp, 'Separate domains? Women and authority in early modern England', in P. Griffiths, A. Fox and S. Hindle, eds, *The Experience of Authority in Early Modern England* (London, 1996), p. 133.

234. W. Shakespeare, *The Merry Wives of Windsor* (1597), ed. H.J. Oliver (London, 1993), II.ii.288–90.

CHAPTER SIX

Conclusion: Continuity and change in early modern manhood

> My Dear and only Son,
> Now that thy infant Years are done,
> All childish Toys at once give o're
> To manly Thoughts thy Mind prepare.[1]

> If you can once get into Children a love of Credit, and an apprehension of Shame and Disgrace, you have put into them the true Principle, which will constantly work, and incline them to the right.[2]

This book has argued that learning how to achieve credit and avoid shame was essential in the process of becoming a man in early modern England. A multitude of literary genres, ranging from conduct manuals for the sons of gentry, to ballads selling for less than a penny, taught that a man's honour depended on exercising control over the sexual behaviour of the women with whom he was associated, whether it was his premarital lover, wife, daughters, sisters, or female servants. Honourable manhood was not something which largely came with birth, but rather had to be earned by winning the approval of others. Court records of defamation and marriage separation provide us with evidence of men attempting and sometimes failing to achieve, maintain or restore honour. Rituals which targeted men who failed in their bid for honour ensured that loss of control in the household could also deprive them of power outside it. The importance of sexual honour, and the fear of the consequences which would follow if it was lost, could have a profound effect upon men's behaviour with each other as well as with women. Indeed, the desire to be seen as an honourable man was thought so powerful that it could affect a man's subconscious. Emotions such as jealousy, guilt and fear could be as much the products of this system of gender relations as those of self-worth and personal achievement.

The story that emerges of early modern manhood often appears to be one of continuity rather than change. It is striking how fictional literature continues to relate the same male fears about women at the end of the seventeenth century as at its beginning. The harm caused by women's talk, the dangers women posed to men by their sexual activities, and the potential for women to challenge men's position of power were all themes which were repeatedly aired. The double sexual standard and the level at which male domestic violence could be deemed intolerable remained two of the key areas of literary debate which centred on male marital behaviour. Both tested the limits of acceptable male behaviour: discussion of the double sexual standard questioned how lax or libertine men could be in their conjugal fidelity, that of violence revolved around the issue of how strictly or how far men could apply their conjugal rights.[3] In the church courts, across the seventeenth century, the accounts by men and married women of their experiences of gender relations form a familiar and usually predictable pattern. Aside from differences in geographical location, the content of the stories told in the Restoration court of Arches differs little from that of those cases heard in the early seventeenth-century Durham consistory court. At the end of the day, are we left with evidence of nothing but timeless, even transhistorical concerns about being a man?

Recently historians have begun to question how far gender relations need be subject to the same degree or scale of change, as aspects of economic, social or political history. Those who in the 1970s boldly suggested all-encompassing theories of change in gender relations, for example Lawrence Stone, whose study traced how supposedly brutal patriarchal family relationships in the early modern period were transformed into the companionate and loving ones of the modern world, have been subject to a great deal of scepticism and criticism.[4] Yet perhaps because the subject of women's history was for so long dismissed as it was argued that women's lives were unchanging, some still feel that if the subject is to deserve serious study then uncovering and explaining change has to play a part. A heated debate between two historians of women, Judith Bennett and Bridget Hill, brought to centre-stage the issue of whether history as the story of the past has to be one that narrates change. In a dispute about the impact of capitalism and industrialisation on women's lives, by proposing that there was no 'golden age' of women's work, and that instead women's history was marked by a continuity of subordination to men through low-paid and low-skilled labour, Bennett found herself defending her work against the charge of being 'a-historical'.[5]

Of those who advocate change in gender relations, some have gone further to consider why change was brought about at certain historical junctures. One theory is that periods of gender 'crisis' are instrumental to change. Several historians have suggested that at the start of the seventeenth century, and at its end, men experienced a 'crisis' of gender relations in which women threatened to overturn the gender order. For example, David Underdown has argued that concern about unruly women was part of the wider 'crisis of order' which led up to the civil war, and was reflected by an increase in the prosecutions of scolds and witches in the courts. The civil war itself gave women unprecedented opportunity for political and religious expression, but arguably precipitated a second crisis in gender relations when peace was restored. Michael Kimmel has argued that men never regained their ascendancy over women, and that particularly with the changes in patterns of work which followed the war, many men abandoned 'traditional masculinity', becoming as effeminate fops the target of pamphlet criticism. Mary Fissell's recent study of gender is a thoughtful discussion of prescriptive literature which emphasises the possibility of multiple readings of texts, and avoids the use of the term 'crisis'. Nevertheless, Fissell also argues that the civil war led to a shake-up in gender relations. In contrast with Kimmel, she has found evidence in popular health texts and conduct books that in the Restoration period men were able to recover their authority over women, and that this was achieved by reconstructing both women's bodies and their part in the reproductive process, and at another level by restricting women's activities and their access to public spaces.[6]

But there are several reasons why applying the term 'crisis' in these historical accounts, or writing of 'a world turned upside down' as Fissell does, is both problematic and inappropriate. First, the word 'crisis' suggests that sudden and dramatic change disrupts formerly static and stable gender relations. Secondly, those who have suggested a 'crisis' in gender relations have tended to assume that it represented a particular historical period for change which had universal effect, regardless of other contingencies such as sex, age or class. Finally, writing gender history which charts changes which are parallel to the great turning points of political history, such as the civil war, limits us to traditional chronologies when so much of women's history has shown us that they can bear little relevance to the rhythms or patterns of everyday life. Linking changes in the wider political, economic and social structure to those in personal relationships is not only extremely complex, but also tends to subsume gender to those structures rather than seeing gender itself as a force for change in people's lives.

Manhood in the seventeenth century was characterised by neither sudden transformation caused by crisis, nor by stasis. Rather, it was a history marked by the endurance of patriarchal ideology, which overlay the constantly shifting daily practice of gender relations. It was this mix of 'small shifts, short-term changes and enduring continuities' which Bennett tried to explain in her work, but which it seems was misunderstood by Hill.[7] This book has shown how in practice gender relations were never stable, were always in contest, and that as a result men had continually to assert their difference from women and their position over them. Although power over women continued to be regarded as fundamental to the experience of being 'male', the attainment of that power was never guaranteed. In their bid for power men in the seventeenth century constructed a language of honour which rewarded those who attained sexual control over women, and could be employed to insult those who challenged or undermined male authority. There are indicators that this was a highly effective system; across the country large numbers of women filled the church courts to defend sexual reputation. Legal records also bear witness to the men who took a variety of actions to exhibit their honour to others, and to restore damaged honour. But by resting male power on female chastity this system was also one which was characterised by instability. Female chastity was an enigma which could not be seen or proved. Men struggled to make sexual dishonour visible; they tried potions to expose maids who were not virgins, attached horns to the entrances of houses owned by cuckolds, examined the faces of their children for signs of paternity, and threatened to mark whores with slit noses. But unless a man trusted his wife's word, or caught her *in flagrante delicto,* he would never know for certain whether she was a virgin on her wedding day, and if she had remained constant to him throughout their marriage.

The irony was that a system designed to give men power, often gave opportunity for women to gain that power over men by shaming their husbands and questioning their manhood. What is more, it created 'subordinate masculinities'.[8] In seventeenth-century England the cuckold and the wittol were targeted for derision, as were those who exhibited signs of effeminacy at one extreme, and pathological jealousy at the other. These individuals and behavioural tendencies were variously slandered, rejected and condemned, yet they were the inevitable products of a system of gender relations which insisted on male self-control and male control of female chastity. Crisis models tend to suggest that it was only women who threatened to disrupt the status quo, but this book has shown how at both the level of men's fears, and in practice, it was frequently the failings of men which led to a breakdown in the gender order. It was particularly through their inability to control their own bodies, exposed by drunkenness, impotence or violence, that men betrayed their weakness. Just as women's history is revealing that all women were not as subordinate or powerless as was once thought, so men's history can expose the relative powerlessness of many men.

By examining the records of marriage breakdown, this book has shown how the balance of power within individual relationships altered and was renegotiated at different points and with varying speed. At this personal level we can see how when faced with crisis some men could promise to change. When Cecily Bradley fled from John, her violent and adulterous husband, in the early 1670s, he begged her to return, sending messages to her that 'he would become a new man and leave the Company of loose women'. His promise to 'become a new man' shows an understanding of what is normally associated with twentieth-century thinking, that men at will could reform or even reconstruct themselves in line with women's expectations. John Bradley's promises were short-lived, and once Cecilia returned to the household he resumed his former pattern of behaviour, leaving her witnesses in the separation case that followed to tell the court of how John had failed to make himself a 'new man'. In the short-term, however, his ploy to promise change had worked as Cecilia had returned and he had been able to continue in his position as household head. In this case, and from many of the others which have been described in this book, we can see how although in general male dominance endured over time, patriarchy still has a history which is made up of the diverse and changing ways in which men attempted to achieve and maintain control of power over women.[9]

Over the next 150 years ideas both about how men could subordinate women, and what constituted manhood, were to change significantly. A distinctive feature of the ideas of manhood, sexual honour and marriage in the seventeenth century described in this book was that they were largely held in common across the social scale, although the ways that male sexual honour was subsequently exhibited, defended and restored could vary according to social class. The eighteenth century, however, was to see a divergence of both the ideas and the practice of manhood which came to be loosely associated with different social groups. John Tosh has convincingly argued in an important essay that matching shifts in ideas about masculinity between 1750 and 1850 with that of changes in the class structure is complicated by the fact that no one class had a monopoly of ideas about gender, and that the desire for household authority continued to be shared by men from all social backgrounds.[10] Nevertheless, it can still be argued, and in contrast with the situation in the seventeenth century, that in the eighteenth century there was divergence about how that household authority could be achieved as new ideas gained currency amongst the burgeoning middle class. Of course, the middle class had always been articulate and supportive of patriarchal ideology, and as Leonore Davidoff and Catherine Hall emphasise in their influential book on this social group, many ideas about household government in the eighteenth century were inherited from their Puritan forefathers. But whereas talk of separate spheres as a means to contain and control women had remained largely at the level of wishful thinking in the seventeenth century, with industrial and commercial expansion in the eighteenth century for some it became a practical possibility. In writings addressed to the middle class, 'domesticity shifted from an abstract utopia to practical wisdom', and the belief that married women should remain within the home became so fundamental that by the nineteenth century 'it was increasingly assumed that a woman engaged in business was a woman without either an income of her own or a man to support her'.[11] Margaret Hunt has qualified Davidoff and Hall's thesis by showing how in practice the separation of the spheres was never complete since the market often '*transcended* the so-called "public sphere" and went to the heart of family life', and because economic partnership remained an important feature of many marriages.[12]

Within the ideology of separate spheres, however, a new idea of womanhood emerged which was to be even more influential. Rather than imagined as sexually voracious and dangerous, the domesticated woman was sexually passive, even innocent. Advocates of new theories of reproduction no longer thought both women and men had to produce 'seed' for conception to occur, and so reduced the importance of female arousal in sexual activity. Whereas religious writings, particularly those associated with Evangelicalism, continued to insist on women's submission to men, in contrast with the seventeenth century, in most prescriptive literature the justification for women's subordination became less dependent upon the scriptures. Even as the political theory of patriarchy was being questioned by John Locke, new ideas about the body gave men's subordination of women an alternative and arguably more powerful basis. The work of Thomas Willis begun in the 1660s on the nervous system, followed by closer studies of human anatomy, enabled men to construct women as fundamentally different from themselves, something they had never been able to achieve fully with the graduated humoural model of the body. Within the wider 'culture of sensibility' which stemmed from these medical discoveries, women were now regarded as not only physiologically, but also psychologically different from men. As conduct books written specifically for, and sometimes by, women multiplied in the eighteenth century, the ideal woman was constructed as 'naturally' different from men, and assigned the qualities of virtue and chastity which were now thought to be innate to her. The establishment of different but complementary gender roles for men and women within this literature allowed the ideal of companionate marriage within a patriarchal system to appear more attainable than ever before.[13]

The brief survey above cannot do justice to the complexities of eighteenth-century thought about gender, and it does not begin to unravel the multiple reasons why and how these ideas arose. But it is intended to highlight how the general social consensus behind ideas of manhood, honour, sex and marriage which has been described in this book was not timeless, but was particular to the seventeenth century. It is true that the concern to achieve domination over women continued to be shared across the social scale. The honour of a man could still be defined in relation to the sexual virtue of his wife. More than ever, a man had a duty to protect the innocence, modesty and chastity of his wife and daughters. Equally, his role within the home could still be seen to determine his success in the world of business or commerce outside.[14] The essentials of hegemonic masculinity in this sense remained intact. But as middle-class men became more confident and certain of the naturalness of their gender difference from women, the personas and behaviours which were relegated as subordinate masculinities altered significantly. In place of concern about failed manhood which we have seen led to the targeting of cuckolds and wittols, there was increased anxiety about the attractiveness to men of the alternatives to heterosexual marital relationships. Masturbation, pornography, sex with prostitutes, and sex with other men became the focus of eighteenth-century concern.[15] Instead of the sexual dangers to manhood being exhibited by women, they came from men themselves. Constructing women as sexually passive had reversed the direction of male fears; now there was the possibility that wives would be unable to satisfy their libidinous husbands, rather than vice versa.

As the ideal of womanhood within the home gained greater currency, notions of desirable manhood widened to give new emphasis to male conduct outside the home. In a 'civil' or 'polite' age knowing what manners were appropriate for company was crucial. The pursuit of politeness 'in some measure united a class which in other respects appeared diverse and divided', Paul Langford has remarked in his comments on the middle class.[16] Within urban society a man could earn and lose honour according to his ability to display signs of social refinement. Concern that young men from the middling sorts should find ways of asserting their manhood and spending their leisure time in social rather than sexual pursuits occupied the minds of those who established the all-male religious Societies for the Reformation of Manners at the turn of the seventeenth century.[17] As Philip Carter has shown, anxiety about male sociability led to the popularisation of a new deviant type of masculinity within early eighteenth-century culture, the 'fop', who was ridiculed for his social rather than sexual misdeeds.[18]

Discussion of middle-class notions of civility and politeness, many of which had originated from courtesy books written for the social elite, should remind us that ideas circulating about manhood were never rigidly demarcated by social class.[19] Nevertheless, as historians of middle-class culture have shown, rather than emulate their betters, many within this social group sought to differentiate themselves from what they saw as the vices of aristocratic culture. Whereas the campaigners of the Reformation of Manners tended to concentrate their efforts on arresting prostitutes and street walkers, by the 1740s blame for this crime had shifted to their clients. A range of moral discourses 'all assumed that criminal lust, that ravager of average families, stemmed either from the upper classes themselves or from efforts to emulate them'.[20] By the late eighteenth century discussions both in London's debating societies and within Parliament concentrated on private adultery rather than public prostitution, but it was still the rakish upper-class male who was held responsible for the rising numbers of marriages ending in divorce. Increasing resentment at the elite's access to the costly parliamentary divorce which allowed for remarriage, and crim. con. actions which could prove lucrative, led to proposals for legislation to curb these elite privileges and punish adultery more severely. Attacks on the aristocratic honour code also led to condemnation of the practice of duelling, which was increasingly seen as out of place in an 'enlightened' world where reasonable men settled their differences without recourse to violence.[21]

Changing ideas about manhood were reflected in social practice. The influence of the church courts had been waning since the civil war, although as we have seen in this book, the work of the Restoration court of Arches showed that there were aspects of church court business which remained active and in demand. However, the position of the courts was further weakened with the 1689 Toleration Act which left dissenters outside its jurisdiction, and rendered the punishment of excommunication largely redundant. The decision by the Societies for the Reformation of Manners from the 1690s to bypass the church courts and use secular jurisdiction for their prosecution of moral offences was a sign that the disciplinary work of the courts had lost its force.[22] Whereas Tim Meldrum's work on the London consistory court in the early eighteenth century shows that there was still demand from women within the middling sorts for personal or instance cases to be settled by the church, Polly Morris's excellent study of the Somerset church courts has revealed that by the close of the eighteenth century the majority of female plaintiffs were from the lower rather than the middle classes. Married women pursuing sexual defamation cases had become distasteful to polite sensibilities. When there was a parliamentary inquiry into the church courts in 1831–32, 'the commissioners and court personnel they interviewed reacted with embarrassment and revulsion to the sexual content of defamation, to the sorts of people who brought these suits and to the survival of public penance for such a crime'.[23] But middle-class offence at those who took legal action after sexual defamation did not prevent them from recognising the power of sexual insult. Both Morris and Anna Clark have found evidence of plebeian women being subject to sexual slander and censure by middle-class men. Working and socialising in the streets, these women were vulnerable to insult because they did not conform to middle-class notions of female 'respectability', and threatened to undermine their ideal of separate spheres for men and women. The middle-class men who were the courts' personnel, furthermore, found that they were increasingly alien to the values of its litigants. According to Clark, plebeian women no longer shared the same notions of female honour as their social superiors, since definitions of female sexual honour had begun to vary along class lines.[24]

The increased diversity of ideas about manhood and sexual honour is reflected in eighteenth-century culture. The novel was *the* literary innovation of this period, which Michael McKeon has argued emerged out of the disintegration of old systems of aristocratic honour, and which sought to address new concerns in an era of considerable social instability. The novel was written, produced, and came to be largely consumed by the middle class.[25] Its subject matter can provide us with an index of some of this group's preoccupations, and can indicate their changing ideas about gender relations. Whereas Daniel Defoe's *Moll Flanders* (1722) indulges in stories of female sexual promiscuity to teach moral lessons, the two most famous novels of Samuel Richardson, *Pamela* (1740–41) and *Clarissa* (1747–48), contrast female virtue with male sexual voraciousness. Narratives of seduction, fornication and rape make it clear that by this period it was thought that the dangers of sexual relations originated from men rather than from women. Whereas the second half of *Pamela* deals with her marriage to Mr B, Richardson's chief interest in youth and in relations between the sexes before marriage was shared by Henry Fielding, whose *Joseph Andrews* (1742) and *The History of Tom Jones, A Foundling* (1749) focus on the adventures and love intrigues of two unmarried men. The absence of stories of adulterous women and cuckolded men is noticeable in these English novels, and by the start of the nineteenth century would contrast with the 'High Age of Adultery' which characterised other European literature.[26] 'Among the eccentricities of English literature is its lack of an adultery novel', Alison Sinclair has noted; in novels such as Jane Austen's *Mansfield Park* (1814) and Charles Dickens's *Dombey and Son* (1846–47) adultery is only incidental to the storyline. By this time, it appears that the notion of female sexual passivity could be taken so much for granted that a novelist such as Austen could portray men and women who were valued for their non-sexual virtues. Anthony Trollope's *He Knew He Was Right* (1868–69) marked a break from the past, and a new willingness in Victorian society to examine the role of men's behaviour in marriage breakdown. It dealt with the fate of a husband, Louis Trevelyan, who, unable to be both masterly and companionate, wrongly believed that his wife had been unfaithful. As a portrayal of jealousy, the novel demands sympathy not ridicule for Trevelyan, who suffers a complete mental and physical breakdown, and whose loss of reason renders him childlike and ultimately dependent upon his wife.[27]

In sharp contrast with the subject matter of the novel, eighteenth- and early nineteenth-century ballads and chapbooks continued to relate stories of scolding and adulterous wives and cuckolded husbands. The price of broadside ballads remained stable, remaining at a penny or halfpenny well into the nineteenth century. By the start of the eighteenth century, however, its audience had become overwhelmingly working class. London still dominated the ballad trade; at the start of the nineteenth century there were at least seventy-five printers based there with chapmen travelling out from the city. But there had also been the establishment of trade in the provincial towns, such as Preston, Manchester and Newcastle in the north, with each forming distinctive regional and local traditions. The subject matter of ballads did diversify, and often reflected changes in working-class life, with accounts of factory work, railways, and working women. The nineteenth century also saw the advent of the music hall, a bastion of working-class culture, which drew upon traditional ballads, and saw the creation of new songs for performance.[28]

Working-class men, as Clark has shown us in her study of artisans and textile workers between 1780 and 1825, were far from being a homogenous group. The form which ideas about manhood and consequential gender struggles took could vary according to occupation, and individual religious and sexual values. But whilst much of male working-class culture continued to be centred around drinking, fighting, and sometimes violent misogyny, 'marriage and fatherhood' still 'marked the state of true manhood'.[29] The most popular themes for ballads sung on the street corner and in the music hall remained love, sex and marriage. Metaphors for sex were now derived from the new industrial scene with ballads such as 'New Bury Loom' (*c.*1800) using terms from weaving, although those from rural work (ploughing and sowing) also continued. 'The Mower' told of male impotence (he could not mow a maid's meadow down with his scythe), whereas the ballad 'He's got no courage in him' was the lament of a wife who promised that if her husband 'does not shortly try' to please her in bed 'a cuckold I am sure to make him'. The stock comic figure of the cuckold lived on in working-class literature.[30] In ballads about marital violence, wives continued to be portrayed as pleading with their drunken husbands to withhold their fists, as well as spare the household income.[31]

Why these popular forms of culture retained the same concerns about manhood as those described in this book remains unanswered. But the differences between the old-style cultures of 'rough' manhood which these cultural forms came to represent, and the new and developing notions of 'respectable' and 'refined' middle-class manhood, were highlighted as they came into conflict. The frank discussion of marital problems, and the bawdy language frequently employed to describe sexual relations both in ballads and by their consumers in the courtroom, offended the sensibilities of the middle classes. There were repeated attempts by these middling groups to reform and change working-class culture, and rituals associated with past times such as horn fairs and charivari came under attack. But as E.P. Thompson has vividly illustrated, customs such as these proved remarkably resilient to reform, even if their original meaning was lost, as in the case of horn fairs, or if they were sometimes adapted to shame different offenders of community norms, as ridings came to be directed against wife- as well as husband-beaters.[32] Working-class culture may have appeared to be espousing traditional notions about manhood, but it had lost none of its dynamism. The irony was that many of the problems and conflicts of manhood which were represented in plebeian culture were in fact shared and experienced by men across the social scale, and would continue to be so whilst the patriarchal ideal of male rule and female subordination remained in place. But whilst plebeian culture confronted the problems of manhood, sex and marriage, albeit in a crude and often comic form, that of the bourgeoisie or social elite variously denied or ignored them, often dismissing them as vices peculiar to their social inferiors. This was particularly noticeable over the issue of male violence within marriage. Only in the late nineteenth century did the middle classes again openly acknowledge the difficulties of reconciling the contradictions between the demands of being both a companionate and patriarchal husband.[33] Until then, the widespread public discussion and cultural representation of the vulnerability of male power in marriage which has been described in this book would be deemed by many vulgar and unseemly.

Notes

1. *A Rational Catechism Or, An Instructive Conference between a Father and a Son* (London, 1687), p. 133.

2. J. Locke, *Some Thoughts Concerning Education* (1693), ed. J.W. and J.S. Yolton (Oxford, 1989), p. 116.

3. James G. Turner also sees libertinism as 'a kind of dramatic testing procedure', 'The properties of libertinism', in R.P. Maccubbin, ed., *'Tis Nature's Fault: Unauthorized Sexuality during the Enlightenment* (Cambridge, 1987), p. 81.

4. L. Stone, *The Family, Sex and Marriage in England 1500–1800* (London, 1977).
5. J.M. Bennett, '"History that stands still": women's work in the European past' *Feminist Studies* 14, 2 (1988), pp. 269–83, and 'Medieval women, modern women: across the great divide', in D. Aers, ed., *Culture and History 1350–1600: Essays on English Communities, Identities and Writing* (London, 1992), ch. 5; B. Hill, 'Women's history: a study in change, continuity or standing still?' *Women's History Review* 2, 1 (1993), pp. 5–22; J.M. Bennett, 'Women's history: a study in continuity and change' *Women's History Review* 2, 2 (1993), pp. 173–84.
6. D.E. Underdown, 'The taming of the scold: the enforcement of patriarchal authority in early modern England', in A. Fletcher and J. Stevenson, eds, *Order and Disorder in Early Modern England* (Cambridge, 1995), ch. 4; M.S. Kimmel, 'From lord and master to cuckold and fop: masculinity in seventeenth-century England' *University of Dayton Review* 18, 2 (1986–87), pp. 93–109, and 'The contemporary "crisis" of masculinity in historical perspective', in H. Brod, ed., *The Making of Masculinities: The New Men's Studies* (Boston MA, 1987), pp. 121–37; M. Fissell, 'Gender and generation: representing reproduction in early modern England' *GH* 7 (1995), pp. 433–56.
7. Bennett, 'Medieval women', p. 164.
8. R.W. Connell, *Masculinities* (Cambridge, 1995), pp. 76–9.
9. CA, Case 1128 (1675), Eee5, ff. 573r–574r, 576v–577v, 595r–596r, 604v–607v.
10. J. Tosh, 'The old Adam and the new man: emerging themes in the history of English masculinities, 1750–1850', in M. Cohen and T. Hitchcock, eds, *English Masculinities 1660–1800* (forthcoming from Longman); I am very grateful to John Tosh for allowing me to read a copy of his unpublished manuscript.
11. L. Davidoff and C. Hall, *Family Fortunes: Men and Women of the English Middle Class 1780–1850* (London, 1987), pp. 172, 272.
12. M.R. Hunt, *The Middling Sort: Commerce, Gender, and the Family in England, 1680–1780* (Berkeley CA, 1996), p. 9; the italics are Hunt's.
13. There is an extensive literature on these topics, for initial reading see F.A. Childs, 'Prescriptions for manners in English courtesy literature, 1690–1760, and their social implications' (unpublished D.Phil. thesis, Oxford University, 1984); N. Armstrong, *Desire and Domestic Fiction: A Political History of the Novel* (Oxford, 1987); L. Jordanova, *Sexual Visions: Images of Gender in Science and Medicine between the Eighteenth and Twentieth Centuries* (Madison WI, 1989); T. Laqueur, *Making Sex: Body and Gender from the Greeks to Freud* (Cambridge MA, 1990); G.J. Barker-Benfield, *The Culture of Sensibility: Sex and Society in Eighteenth-Century Britain* (Chicago, 1992); R. Martensen, 'The transformation of Eve: Women's bodies, medicine and culture in early modern England', in R. Porter and M. Teich, eds, *Sexual Knowledge, Sexual Science: The History of Attitudes to Sexuality* (Cambridge, 1994); M. McKeon, 'Historicizing patriarchy: the emergence of gender difference in England, 1660–1760' *Eighteenth-Century Studies* 28, 3 (1995), pp. 295–322; A. Fletcher, *Gender, Sex and Subordination in England 1500–1800* (New Haven, 1995); and R.B. Shoemaker, *Gender in English Society 1650–1850* (London, 1998).
14. See, for example, Hunt, *The Middling Sort*, p. 162.
15. See, for example, P. Wagner, *Eros Revived: Erotica of the Enlightenment in England and America* (London, 1988); R. Trumbach, 'Sex, gender, and sexual identity in modern culture: male sodomy and female prostitution in eighteenth-century London' *Journal of the History of Sexuality* 2, 2 (1991), pp. 186–203; F.N. Dabhoiwala, 'Prostitution and police in London, *c.*1660–*c.*1760' (unpublished D.Phil. thesis, Oxford University, 1995); and T. Hitchcock, *English Sexualities, 1700–1800* (London, 1997), chs 2, 3, 5.
16. P. Langford, *A Polite and Commercial People: England 1727–1783* (Oxford, 1989), p. 59.
17. Hunt, *The Middling Sort*, pp. 70, 104–11.
18. P. Carter, 'Men about town: representations of foppery and masculinity in early eighteenth-century urban society', in H. Barker and E. Chalus, eds, *Gender in Eighteenth-Century England: Roles, Representations and Responsibilities* (London, 1997), ch. 2.

19. Childs, 'Prescriptions for manners', pp. 94–101, 110–12, and ch. 4; L.E. Klein, 'Politeness for plebes: consumption and social identity in early eighteenth-century England', in A. Bermingham and J. Brewer, eds, *The Consumption of Culture 1600–1800: Image, Object, Text* (London, 1995), ch. 19.

20. Hunt, *The Middling Sort*, p. 199.

21. D.T. Andrew, '"Adultery à-la-Mode": Privilege, the law and attitudes to adultery 1770–1809' *History* 82 (1997), pp. 5–23, and 'The code of honour and its critics: the opposition to duelling in England, 1700–1850' *Social History* 5, 3 (1980), pp. 409–34.

22. M. Ingram, *Church Courts, Sex and Marriage in England, 1570–1640* (Cambridge, 1987), pp. 372–4; R.B. Shoemaker, *Prosecution and Punishment: Petty Crime and the Law in London and Rural Middlesex, c.1660–1725* (Cambridge, 1991), p. 21, ch. 9.

23. T. Meldrum, 'A women's court in London: defamation at the Bishop of London's consistory court, 1700–1745' *London Journal* 19, 1 (1994), pp. 1–20; P. Morris, 'Defamation and sexual reputation in Somerset, 1733–1850' (unpublished Ph.D. thesis, Warwick University, 1985), pp. 236–42.

24. Morris, 'Defamation', ch. 6; A. Clark, 'Whores and gossips: sexual reputation in London 1770–1825', in A. Angerman, G. Binnema, V. Poels and J. Zirkzee, eds, *Current Issues in Women's History* (London, 1989), pp. 231–48, and *The Struggle for the Breeches: Gender and the Making of the British Working Class* (London, 1995), pp. 48–62.

25. M. McKeon, *The Origins of the English Novel 1600–1740* (London, 1988); I. Watt, *The Rise of the Novel* (London, 1987).

26. For European comparisons see J. Armstrong, *The Novel of Adultery* (London, 1976); T. Tanner, *Adultery in the Novel: Contract and Transgression* (Baltimore, 1979); and N. White and N. Segal, eds, *Scarlet Letters: Fictions of Adultery from Antiquity to the 1990s* (London, 1997).

27. A. Sinclair, *The Deceived Husband: A Kleinian Approach to the Literature of Infidelity* (Oxford, 1993), pp. 48, 186–7, 217–26; Claire Lamont, '"Let other pens dwell on guilt and misery": Adultery in Jane Austen', and M. Hamer, 'No fairy tale: the story of marriage in Trollope's *He Knew He Was Right*', in White and Segal, eds, *Scarlet Letters*; A.J. Hammerton, *Cruelty and Companionship: Conflict in Nineteenth-Century Married Life* (London, 1992), pp. 153–5.

28. M. Vicinus, *Broadsides of the Industrial North* (Newcastle, 1975), pp. 7–17; J.S. Bratton, *The Victorian Popular Ballad* (London, 1975), ch. 6; P. Joyce, *Visions of the People: Industrial England and the Question of Class 1848–1914* (Cambridge, 1991), ch. 10; D. Kift, *The Victorian Music Hall: Culture, Class and Conflict* (Cambridge, 1996).

29. Clark, *The Struggle for the Breeches*, pp. 8, 14, 25–6, 30–4.

30. Vicinus, *Broadsides*, pp. 16–17, 30, 32, 76.

31. Vicinus, *Broadsides*, p. 39; Clark, *The Struggle for the Breeches*, pp. 67–71.

32. E.P. Thompson, *Customs in Common* (London, 1991), chs 1, 8; for the fate of horn fairs see above, ch. 4.

33. M. Hunt, 'Wife beating, domesticity and women's independence in eighteenth-century London' *GH* 4, 1 (1992), pp. 25–8; Hammerton, *Cruelty and Companionship*, passim.

Further Reading

The following list of titles is intended to act as a guide for further reading into some of the issues which this book has discussed. It is in no way an exhaustive list of all the sources used in preparing the book, and focuses on secondary works.

Approaches to Studying Manhood and Gender History

N.Z. Davis, in '"Women's history": in transition: the European case' *Feminist Studies* 3 (1975), was one of the earliest historians to argue for the study of men as well as women. J.W. Scott provided a strong theoretical basis for the study of gender history in 'Gender: a useful category of historical analysis' *American Historical Review* 91, 5 (1986), reprinted in *Gender and the Politics of History* (New York, 1988), and G. Bock, 'Women's history and gender history: aspects of an international debate' *GH* 1, 1 (1989) provides a useful overview of the developing relationship between women's and gender history, and some of the themes which are of current interest in these fields. Masculinity is a subject which is receiving much attention from sociologists, psychologists and philosophers, with 'men's studies' flourishing as a new academic subject. Although this work is mainly concerned with modern day concerns of men, particularly with their responses to twentieth-century feminism, work by sociologists which reflects on changing male roles and gender relations such as R.W. Connell, in his *Gender and Power: Society, the Person and Sexual Politics* (Cambridge, 1987) and *Masculinities* (Cambridge, 1995), and the collection of essays in H. Brod, ed., *The Making of Masculinities: The New Men's Studies* (Boston MA, 1987) can be thought-provoking for the historian. M. Roper and J. Tosh, 'Introduction: historians and the politics of masculinity', in M. Roper and J. Tosh, eds, *Manful Assertions: Masculinities in Britain since 1800* (London, 1991), and J. Tosh, 'What should historians do with masculinity? Reflections on nineteenth-century Britain' *HWJ* 33 (1994), remain the best introductions to the history of masculinity.

General Introductions to Early Modern Manhood

A. Fletcher's *Gender, Sex and Subordination in England 1500–1800* (New Haven, 1995) is the first to survey both boys' upbringing and their subsequent experiences as adults. Although the focus of the work in H. Barker and E. Chalus, eds, *Gender in Eighteenth-Century England: Roles, Representations and Responsibilities* (London, 1997), and R.B. Shoemaker, *Gender in English Society 1650–1850* (London, 1998), is mainly upon a later chronological period compared to this book, the Introductions to both books provide interesting overviews to recent work and debates within gender history. Shoemaker's book examines how far the lives of men were conducted in 'separate spheres' from women, and his chapters on 'Ideas about Gender', 'Sexuality' and 'Family and Household Life' all contain material which is relevant to the history of manhood in the early modern period. For other studies on early modern manhood see K. Hodgkin, 'Thomas Whythorne and the problems of mastery' *HWJ* 29 (1990); S.D. Amussen, '"The part of a Christian man": the cultural politics of manhood in early modern England', in S.D. Amussen and M.A. Kishlansky, eds, *Political Culture and Cultural Politics in Early Modern England: Essays Presented to David Underdown* (Manchester, 1995); A. Bray, 'To be a man in early modern society. The curious case of Michael Wigglesworth' *HWJ* 41 (1996); F. Dabhoiwala, 'The construction of honour, reputation and status in late seventeenth- and early eighteenth-century England' *TRHS* Sixth Series, VI (1996); M.R. Hunt, *The Middling Sort: Commerce, Gender, and the Family in England, 1680–1780* (Berkeley CA, 1996); and P. Carter, 'Men about town: representations of foppery and masculinity in early eighteenth-century urban society', in H. Barker and E. Chalus, eds, *Gender in Eighteenth-Century England* (London, 1997).

Prescriptive Codes for Manhood

Studies that look at codes which were constructed for the social elite include L.B. Wright, ed., *Advice to a Son: Precepts of Lord Burghley, Sir Walter Raleigh, and Francis Osborne* (Ithaca NY, 1962), which provides some good primary material, and R. Kelso, *The Doctrine of the English Gentleman in the Sixteenth Century* (Gloucester MA, 1964), which contains a wealth of detail. F. Heal and C. Holmes, in *The Gentry in England and Wales 1500–1700* (London, 1994), have placed these prescriptive codes into their historical context, and outline the contemporary debates over what qualities made an 'honourable gentleman'.

For work which looks at the theoretical basis of male power over women in this period see M.L. Shanley, 'Marriage contract and social contract in seventeenth century English political thought' *Western Political Quarterly* 32, 1 (1979); S.D. Amussen, 'Gender, family and the social order, 1560–1725', in A. Fletcher and J. Stevenson, eds, *Order and Disorder in Early Modern England* (Cambridge, 1987), and *An Ordered Society: Gender and Class in Early Modern England* (Oxford, 1988), ch. 2; and M.R. Sommerville, *Sex and Subjection: Attitudes to Women in Early-Modern Society* (London, 1995). The concept that society should be ordered along gender as well as class lines was to have a huge impact upon the authors of prescriptive literature who addressed courting and married couples. The basis of a successful marriage, according to these authors, was a clear demarcation of gender roles within and outside the household. K.M. Davies, 'Continuity and change in literary advice on marriage', in R.B. Outhwaite, ed., *Marriage and Society* (London, 1981), and A. Fletcher, 'The Protestant idea of marriage in early modern England', in A. Fletcher and P. Roberts, eds, *Religion, Culture and Society in Early Modern Britain: Essays in Honour of Patrick Collinson* (Cambridge, 1994), examine the different roles which men and women were expected to adopt, and debate the extent to which conduct literature written after the Reformation was prescribing a particularly 'Protestant' pattern of marriage compared to pre-Reformation texts. K. Wrightson, *English Society 1580–1680* (London, 1982), chs 3–4, and R. Houlbrooke, *The English Family 1450–1700* (London, 1984), chs 4–5, provide excellent general introductions to the formation and pattern of marriages in this period, and contrast the ideal pattern of marital relationships with their realities.

Church Court Records, Defamation and Marital Separation

M. Ingram, *Church Courts, Sex and Marriage in England, 1570–1640* (Cambridge, 1987) provides by far the clearest introduction to church court procedure. Chapter 10 considers records of sexual slander, Chapters 5 and 8 those of marriage breakdown. R. Phillips, *Putting Asunder: A History of Divorce in Western Society* (Cambridge, 1988), and *Untying the Knot: A Short History of Divorce* (Cambridge, 1991), both provide excellent introductions to the legal position on marriage separation and divorce. L. Stone's *Road to Divorce: England 1530–1987* (Oxford, 1990), and his narratives of marriage breakdown in *Uncertain Unions and Broken Lives: Intimate and Revealing Accounts of Marriage and Divorce in England* (Oxford, 1995), have proved controversial, not least because the latter is so loosely based on the actual court records. In contrast, N.Z. Davis, *Fiction in the Archives: Pardon Tales and their Tellers in Sixteenth-Century France* (Cambridge, 1987) was one of the earliest studies to look seriously at how legal records or 'narratives' were constructed, and has been enormously influential upon the way that many historians have subsequently interpreted legal documents. V. Frith, ed., *Women and History: Voices of Early Modern England* (Toronto, 1995) contains some useful extracts of church court records.

L. Gowing, *Domestic Dangers: Women, Words, and Sex in Early Modern London* (Oxford, 1996) is the first account of sexual slander and marriage breakdown which approaches the legal records from a gender perspective, and provides stimulating reading. 'Gender and the language of insult in early modern London' *HWJ* 35 (1993), and 'Language, power and the law: women's slander litigation in early modern London', in J. Kermode and G. Walker, eds, *Women, Crime and the Courts in Early Modern England* (London, 1994), are also by L. Gowing and focus on women and their sexual language of insult. J.A. Sharpe, *Defamation and Sexual Slander in Early Modern England: The Church Courts at York*, Borthwick Papers 58 (York, 1980) is an important work which considers the nature of sexual honour, and also examines how gossip operated in early modern England. J.A. Sharpe continued his work on defamation suits in '"Such disagreement betwyx neighbours": litigation and human relations in early modern England', in J. Bossy, ed., *Disputes and Settlements: Law and Human Relations in the West* (Cambridge, 1983), where he argued that the initiation of these legal cases often triggered communities to pursue informal means of arbitration between the parties, enabling disputes to be settled and legal action to be abandoned. S.D. Amussen surveyed the records of the Norwich church courts in *An Ordered Society: Gender and Class in Early Modern England* (Oxford, 1988), and Chapter 4 examines the differences between the defamation cases brought by men and women. M. Chaytor,

'Household and kinship: Ryton in the late 16th and early 17th centuries' *HWJ* 10 (1980), and P. Rushton, 'Women, witchcraft, and slander in early modern England: cases from the church courts of Durham, 1560–1675' *Northern History* 18 (1982), are both articles which, like this book, have drawn upon the defamation records of Durham consistory court. T. Meldrum's 'A women's court in London: defamation at the Bishop of London's consistory court' *London Journal* 19, 1 (1994) is one of the few published pieces of research which looks at defamation cases in the early eighteenth century.

S. Staves, 'Money for honor: damages for criminal conversation' *Studies in Eighteenth-Century Culture* 11 (1982), and L. Stone, 'Honor, morals, religion, and the law: the action for criminal conversation in England, 1670–1857', in A. Grafton and A. Blair, eds, *The Transmission of Culture in Early Modern Europe* (Philadelphia PA, 1990), both look at an additional remedy to adultery which was very occasionally taken by men outside the church courts.

Drama and Manhood

For introductions to the Renaissance theatre see A. Gurr, *The Shakespearean Stage 1574–1642* (Cambridge, 1992), and P. Thomason, 'Playhouses and players in the time of Shakespeare', in S. Wells, ed., *The Cambridge Companion to Shakespeare Studies* (Cambridge, 1992). The composition of audiences and their playgoing experiences are discussed in A. Gurr, *Playgoing in Shakespeare's London* (Cambridge, 1987), and G. Salgado, *Eyewitnesses of Shakespeare: First Hand Accounts of Performances 1590–1890* (Sussex, 1975), part I, which provides some primary material. The histories of the acting companies are surveyed in A. Gurr, *The Shakespearian Playing Companies* (Oxford, 1996). A.R. Braunmuller and M. Hattaway, eds, *The Cambridge Companion to English Renaissance Drama* (Cambridge, 1990), and G.K. Hunter, *English Drama, 1558–1642* (Oxford, 1997) are both textbooks which provide broad overviews of the context and subjects of the Renaissance stage.

The range of meanings attached to the concept of male honour on the Renaissance stage are explored in C.L. Barber, *The Idea of Honour in the English Drama 1591–1700* (Göteborg, 1957) and *The Theme of Honour's Tongue: A Study of Social Attitudes in English Drama from Shakespeare to Dryden* (Götenborg, 1985); C.B. Watson, *Shakespeare and the Renaissance Concept of Honour* (Princeton NJ, 1960); and N. Council, *When Honour's at the Stake: Ideas of Honour in Shakespeare's*

Plays (London, 1973). The sexual dimension of male and female honour fascinated dramatists. At a time when men's sexual honour depended so heavily on a woman's chastity, dramatists frequently depicted the women that men most feared: the scold and adulteress. The portrayal of actors in these female roles, and the significance of drama in the construction of early modern notions of femininity, is discussed in L. Jardine, *Still Harping on Daughters: Women and Drama in the Age of Shakespeare* (New York, 1983); K. Newman, *Fashioning Femininity and English Renaissance Drama* (Chicago IL, 1991); and D. Kehler and S. Baker, eds, *In Another Country: Feminist Perspectives on Renaissance Drama* (London, 1991). Men who were married to adulteresses or scolds, and had lost their sexual honour, or who were obsessed with the fear of its loss, were common figures on the seventeenth-century stage. The stage representations of the cuckold, wittol and jealous husband, and what these stereotypes tell us about contemporary understandings of manhood and gender relations are discussed in C. Kahn, *Man's Estate: Masculine Identity in Shakespeare* (Berkeley CA, 1981) and *Roman Shakespeare: Warriors, Wounds, and Women* (London, 1997); P. Erickson, *Patriarchal Structures in Shakespeare's Drama* (London, 1985); S. Greenblatt, *Renaissance Self-Fashioning* (London, 1984), especially ch. 6; and M. Breitenberg, *Anxious Masculinity in Early Modern England* (Cambridge, 1996), especially ch. 6. L. Jardine's, '"Why should he call her whore?" Defamation and Desdemona's case', in M. Tudeau-Clayton and M. Warner, eds, *Addressing Frank Kermode: Essays in Criticism and Interpretation* (Urbana IL, 1991), and revised in her *Reading Shakespeare Historically* (London, 1996), uses printed defamation records of the Durham consistory court to interpret Othello's jealousy and the fate of Desdemona, and is an excellent example of how a study of legal sources, in conjunction with fictional texts, can help us to gain a closer understanding of how narratives in both settings were constructed.

For introductions to the Restoration theatre, its audiences and themes see N.N. Holland, *The First Modern Comedies: The Significance of Etherege, Wycherley and Congreve* (Cambridge MA, 1959); I. Donaldson, *The World Upside Down: Comedy from Jonson to Fielding* (Oxford, 1970); R.D. Hume, ed., *The Rakish Stage: Studies in English Drama 1660–1800* (Carbondale IL, 1983); R.W. Bevis, *English Drama: Restoration and Eighteenth Century, 1660–1789* (London, 1988); and D. Roberts, *The Ladies: Female Patronage of Restoration Drama 1660–1700* (Oxford, 1989). E. Howe considers the importance of the arrival of women on the English stage in *The First English Actresses: Women and Drama*

1660–1700 (Cambridge, 1992). G.S. Alleman, *Matrimonial Law and the Materials of Restoration Comedy* (Philadelphia, PA, 1942) puts into context the many references which are made by characters in Restoration plays to the legal processes concerned with marriage separation.

The titles above represent just a small fraction of the work by literary scholars on the themes introduced in this book. The journals *English Literary Renaissance, Shakespeare Studies, Shakespeare Survey, Studies in English Literature 1500–1900* and *Studies in Philology* contain numerous articles of interest and relevance to historians of gender relations.

Broadside Ballads and Manhood

Ballad production, distribution and audience are described in L. Shepard, *The Broadside Ballad: A Study of Origins and Meaning* (London, 1962) and *The History of Street Literature* (Newton Abbot, 1973); M. Spufford, *Small Books and Pleasant Histories: Popular Fiction and its Readership in Seventeenth-Century England* (London, 1981); and N. Wurzbach, *The Rise of the English Street Ballad 1550–1650* (Cambridge, 1990). B. Capp provides a broad survey of this literature in 'Popular literature', in B. Reay, ed., *Popular Culture in Seventeenth-Century England* (London, 1985), and an excellent case study of the life and works of one writer of popular literature in *The World of John Taylor the Water Poet 1578–1653* (Oxford, 1994). T. Watt's *Cheap Print and Popular Piety, 1550–1640* (Cambridge, 1991) is chiefly a study of ballads which had a pious theme, but it is a scholarly volume which contains a wealth of detail about the ballad trade.

The content of ballads which focused on courtship, sex and marriage is analysed in J.A. Sharpe, 'Plebeian marriage in Stuart England: some evidence from popular literature' *TRHS* Fifth Series, 36 (1986); J. Wiltenburg, *Disorderly Women and Female Power in the Street Literature of Early Modern England and Germany* (Charlottesville VA, 1992); and E.A. Foyster, 'A laughing matter? Marital discord and gender control in seventeenth-century England' *Rural History* 4, 1 (1993). D. Dugaw, *Warrior Women and Popular Balladry 1650–1850* (Cambridge, 1989) looks at ballads which told stories of adventurous women who abandoned their conventional roles of maid, wife and mother, and suggests reasons why this should have been such a popular theme for songs at this time. A. Fox has shown how commercially produced ballads were not the only songs available to the lower orders of society. In 'Ballads, libels and popular ridicule in Jacobean England' *PP* 146 (1994) he details how the semi-literate composed their own rhymes or songs to spread news, or target insults at unpopular members of their communities.

Details of published collections of broadside ballads are given in the Abbreviations at the start of this book.

Using Fictional Sources

A summary of the objections made by some historians about the use of fictional sources in historical writing is in C. Hill, 'Literature and the English Revolution' *The Seventeenth Century* 1, (1986), p. 15. An excellent defence of the use of literature as a historical source is K. Thomas, *History and Literature* (Swansea, 1988), and the clearest introductions to new historicism are the essays contained within R. Wilson and R. Dutton, eds, *New Historicism and Renaissance Drama* (New York, 1992).

Interpreting the humour which often features in the popular literature of this period is extremely difficult. A.A. Berger, *An Anatomy of Humor* (New Brunswick, 1993) provides a useful summary of theories which have been advanced to explain why people laugh. K. Thomas, 'The place of laughter in Tudor and Stuart England' *Times Literary Supplement* (21 January 1977), and J. Bremmer and H. Roodenberg, eds, *A Cultural History of Humour* (Cambridge, 1997) both look at humour in its historical context. Understanding the sexual jokes and innuendo of the period is greatly helped by the use of the following books and glossaries: E. Partridge, *Shakespeare's Bawdy* (London, 1968) and E.A.M. Colman, *The Dramatic Use of Bawdy in Shakespeare* (London, 1974).

The Gentry and Honour

M. James, *English Politics and the Concept of Honour 1485–1642*, Past and Present Supplement 3 (The Past and Present Society, 1978), reprinted in his *Society, Politics and Culture in Early Modern England* (Cambridge, 1996) was the first to suggest that the gentry had distinctive honour systems. For other work on the gentry and male honour see A.J. Fletcher, 'Honour, reputation and local officeholding in Elizabethan and Stuart England', in A.J. Fletcher and J. Stevenson, eds, *Order and Disorder in Early Modern England*

(Cambridge, 1987); R. Cust, 'Honour and politics in early Stuart England: the case of Beaumont v. Hastings' *PP* 149 (1995); F. Heal, 'Reputation and honour in court and country: Lady Elizabeth Russell and Sir Thomas Hoby' *TRHS* Sixth Series, VI (1996); C. Herrup, ' "To pluck bright honour from the pale-faced moon": gender and honour in the Castlehaven story' *TRHS* Sixth Series, VI (1996), and 'The patriarch at home: the trial of the 2nd earl of Castlehaven for rape and sodomy' *HWJ* 41 (1996); and D. Lindley, *The Trials of Frances Howard: Fact and Fiction at the Court of King James* (London, 1996).

Youthful Manhood

For diaries written by young men which have been published see W.L. Sachse, ed., *The Diary of Roger Lowe* (London, 1938), and G. Parfitt and R. Houlbrooke, eds, *The Courtship Narrative of Leonard Wheatcroft Derbyshire Yeoman* (Reading, 1986). I.K. Ben-Amos, *Adolescence and Youth in Early Modern England* (New Haven CT, 1994), and P. Griffiths, *Youth and Authority: Formative Experiences in England 1560–1640* (Oxford, 1996) are the best studies on youth, although neither give lengthy consideration to youth as a period of gender construction. L. Roper's 'Blood and codpieces: masculinity in the early modern German town', in *Oedipus and the Devil: Witchcraft, Sexuality and Religion in Early Modern Europe* (London, 1994) is an exceptionally original study which considers youth, gender and the male body. J.R. Gillis, *For Better, For Worse: British Marriage 1600 to the Present* (Oxford, 1985) is an excellent study of courtship practices.

Men and Women's Talk

Historians have benefited greatly from the observations of anthropologists on the operation and function of gossip. A key anthropological article is M. Gluckman, 'Gossip and scandal' *Current Anthropology* 4, 3 (1963). R. Paine's article, 'What is gossip about? An alternative hypothesis' *Man* new series, 2 (1967) was written as a reply to Gluckman and disputes many of Gluckman's findings. Other useful studies on gossip are F.G. Bailey, ed., *Gifts and Poison: The Politics of Reputation* (Oxford, 1971); R.L. Rosnow and G.A. Fine, *Rumor and Gossip: The Social Psychology of Hearsay* (Oxford, 1976); and S.E. Merry, 'Rethinking gossip and scandal', in D. Black, ed., *Toward a General Theory of Social Control* (London, 1984). The portrayal of gossips in literature is surveyed in L. Woodbridge, *Women and the English Renaissance: Literature and the Nature of Womankind, 1540–1620* (Urbana IL, 1986), ch. 9, and P.M. Spacks, *Gossip* (Chicago IL, 1985).

One of the first historians to suggest that women's talk presented particular problems to men in the early modern period was D.E. Underdown, in 'The taming of the scold: the enforcement of patriarchal authority in early modern England', in A. Fletcher and J. Stevenson, eds, *Order and Disorder in Early Modern England* (Cambridge, 1987). M. Ingram suggests that Underdown may have exaggerated the extent to which women's talk and behaviour caused a 'crisis' in gender relations, and examines the circumstances which led to the prosecution of scolds in '"Scolding women cucked or washed": a crisis of gender relations in early modern England?', in J. Kermode and G. Walker, eds, *Women, Crime and the Courts in Early Modern England* (London, 1994). L.E. Boose, 'Scolding bridles and bridling scolds: taming the woman's unruly member' *Shakespeare Quarterly* 42, 2 (1991) contains illustrations of bridles and vivid accounts of women who underwent these punishments. S. Hindle, 'The shaming of Margaret Knowsley: gossip, gender and the experience of authority in early modern England' *CC* 9, 3 (1994) is a superb case study of the fate of one woman who was labelled a scold, and along with B. Capp, 'Separate domains? Women and authority in early modern England', in P. Griffiths, A. Fox and S. Hindle, eds, *The Experience of Authority in Early Modern England* (London, 1996) contains much useful analysis of the workings of gossip.

J. Kamensky's, 'Talk like a man: speech, power, and masculinity in early New England' *GH* 8, 1 (1996) is a fascinating study, and is the only one to date which considers the importance of speech to men.

Male Sexuality

T. Hitchcock, *English Sexualities, 1700–1800* (London, 1997) provides a useful introduction to work on the male body and sexuality, as well as giving an overview and summary of the criticisms which the most controversial book on this subject, T. Laqueur, *Making Sex: Body and Gender from the Greeks to Freud* (Cambridge MA, 1990), has attracted. Male attitudes to sexuality, and contrasts between contemporary medical thought and popular belief, are also discussed in R.P. Maccubbin, ed., *'Tis Nature's Fault: Unauthorized Sexuality*

During the Enlightenment (Cambridge, 1987); V. Fildes, ed., *Women as Mothers in Pre-Industrial England* (London, 1990); R. Porter and M. Teich, eds, *Sexual Knowledge, Sexual Science: The History of Attitudes to Sexuality* (Cambridge, 1994); M. Fissell, 'Gender and generation: representing reproduction in early modern England' *GH* 7 (1995); and R. Porter and L. Hall, *The Facts of Life: The Creation of Sexual Knowledge in Britain, 1650–1950* (New Haven, 1995). K. Thomas, 'The double standard' *Journal of the History of Ideas* 20, 2 (1959) and 'The puritans and adultery: the Act of 1650 reconsidered', in D. Pennington and K. Thomas, eds, *Puritans and Revolutionaries: Essays in Seventeenth-Century History Presented to Christopher Hill* (Oxford, 1978), both consider how far married men escaped the penalties for extra-marital sex which were faced by their wives.

Men's fears of sexual disease are described in R. Anselment, 'Seventeenth-century pox: the medical and literary realities of venereal disease' *The Seventeenth Century* 4, 2 (1989); R. Davenport-Hines, *Sex, Death and Punishment: Attitudes to Sex and Sexuality in Britain since the Renaissance* (London, 1990); and C. Quetel, *History of Syphilis* (Oxford, 1990). For the cure of venereal disease see M. Pelling, 'Appearance and reality: barber-surgeons, the body and disease', in A.L. Beier and R. Finlay, eds, *London 1500–1700: The Making of the Metropolis* (London, 1986), and W.F. Bynum, 'Treating the wages of sin: venereal disease and specialism in eighteenth-century Britain', in W.F. Bynum and R. Porter, eds, *Medical Fringe and Medical Orthodoxy 1750–1850* (London, 1987).

The key work on male homosexuality in the sixteenth and early seventeenth centuries is A. Bray, *Homosexuality in Renaissance England* (London, 1988), and 'Homosexuality and the signs of male friendship in Elizabethan England' *HWJ* 29 (1990). P. Morris concentrates on a later period and her 'Sodomy and male honour: the case of Somerset, 1740–1850', in K. Gerard and G. Hekma, eds, *The Pursuit of Sodomy: Male Homosexuality in Renaissance and Enlightenment Europe* (New York, 1989) shows how once homosexuality had become 'a vice pertaining to persons rather than acts', prosecution patterns could be more systematic and brutal, and male sexual reputation more vulnerable to accusations of sodomy.

Men and Violence

The history of attitudes to duelling, and the patterns of more disorderly male fighting and brawls, are outlined in R. Baldick, *The Duel:*

A History of Duelling, 2nd edn (London, 1970); D.T. Andrew, 'The code of honour and its critics: the opposition to duelling in England, 1700–1850' *Social History* 5, 3 (1980); J.M. Beattie, *Crime and the Courts in England 1660–1800* (Princeton, 1986); V.G. Kiernan, *The Duel in European History: Honour and the Reign of the Aristocracy* (Oxford, 1988); and S. Anglo, 'How to kill a man at your ease: fencing books and the duelling ethic', in S. Anglo, ed., *Chivalry in the Renaissance* (Woodbridge, 1990).

For discussion of attitudes towards men who were violent towards their wives see M. Hunt, 'Wife beating, domesticity and women's independence in eighteenth-century London' *GH* 4, 1 (1992); S.D. Amussen, '"Being stirred to much unquietness": violence and domestic violence in early modern England' *Journal of Women's History* 6, 2 (1994), and 'Punishment, discipline, and power: the social meanings of violence in early modern England' *Journal of British Studies* 34 (1995); and E. Foyster, 'Male honour, social control, and wife beating in late Stuart England' *TRHS* Sixth Series, VI (1996).

Women who were violent towards their husbands could find that they and their spouses were subject to neighbourhood censure. The rituals targeted against these couples are described in M. Ingram, 'Ridings, rough music and "the reform of popular culture" in early modern England' *PP* 105 (1984), 'Ridings, rough music and mocking rhymes in early modern England', in B. Reay, ed., *Popular Culture in Seventeenth-Century England* (London, 1985), and 'Juridical folklore in England illustrated by rough music', in C. Brooks and M. Lobban, eds, *Communities and Courts in Britain 1150–1900* (London, 1997). F.E. Dolan, *Dangerous Familiars: Representations of Domestic Crime in England 1550–1700* (Ithaca NY, 1994), and G. Walker, '"Demons in female form": representations of women and gender in murder pamphlets of the late sixteenth and early seventeenth centuries', in W. Zunder and S. Trill, eds, *Writing and the English Renaissance* (London, 1996), both consider popular male representations of these violent women.

Index